For Gwen Hebert —
Bon Appetit!

NEW ORLEANS CHEFS COOKBOOK

New Orleans Chefs Cookbook

Edited by Phil Johnson

PELICAN PUBLISHING COMPANY
GRETNA 1988

First printing, January 1988
Second printing, April 1988

Library of Congress Cataloging-in-Publication Data

The New Orleans chefs cookbook.
   Includes index.
     1. Cookery, American – Louisiana style.   2. Cookery –
Louisiana – New Orleans.   3. Cookery, International.
I. Johnson, Phil.
TX715.N5253   1988   641.59763'35   87-7243
ISBN 0-88289-666-0

Published by Pelican Publishing Company, Inc.
1101 Monroe Street, Gretna, Louisiana 70053
Manufactured in the United States of America

Contents

Acknowledgments

Many hands have touched this book to make it what it is. We must thank, first of all, the chefs of New Orleans who have given so freely of themselves and their talents; not just in making this book, but in raising over a half-million dollars in ten years to help the children of St. Michael's School. We must also thank the ladies of St. Michael's, the Guild, which plays such an important role in the Chefs' Charity. We quite literally could not do it without them. And we must thank Bernd Wohlschlaeger, Jerry Ursin, and Leo Grabler of the New Orleans Fairmont Hotel for their unflagging help and support. And most of all, we give prayerful thanks and praise to Mrs. Hilda Crochet of WWL-TV, who really "wrote the book." She, quite literally, typed out over the years each and every recipe, each ingredient, each measurement; in fact, each and every paragraph and sentence and word in all the hundreds of pages that make up this book. She is an amazing lady. And St. Michael's is forever in her debt.

Foreword

The recipes in this book are the end results of a labor of love, a testament to the chefs of New Orleans and their very special mission: the education of retarded children.

It was in pursuit of that mission in 1978 that the "Chefs' Charity for Children" was born. The "Chefs' Charity" is a two-day cooking extravaganza held each January in New Orleans, with the entire proceeds going to help the children of St. Michael's Special School.

It is a labor of love in the truest sense. The chefs give their time and talents, and some even close their restaurants so their staffs can be free to assist. After all, they will serve 1,000 meals each day. The chefs provide all the food; some of it given by suppliers, and much of it is bought by the chefs themselves.

In essence, the "Chefs' Charity for Children" is a classic charity. Nothing comes off the top. There are no hidden charges, no promotion fees, no salaries, and no commissions. Everything that is collected goes to St. Michael's. In the last 10 years the "Chefs' Charity" has raised over a half million dollars for the school, enabling it to double in size, to eliminate – almost – a sizable waiting list for entrance, and to establish a sheltered workshop. In this workshop, teenage graduates can learn to work at small tasks and be trained to enter the outside world, where they will be able to cope in a special way with what they find there.

The idea for the "Chefs' Charity" came from Warren Leruth, founder of the fabled LeRuth's Restaurant in New Orleans. Quite obviously, it was an idea whose time had come. It grew out of a need to do something to help someone. Leruth puts it very simply: "God has been very good to me. I wanted to do something in return." He found that his friends, other chefs in New Orleans, felt the same way: they all wanted to help. The problem was finding someone who *needed* their help.

They found that someone in Sister Lillian McCormick of the School Sisters of Notre Dame, a Roman Catholic nun who began St. Michael's in 1965 in an old, run-down school on the edge of New Orleans' Irish Channel neighborhood. Sister Lillian had struggled with problems of finance and space, and the heartbreaking realization that a place on the waiting list was all she could offer to many of the retarded children of New Orleans. The "Chefs' Charity" dedicated itself to the elimination of that waiting list.

Over the years, special "guest chefs" have come down to share with their counterparts in New Orleans the pride of working for a very special cause. Louis Szathmary of The Bakery Restaurant in Chicago has made three appearances, in 1978, 1982 and 1987. Others include Pierre Franey of the *New York Times*; Jacques Pepin, chef and food writer; Merle Ellis, "The Butcher" of TV and newspaper fame; Jacques Blanc, of Washington's Le Provençal Restaurant. Movie star Jane Powell came to cook her favorite dishes, and Pete Fountain fried trout. And in 1980, John Arena, owner of Winston's Restaurant in Toronto, Canada, flew down with his executive chef and a staff of seven.

The format is simplicity itself. They picked the biggest ballroom in town – the Imperial Room of the Fairmont Hotel. Guests are limited to 1,000 each day. Tickets cost $30 each. Each chef demonstrates how to cook one dish: seafood, soup, chicken, beef, appetizer, or dessert. A special closed-circuit television system, provided free of charge by WWL-TV (the CBS affiliate in New Orleans), enables all the guests to watch the chefs on hotel monitors. No guest is more than 12 feet from a monitor, and when all the demonstrations are finished, dinner is served. The menu is everything the chefs cooked that day because, while they were on stage, their staffs were busy in the Fairmont's banquet kitchen, cooking their special dish for the multitudes. Complimentary wine, red and white, is provided by various wine distributors of New Orleans.

Visiting chefs from major cities are awed by the sense of camaraderie and cooperation they see among the chefs working for St. Michael's. Jacques Pepin said, "I don't know of any other major city where chefs of competing restaurants could get together and work together like this, helping each other, sharing recipes, pots, knives . . . you name it. It's a miracle."

If you walk into the Fairmont's banquet kitchen during the "Chefs' Charity," you will hear chefs talking in French, German, Spanish, English, Greek, Cajun patois, Italian, and Chinese. But, as it turns out, they are all speaking the same language – the language of love – love for special children and for St. Michael's School.

And it is to all the children of St. Michael's and to Sister Lillian, who loves them and cares for them and educates them, that the chefs of New Orleans dedicate this book.

NEW ORLEANS CHEFS COOKBOOK

Biographies

Identifying the Chefs

The following list of initials identifies the chef, or chefs, responsible for each recipe in this book. The identifying letters can be found at the end of each recipe:

JLA	Jean Luc Albin
WC	Willy Coln
LE	Louis Evans
GF	Goffredo Fraccaro
JGF	Justin Galatoire Frey
RH	Roland Huet
CK	Chris Kerageorgiou
LED	André Ledoux
LLL	Larry and Lee Leruth
WL	Warren Leruth
AL	Austin Leslie
GP	Gunter Preuss
PP	Paul Prudhomme
MR	Mike Roussel
TW	The Wongs

Jean Luc Albin was born in France, and he began his career in the gastronomic center of that country, the city of Lyon. As he toiled in the kitchens of restaurants and hotels around Lyon, he considered himself most fortunate, being only a few hours' drive from the Riviera beaches in the summer, and only a few hours' drive to alpine ski resorts in the winter. But despite these advantages, he yearned to be more than a cook. He wanted to be a chef, and a *chef de cuisine* most of all.

Realizing the truth of an old French saying, "A chef isn't a chef until he has worked in Paris," he bought a Michelin Guide and wrote to all the great hotels in Paris: the Crillon, the Bristol, the Plaza-Athenee, the Georges V. Only the Georges V replied, and he set out for Paris to work in one of the great hotel kitchens of the world.

The operation of the Georges V fascinated him. "Can you imagine 50 cooks in one kitchen?" he asked. He began as a rotisseur, then worked as assistant to the Garde Manger, and for a year and a half worked as a Saucier. In 1974 he left Paris to become chef at the Princess Hotel in Bermuda.

Albin came to New Orleans in 1979, where he became Chef de Cuisine at the Fairmont Hotel. He brought a new sense of style and lightness to that already first-rate kitchen, and a few years later was brought upstairs to become the hotel's Director of Food and Beverage. Two years after that he moved to Dallas, to oversee the food and beverage operation of the Fairmont there. Currently he is in Los Angeles, masterminding the building and operation of seven restaurants in a mammoth new building development in Studio City.

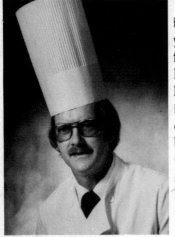

Chef **Willy Coln** is one of the most imaginative chefs in New Orleans, which you might expect of a man who has cooked for Chancellor Konrad Adenauer, Prince Bernhard of the Netherlands, and Henry Kissinger. He has also cooked for two Presidents – Richard Nixon who ate cottage cheese, and Lyndon Johnson who ordered beans and barbecue. Chef Coln has also worked his culinary magic around the world, serving as chef on many Dutch cruise liners, and in hotels in Germany, Switzerland and the U.S.

He gets his name from his birthplace, Cologne, West Germany. He came to America in 1964 and quickly became the star of the Sonesta Hotel chain. He lived in New Orleans briefly when he worked as a chef at the Royal Orleans Hotel, and he returned for good in 1972 when he was named Executive Chef of the Royal Sonesta Hotel on Bourbon Street. It was a time of great cuisine and great chefs. His sous-chef at the time was Gerard Crozier, who also owns one of New Orleans' best restaurants.

Chef Coln left the Royal Sonesta in 1976 to open his own restaurant across the Mississippi River from New Orleans, in a chalet-style house in Gretna. That year he was named "Chef of the Year" by his fellows of the Chefs de Cuisine de la Louisiane.

He does remarkable things with seafood and veal. His *seviche*, or marinated fish and shellfish, is delectable, and his Bahamian chowder a minor miracle of the chef's art. And he, too, has fallen under the spell of New Orleans cuisine: even his schnitzels reflect a little of the Creole influence.

Chef **Louis Evans** is a walking, talking example of the popularity of New Orleans cooking.

He is the chef upon whose broad shoulders the reputation of the fabled Caribbean Room of the Pontchartrain Hotel rested for so many years. He succeeded the legendary Nathaniel Burton, and through hard work and a feel for Creole cuisine, he added to the repertoire of the Pontchartrain's kitchen. Chef Louis continued its glory to still another generation.

But when he left the Pontchartrain in late 1987, he didn't even have time to take a vacation. The manager of the New Orleans Hilton heard he was free on a Sunday; by Monday Chef Louis was in his office. Within a week he was installed as Executive Chef of Kabby's, the Hilton's riverside restaurant overlooking the broad Mississippi River.

And once again he is working his Creole magic, bringing that kitchen into the fold. He enjoys using his menu as a pulpit to preach the glories of Louisiana crabs, oysters, and shrimp, and showing how judicious use of the proper seasonings – a little cayenne here, a little bell pepper there – can transform them all into something magical.

Chef Louis has been working that magic for three decades now, with a firm foundation in the basics. He studied at the Culinary Institute of America in Hyde Park, New York. And, a few years ago, he was awarded the Order of the Golden Toque, one of only two chefs in New Orleans to achieve that honor – the other being Warren Leruth. He is a native of Mississippi, married, and the father of three children.

Chef **Goffredo Fraccaro's** renown as a Master Chef has reached all the way across the Atlantic back to his birthplace – Italy. Twice in the past several years the chef has been honored by his native land. In 1983 he was knighted by the Republic of Italy and given the title "Cavalieri" for his talents in furthering the *cucina d'Italia*. And two years later, together with Giovanni Agnelli, President of Fiat, he was honored by the President of Italy and presented on nationwide television with a small reproduction of Michelangelo's statue *David*, the Italian equivalent of the Oscar, for "exemplifying the ideals of Italy to the world."

Goffredo is by nature a happy, outgoing man. He only gets serious when he begins to cook. We can be happy for that because the products of his kitchen are marvelous. His veal dishes are classics – never heavy, but tasteful and exciting. His Calimari Frito is exquisite and always fresh. And his Pasta al Pesto, with a paste made from fresh basil, is unique in New Orleans.

Goffredo is Genovese, born in Tortona, a small town near Genoa. He would have been a singer, but his voice changed. He could have been a comedian, but he chose cooking instead – for which we can all give thanks.

He has cooked at all the grand hotels of Italy and throughout Europe. And as chief steward of the Italian Merchant Marine, he has cooked around the world. He came to Louisiana in 1961 to cook for The Village Restaurant in Baton Rouge, and he came to New Orleans eleven years later to work at Tre Fontana. Then, several years ago, he opened La Riviera. Italian cooking in Greater New Orleans has never been the same since.

He was just another youngster, like thousands of others, growing up in the Mid-City area, near City Park, riding his bike along the Bayou, heading for the lake front in the summer to swim or to sail. He graduated from Brother Martin High School and then Nicholls State College in Thibodaux, and he came back to New Orleans to begin his career.

A typical story, right? Happens to thousands of kids every year, right?

Well, not exactly.

Because this kid was a Galatoire . . . **Justin Galatoire Frey**. And his career wasn't just any career. He was destined for a very special career . . . to carry on the name – and the fame – of Restaurant Galatoire, a New Orleans tradition and one of America's finest eating establishments.

Justin Galatoire Frey is the son of Leona Galatoire Frey, daughter of the famed Justin Galatoire, who for decades ruled the dining room from his perch behind the cash drawer against the far wall. And since Justin Galatoire was the nephew of Jean Galatoire, the tiny Frenchman who started it all over 80 years ago, that makes Justin Frey the fourth generation of Galatoires to carry on the traditions and the cuisine of this most special restaurant.

His name didn't mean a thing when he began. He was just another member of the *brigade de cuisine*, cleaning up, learning, watching, taking notes. But now, an accomplished chef in his own right, he wears proudly the *toque blanche* he so truly earned when he steps behind the big black ranges in Galatoire's kitchen. He and a cousin, David Gooch, are the latest generation operating Galatoire's. As you will see, the fine old restaurant is in good hands.

Chef **Roland Huet**, with his trim mustache and white toque, is not your everyday idea of a wild adventurer. Yet in mid-career, as one of the most successful chefs in Paris, he tossed aside honors and success to set off on an adventure and a goal – to come to America and cook, and prove himself in another country.

What was he walking away from? Well, he was "born cooking" in France, and since his teens had worked in restaurants in the provinces. He moved on to Paris and cooked in such famous kitchens as Drouant and Lucas Corton. Before long, the word was out about this new, impressive young chef, and he was hired to become Executive Chef at the Veau D'Or in Paris, where he reigned for 18 years.

Why would he leave such success? Well, there was the challenge. Galatoire's, the venerable, almost-hallowed restaurant in New Orleans, had lost its long-time chef, and had heard of Huet. They talked to him about the job, and before long, he was in New Orleans. Also at Galatoire's was the founder's grandson, Chris Ansel, an engineer by training with years of schooling and work in France behind him. He had given up his engineering to manage the family restaurant, and he and Roland got along well. In 1973, when Chris left to start his own restaurant, he wanted no one for his head chef but Roland, and the two have been together ever since.

There are rumors that Roland has been "captured" by the old New Orleans culinary mystique. His sauces, once militantly French in taste and texture, are becoming more and more Creole, with a little of the Cajun seasonings mixed in. How did such a rumor get started? When Chef Roland returned from a vacation two years ago in France, he was heard telling one of his kitchen helpers, "The food in France is good, but they don't season it enough . . . not like New Orleans."

Chef **Chris Kerageorgiou** is one of those rare ideas whose time has come. In his time, he has roamed the world, at sea, across the land. He baked. He cooked. He worked as a maitre d'hôtel, always moving but always learning.

Then about fifteen years ago, he stopped. Apparently, all those years he had been looking, and finally he found what he had been looking for. It was a small opening in the pines just off the highway connecting Lacombe to Mandeville. Nowhere, really. But at sunset, when the light turns to amber as it filters through the tall long-leaf pines, he was reminded of another special light, the umber earth tones of his native Provence. So he stopped and built a restaurant and he called it La Provence. From then till now, La Provence has been one of the premier dining experiences of America.

People travel from all over southeast Louisiana to eat at Chris' table, and they always eat well. His Shrimp Armoricaine are divine, definitely habit-forming. And a new sauce for shrimp, fresh tomatoes with equally fresh basil, is as good. He does things with chicken few can match, and his pâtés are all homemade.

The genius of Chef Chris is that he never stands still. He is always experimenting . . . with tastes, with textures. He agrees with the aphorism of the master, Brillat-Savarin, who held that "The discovery of a new dish does more for human happiness than the discovery of a new star."

Recently Chris conceived a bold new way of making crab soup, which is a terribly simple way to describe what he does with stock, crabmeat, fresh vegetables and saffron. His soup was a prize-winner in the Crab Olympics in San Francisco.

Chris himself is an old star, still shining brightly. His new dishes reflect his quest for perfection. He will never find it, of course, but aren't we lucky to be around while he looks.

It's a long way from the storied Pied de Cochon Restaurant in Paris to the Fairmont in New Orleans. But Executive Chef **André Ledoux** has made the trip in fine style, with some interesting excursions along the way.

He is a graduate of the Ecole Hôtelière de Versailles in Paris. He has cooked at many fine Paris restaurants. In 1965, he hit the culinary jackpot: he came to America to work for the legendary Henri Soule at his equally legendary restaurant, Le Côte Basque. He worked as sous-chef under Roland Chanus, a magnificently talented man, who was the last Executive Chef at Le Pavillon and is now the owner-chef of Le Chantilly in New York.

Other gastronomic excursions included the Hotel Pierre, the St. Regis and the Sheraton in New York, the Cricket Club in Miami, and the Marina City Club in Marina del Rey, California. Now he is with us in New Orleans at the Fairmont.

His job is a tough one. In addition to creating new and intriguing menus for the hotel, he must oversee an enormous staff, working in several kitchens. His banquet staff and production are renowned across America, and the Fairmont is one of the few hotels in the country which maintains the highest quality whether serving five or five hundred.

First and foremost, however, André Ledoux is a cook and is happiest when he steps before a range to make magic with a mirepoix, a cut of meat, or a fish and lots of extraordinary talent. He is a welcome addition to the New Orleans culinary scene.

When Warren Leruth opened his now legendary restaurant in a small house on the "wrong" side of the river from New Orleans, his two sons, Larry and Lee, were only nine and seven years old. On Friday nights, sometimes, and some Saturdays, they would come to the restaurant to help. Lee might slice bread for the toasted croutons; Larry would peel the lettuce for the salad.

Over the years, as LeRuth's grew in size and in stature, the two Leruth boys grew too. And now they have taken up the challenge to maintain the LeRuth quality and that unique LeRuth taste, to enlarge upon the LeRuth repertoire, and to build and create ever anew.

Like their father, both **Lee and Larry Leruth** began as bakers, pastry chefs, with the pastry man's innate sense of balance and scale. No "pinch of this" or "a little of that" with these chefs. They have learned from the master, and everything in every recipe is measured out to the minutest amount. To Leruth, his recipes are not mere arrows, pointing out a vague location; they are minute road maps, leading to a very specific destination.

The restaurant bears out this care. In Leruth's long reign, he personally changed the face of cuisine in this city, adding to the traditional Creole cookery and transforming it into something very personal and very special. It is good to know that there are two more Leruths following him and carrying on the traditions of imagination and taste.

The French, as usual, have the words for it: *Plus ça change, plus c'est la même chose* . . . Everything changes, yet everything stays the same.

That's LeRuth's for you.

Editor's note: The restaurant is spelled "LeRuth's." The family name is spelled "Leruth."

Warren Leruth is a master of good taste and making things taste good. Indeed, it is his awesome sense of taste that remains his secret weapon. He is able to season his creations just below what he calls "the threshold of recognition." You don't quite know what it is, only that it makes the food taste delicious.

He returned home to New Orleans in the mid-1960s, after a decade or more of living and learning – and cooking – literally around the world on cruise ships and freighters. He also cooked in Rio, France, and in the Army in Korea where he was personal chef to a general who kept a platoon of M.P.'s busy hunting down the wild game he loved. He was also a research chef, developing and getting patents for the buttery taste of Chiffon Margarine and Seven Seas salad dressing.

Small wonder that, when he opened his restaurant in a plantation home across the Mississippi River from New Orleans, everything was so good he had sold-out business after only three weeks. It has been like that ever since. Leruth single-handedly changed the face of the traditional Creole cuisine in New Orleans, adding new tastes and textures into a once-fixed repertoire. His marriage of oysters and artichokes into a rich, thick bisque became his trademark, and is now on menus of most New Orleans restaurants.

Dining at his restaurant was always a personal experience, and he made it that way. After all, he baked his own bread, made his own salad dressings, ice cream and ices, and saw to it that everything leaving his kitchen carried his own unique concepts of taste and succulence. He won the Mobil 5-Star award and was a perennial on the *Holiday* magazine list of great American restaurants.

Since turning his restaurant over to his two sons, he has acted as a consultant for Popeye's Fried Chicken in New Orleans and began his own franchise operation, Chelsey's Frozen Custard. It's a soft ice cream and, of course, it is delicious.

Chef **Austin Leslie** is the owner of the finest Creole-Soul restaurant in the South. Where else but at Chez Helene can you get Oysters Rockefeller and black-eyed peas at the same meal, or red beans and rice and trout amandine? At Chez Helene, you get it all . . . and it all tastes good.

There really is a Helene. That would be Austin's Aunt Helen Howard, who ran Howard's Eatery years ago on Perdido Street. That's where Chef Leslie first learned to cook. Then in 1959 he served for a while as assistant chef at D. H. Holmes Restaurant. In 1964, Aunt Helen had moved to 1540 N. Robertson Street, off St. Bernard, and opened Chez Helene. She needed help, and she called Austin to come run the kitchen for her. The rest is history.

Now Austin owns the restaurant and is there usually seven days a week making sure the quality stays high and the portions big.

His menu is a litany of real New Orleans neighborhood cooking. His fried chicken is classic, accompanied by potato salad and greens and cornbread muffins, his barbecue is tart and delicious, and he probably makes the finest stuffed peppers in New Orleans. But one could go on and on. Let's make it simple. At Chez Helene everything is good.

The restaurant's reputation reached all the way to Hollywood where, in the Spring of 1987, CBS bought a brand new situation comedy named "Frank's Place" for its new season in September. It is set in New Orleans at Chez Helene, and on the show they are calling it "Chez Louisiane." The chef is patterned after Austin Leslie, even down to the white yachting cap he wears in the kitchen, and the Hollywood set is a faithful reproduction of Austin's dining room. Is it art copying life – or just TV, copying art?

Chef **Gunter Preuss**, to quote a famous television commercial, got his Toque Blanche and his reputation the old fashioned way – he earned it.

A Berliner born and bred, he began his career in his teens, apprenticed to the finest kitchens in Europe. He worked in Germany, Sweden, Switzerland, France, and England, before coming to the United States. He worked here in the Hilton chain, in New York, Washington, and Kansas City, advancing from apprentice to sous-chef to executive chef.

His talents attracted the attention of the Fairmont Hotel, and he was brought to New Orleans as Executive Chef, where he personally turned that food operation around and established high standards of quality and taste. A few years later, he moved onto St. Charles Avenue into every chef's dream, a restaurant of his own, The Versailles.

"I had always aspired to travel and work in America," he said. "I wanted to bring with me the benefits of my European heritage and to cook and operate my own restaurant. So one day I came to New Orleans. I have lived here and loved it ever since."

In the years he has operated The Versailles, he has won most of the major awards in American gastronomy. He is a member of the Academy of Chefs, an Honor Society of the American Culinary Federation, and has the unique title of "Vice Counseilleur de Culinaire" of the Chaine des Rôtisseurs. He is also a member of the board of the Greater New Orleans Tourist and Convention Commission.

Chef Preuss and his wife Evelyn have two sons, Marc and Andreas, and live in Metairie. They have also acquired a partnership in the famous French Quarter restaurant, Broussard's.

Paul Prudhomme has seen more of America in the last several years than most families would do in several lifetimes. Since the publication of his new cookbook, *Chef Paul Prudhomme's Louisiana Kitchen*, he has been constantly on the go, giving cooking demonstrations, plugging the book, and making personal appearances on all the major television talk shows. It is a best seller, and deservedly so.

His restaurant, K-Paul's Louisiana Kitchen, still boasts long lines as visitors and locals alike line up for his Blackened Redfish and Filé Gumbo and other great Cajun dishes.

He never does anything by halves. First he cooked for President Reagan at the Williamsburg Conference in 1983; then, later, he moved his entire restaurant to San Francisco for a fantastic, sold-out month. In 1986 he moved to New York for a month – again, a complete sellout.

Like most great cooks, he has done it all, from cooking at home (beginning at seven, the youngest of thirteen children) to becoming Corporate Chef for one of the nation's foremost groups of fine restaurants. Along the way he found time to organize and personally stage the Pan-American Culinary Olympics in New Orleans, the first time such a prestigious event was ever held in this city.

His philosophy is simple: make it taste good. To do this he uses fresh ingredients, getting his rabbits and hens from his hometown of Opelousas and his seafood from the Gulf and bays of Louisiana's rich coastline. The result: delicious.

Chef Paul is singularly responsible for the craze for Creole and Cajun food that has swept across America. And he is Louisiana's best ambassador, preaching the merits of the state and its cooking wherever he goes. His blackened redfish has been copied so much all over America that the fish may become an endangered species.

Executive Chef **Mike Roussel** of Brennan's is living proof that Horatio Alger is not only alive and well in New Orleans, but is still up to his old tricks. Because Roussel is the embodiment of the Horatio Alger story.

He started working at Brennan's 30 years ago as a busboy. And after decades of hard work and imagination, he is now head man in the kitchen, and figures to be there for a long time.

Chef Roussel, quite literally, has done everything there is to do at Brennan's, from busboy, to waiter, to wine steward, to Maître d'Hotel. Along the way, he has retained all the little tips and secrets of the cooks he worked with. He credits the Dutch chef Paul Blange for teaching him most of what he knows. He has also cooked under Rheinhold Lucas, Klaus Rossler, Rudy Steinhauer, and Fernando Oca . . . all accomplished chefs.

Now he is the boss. Mike is a native of New Orleans. He is married to the former Josephine Jolibare and they have three children. When he's not working in Brennan's kitchen, his hobby is – you guessed it – cooking.

Lately, however, he has been on the road, demonstrating at Bloomingdale's in New York and in restaurants all across America a new line of spices he and the Brennan boys have developed, as well as a new line of packaged Cajun and Creole dishes.

Question: What do Hammond, Mandeville, and New Orleans have in common, besides the fact that all three are in Louisiana? The answer is delicious, glorious, sumptuous Chinese food, as prepared by **the brothers Wong** – James, Frank, John, Tommy, and Joe. For years they were one of the great culinary secrets of this area, operating out of the tiny China Inn in Hammond near Southeastern Louisiana University.

But now there are three restaurants – a new one in Hammond, Mandeville, and New Orleans. All are called Trey Yuen, Chinese for Jade Green Garden. And they are magnificent temples of oriental magic, where the Wongs transform native Louisiana seafood – soft shell crabs, shrimp, crawfish, and even alligator – into Chinese delicacies.

That is the secret of their magic – the blending of ingredients so familiar to Cajun and Creole cooks into the Chinese culinary ethic. The results are delicious. Imagine soft shell crab in a sweet and sour sauce, minced squab in lettuce leaves, or stir fried alligator.

All of the Wongs are accomplished chefs, and they are constantly seeking out new tastes, new dishes, new experiences. Each year, they go back to the source and one, perhaps two of the brothers, will travel to Taiwan, Hong Kong, or even mainland China, to bring back still more ideas to delight and excite the palates of their adventurous customers.

Phil Johnson is a child of New Orleans; born and raised in the Third Ward, a mid-city enclave of blue collars, baseball fans and the finest poor-boy sandwiches in town. In fact, it was a particularly sloppy hot-dog-with-chili poor-boy at the Home Plate Inn that turned him on to food decades ago. He has been eating his way through New Orleans ever since, blessed with friends who just happen to be chefs at all of the city's great restaurants.

He has been a part of the "Chefs' Charity" since the beginning, helping to make it work by tying up loose ends and tending to details so the chefs can concentrate on cooking.

Johnson is assistant manager and former news director of WWL-TV in New Orleans. By profession, he is a writer and journalist. He has been a merchant seaman, U.S. Navy submariner, newspaperman (old New Orleans *Item*), TV editorialist, and war correspondent reporting from Viet Nam, Israel, and Lebanon. His daily editorial on WWL-TV is the longest running editorial commentary on American television, having begun in March 1962.

He is a specialist in television documentaries, and some he has written or produced have won major awards in American television. These include three Peabody Awards (the television equivalent of the Pulitzer Prize) and an Emmy. He has produced documentaries for the greater New Orleans audience from China, Rome, Viet Nam, Egypt, Paris, and Lebanon.

Johnson is also a chef and a saucier of some repute. He owns a personal wine cellar of several thousand bottles. He was a Nieman Fellow at Harvard University, and he holds a Bachelor of Arts degree from Loyola University of New Orleans. He is 57, married, and the father of five children.

Appetizers

CRABMEAT RAVIGOTTE

1 cup mayonnaise
2 tbsp. minced parsley
2 tbsp. capers, finely
  chopped
1 tbsp. dry mustard
1 tbsp. horseradish

2 tbsp. chopped pimento
1 hard-cooked egg, finely
  chopped
½ tsp. lemon juice
2 cups lump crabmeat

Thoroughly mix first 8 ingredients. Add crabmeat and toss lightly; chill. Heap into shell or ramekin for individual serving. Garnish with crisscross of 2 slices of pimento and half-slices tomato.
Serves 4. – MR

CHICKEN LIVERS ST. PIERRE

½ cup butter
½ cup chopped green
  pepper
½ cup chopped green onion
½ cup finely sliced white
  onion
1½ cups chicken livers

2 tbsp. chopped mushrooms
½ cup lima beans, cooked
  and drained
¼ cup sliced pimento
1 tsp. salt
dash cayenne

In a 9-inch skillet melt butter and sauté green pepper, green onion, and white onion. Add chicken livers and sauté until browned, 8 to 10 minutes. Add mushrooms, lima beans, pimento, salt and pepper. Heat through.
Serves 2. – MR

OYSTERS JEAN BAPTISTE REBOUL

1 lb. fresh mushrooms
½ cup olive oil
3 to 4 shallots, chopped
1 head garlic, chopped

1 tbsp. fresh sweet basil
1 cup dry white wine
1 bunch parsley, chopped

Chop mushrooms; sauté in olive oil till water is evaporated. Add shallots, garlic, half of parsley, and white wine and reduce. Remove from fire when reduced and add fresh basil and remaining parsley and keep refrigerated.

Use as needed, for stuffed baked oysters. Pour sauce over oysters in shell and place in oven to brown. Will cover 12 oysters.   – CK

MOUSSE DE CANETONS
(Duckling Mousse)

meat from 1 duckling
  (skinned, boned, and put
  through a grinder 3
  times)
1 tbsp. chopped dry
  shallots
½ tbsp. garlic

2 tbsp. chopped parsley
salt and white pepper to
  taste
½ cup brandy or cognac
5 egg whites
1 or 1½ cups heavy cream

In a mixing bowl combine and mix well first 6 ingredients. Add egg whites a little at a time. Stir in cream. Fill a buttered mold and place in a pan of water; cook in a 350-degree oven approximately 30 to 35 minutes. Unmold and serve.

Serves 4.   – GP

REDFISH FROID
(Served with horseradish sauce)

6 3-oz. fillets of redfish

(Redfish is a specialty fish of the region, but any boneless fillet of fish will work for this formula.) Poach the fish and cool it in the courtbouillon, preferably overnight in refrigerator. Next day, drain and mask with the horseradish sauce. Serve on beds of shredded lettuce, garnished with finely minced parsley.

Serves 6 as an appetizer.

COURTBOUILLON

1 stalk celery, sliced	**2 qts. water**
3 sprigs parsley	**10 peppercorns, bruised**
1 bay leaf	**1 pinch thyme**
2 carrots, coarsely chopped	**1 large white onion, sliced**
1 lemon, sliced	**1 cup dry white wine**
1 tsp. salt	**¼ cup cider vinegar**

Combine all ingredients in a deep saucepan, and simmer uncovered for 20 minutes. Strain the liquid through a fine sieve. Makes about 1 quart.

HORSERADISH SAUCE

2 cups commercial sour cream, blended well with 1½ cups horseradish, drained thoroughly, with ⅓ cup chopped pecans and salt and pepper to taste.   – RH

OYSTERS ROLAND

1 bunch parsley
1 lb. butter, softened
1 tsp. black pepper
1 tsp. salt
2 cloves garlic
1 12-oz. can mushrooms,
    stems, and pieces, with
    juice

1 cup bread crumbs
¼ tsp. nutmeg
5 doz. parboiled oysters

Blend ingredients in high speed food processor (such as Cuisinart) in the following order: blend well parsley, garlic, mushrooms until parsley is finely chopped; then add butter and spices and blend again; now add mushroom juice and bread crumbs and blend well. If this type of food processor is not available, a meat grinder may be substituted, using the smallest plate for grinding parsley, garlic, and mushrooms and blending after with a mixer.

Place 6 parboiled oysters each in 4½-inch au gratin dish, smooth butter mixture over, and put under broiler until brown and bubbly.

Serves 10.   – RH

SHRIMP MADELEINE

2 tbsp. dry English mustard
4 tbsp. butter
3 lbs. raw shrimp, medium-
    size

⅓ cup brandy
2 cups heavy cream
salt and pepper

Mix the dry mustard with a little water to make a light paste. Melt the butter over high heat and sauté the shrimp until all water has evaporated. Then pour over brandy and ignite. When the flames subside, add the cream and cook, stirring all the time, until a smooth sauce is obtained. Add the mustard paste and season to taste with salt and pepper. Serve in individual casserole dishes or on a platter; garnish with parsley.

Serves 8.   – RH

ZWIEBELKUCHEN
(Onion Cake)

CRUST:

1 cup all-purpose flour   ½ cup melted butter
¼ tsp. salt   2 to 3 tbsp. iced water

Mix the ingredients together gently and put in refrigerator until dough is able to be handled. Roll dough out and put in 8-inch pie tin and bake in 350-degree oven for 10 minutes or until half done.

BATTER:

4 large onions, diced   ¾ cup sour cream
6 strips bacon, diced   1 tsp. chives, chopped
2 whole eggs   pinch of caraway seed
1 egg yolk   salt and pepper to taste

Fry the bacon and when done, drain off the fat and fry the onions in the same fat. When cooked (not brown) drain off the fat and then add the beaten eggs, onions, crumbled bacon, sour cream, salt, pepper, and chives. Pour into pie crust already baked, add caraway seeds and bake in 350- to 375-degree oven for 15 minutes. Serve warm.
Serves 8 to 10.   – WC

OYSTERS BIENVILLE

3 doz. oysters, boiled   ½ cup grated Parmesan
3 doz. clean oyster shells   cheese
½ cup Hollandaise sauce   1 oz. butter, melted
½ cup bread crumbs   (margarine, if preferred)

Preheat broiler at high flame, or oven to 500°. Place boiled oysters in shells and cover with cold Hollandaise sauce. Top with the bread crumbs and cheese and place on cookie sheet. Pour melted butter over oysters to moisten and place under broiler for 4 to 5 minutes, or in oven for 7 to 10 minutes.
Serves 6.   – AL

OYSTERS ROCKEFELLER

½ lb. butter (or margarine, if preferred)
3 lbs. fresh spinach
4 stalks green onion
4 sprigs parsley and leaves
½ head iceberg lettuce
½ cup bread crumbs

1 tsp. green food coloring
½ cup Herbsaint liqueur
3 doz. oysters, boiled*
3 doz. clean oyster shells
½ cup grated Parmesan cheese

*To cook oysters, bring them to a boil in their own liquid. As soon as boiling point is reached, remove from heat. Let oysters sit in the hot liquid until you are ready to use them.

Preheat broiler to medium heat. Melt butter and set aside. Grind spinach, onions, parsley, and lettuce in a food processor and place in a mixing bowl. Stir in bread crumbs (reserving a small amount for later), the food coloring, and Herbsaint, and place mixture in a blender. Puree at fast speed until creamy (about 2 minutes). Place the boiled oysters in the shells and cover with the pureed mixture. Sprinkle with cheese and reserved bread crumbs. Place under the broiler for 20 minutes. Dot with a little melted butter before serving.

Serves 6.

– AL

CRABMEAT AND OYSTERS AU GRATIN

1 lb. crabmeat
1 qt. oysters
2 tbsp. butter
½ onion, grated
1 tbsp. chopped green peppers

2 tbsp. flour
cream
lemon juice
salt
bread crumbs

Cook oysters in their liquor until edges curl; strain, reserving liquor. Sauté onion and green peppers lightly in butter. Add flour, oyster liquid, and enough cream to make a thick sauce. Season with salt and lemon; add oysters and crabmeat. Place in a baking dish, sprinkle with buttered crumbs, and bake until heated.

– LE

DEVILED OYSTERS
ON HALF SHELL
(Oysters Diablo)

3 doz. oysters
1 tbsp. butter
3 shallots, finely chopped
2 tbsp. flour
⅛ tsp. nutmeg
few grains cayenne
½ tsp. salt

½ tsp. prepared mustard
1 tbsp. Worcestershire sauce
1 can chopped mushrooms
  (small)
½ tsp. chopped parsley
1 egg yolk, whipped
buttered cracker crumbs

Wash and chop oysters. Cook shallots in butter; add flour and brown. Add the rest of seasoning, oysters, and mushrooms; cook few minutes. Remove from fire and add egg yolk. Put mixture in deep halves of oyster shells, cover with crumbs and bake 15 minutes at 350°F.   – LE

HUÎTRES FARCIES AU BEURRE AIL
(Baked Oysters on Half-Shell)

24 large fresh oysters on
  half-shell
1 lb. butter
1 tsp. thyme
2 oz. dry shallots or white
  of green onions
½ bunch fresh parsley

2 oz. fresh garlic
1 pinch nutmeg
1 oz. cognac
fresh black peppercorn,
  crushed
salt
ice cream salt

Make paste of butter, thyme, shallots, parsley, garlic, nutmeg, cognac, and pepper (butter should be room temperature). Then refrigerate until needed. Open oysters, leaving oyster attached to one side of shell. Use approximately 1 teaspoon of butter preparation on top of each oyster. Bake in 500-degree oven approximately 10 minutes. *Do not overcook!* Serve while hot.

Note: Place shells in pan of ice cream salt to bake. Do not remove water from fresh oysters.

Serves 4.   – CK

PÂTÉ DE CAMPAGNE BERNE

3 lbs. pork from around
  neck or shoulder
1 lb. pork liver (*pork* only)
2 tbsp. salt per 2 lbs.
2 tsp. pepper per 2 lbs.
1 tsp. thyme
⅓ tsp. saltpeter per 2 lbs.

dry shallots or onions,
  chopped fine
3 cloves garlic
3 oz. cognac
3 oz. madeira or port
3 eggs

Note: Use 2 lbs. lean pork, 1 lb. fat, and 1 lb. liver ground through largest hole of grinder.

Combine all ingredients. Use thin layer of fresh back fat, approximately 3 inches wide. Line 4" × 8" loaf pan, then fill with stuffing. Cover with thin layer of fat. Place in pan of water in 275-degree oven. Bake approximately 3 hours. Do not remove grease that comes to top. Set aside to cool. When cool, refrigerate. Press top down with some weights. Suggest making 2 pans of 2 pounds each.   – CK

DAUBE GLACE

3 lbs. lean veal
3 qts. water
6 dill pickles
2 leeks (white only)
4 carrots
2 large onions
3 bay leaves

1 tsp. caraway seeds
¼ tsp. chopped garlic
2 cups white wine
1 cup plain gelatin
salt and white pepper to
  taste

Cut veal in ½-inch cubes and simmer in water with bay leaves, caraway seeds, garlic, salt, and pepper until tender. (Keep skimming mixture.) Cube vegetables and pickles and slice leeks. Blanch for 3 to 5 minutes until crunchy. Strain and add to veal mixture. Dissolve gelatin in wine. Also add to mixture. Very slowly boil for 1 to 2 more minutes. Pour in forms. Chill overnight and serve with vinaigrette sauce.

Serves 12.   – GP

SHRIMP REMOULADE

2 lbs. boiled shrimp, peeled
and deveined

8 leaves of crisp romaine
lettuce

REMOULADE SAUCE:

1 cup finely minced celery
1 cup finely minced green
onion
1 cup finely minced parsley
1 cup finely minced dill
pickle
3 tbsp. finely minced garlic

2 cups Creole hot mustard
4 tbsp. horseradish
½ cup vegetable oil
½ cup red wine vinegar
about 1¾ tsp. salt
2 tbsp. Worcestershire sauce

To prepare the sauce, combine all the ingredients in a mixing bowl and mix thoroughly with a whisk until very well blended. Using 8 chilled salad plates, place a lettuce leaf on each one, then top with ⅛ of the boiled shrimp. To serve, ladle about ½ cup sauce evenly over each portion.

Serves 8.

– MR

SINGING SHRIMP

3 tbsp. butter
½ cup chopped green
onions
1 cup sliced fresh
mushrooms

¼ cup finely chopped garlic
2 lbs. peeled fresh shrimp
½ cup dry white wine
8 rounds of Holland rusk

Melt the butter in a chafing dish or an attractive skillet over an alcohol burner. Add the green onions and mushrooms and sauté for about 3 to 4 minutes, then add the garlic and shrimp. Sauté about 4 minutes more. Add the wine and simmer briefly. To serve, place a Holland rusk on each of 8 heated individual ramekins, then top with equal portions of shrimp and generous amounts of sauce from the chafing dish. Set the ramekins on plates to serve.

Serves 8.

– MR

EGG ROLLS

6 oz. lean pork (or ham or
    roast beef)
4 oz. shrimp, shredded
½ lb. cabbage or bean
    sprouts
2 oz. spring onions,
    shredded

20 pieces spring roll skins
6 cups oil
cornstarch (make a paste)
1 tbsp. soy sauce
1 tbsp. salt
½ cup soup stock
flour

MARINADE:

soy sauce
cornstarch

salt

After cutting the pork into string shapes, marinate with soy sauce and cornstarch. In another bowl marinate shrimp with salt and cornstarch. Shred cabbage into string shapes about 1½ inches long.

Heat 5 tablespoons oil in frying pan, stir fry the pork about ½ minute, drain and put it aside. Use the same oil to fry shrimp until well done. Remove to bowl with pork. Add the shredded cabbage to the frying pan and stir fry a moment. Add soy sauce, salt, and soup stock; cover with lid and cook about 2 minutes. Then add pork, shrimp, and spring onions; stir fry another ½ minute over high heat. Stir in the cornstarch paste until thickened and remove to another bowl.

Place 2 tablespoons filling on the egg roll skin, about 1 inch from the edge that is toward you. Roll once or twice, then fold right side toward center, then left side toward center, continue rolling into a tight roll. Brush outer edge of skin roll with flour paste (to 1 tablespoon flour add 1½ tablespoons of water). Place this side face down to hold tightly and to keep its shape until time for frying.

Heat the oil in pan; deep fry egg rolls 10 at a time. Use high heat and fry about 3 minutes or until golden. Serve with some soy sauce and brown vinegar.   — TW

SHRIMP REMOULADE

1 lb. shrimp
⅔ cup olive oil
5 tbsp. Creole mustard
1 bunch green onions
2 tbsp. paprika
⅓ cup vinegar

1 stalk celery
2 cloves garlic
1 bunch parsley
dash Tabasco
1 tbsp. horseradish
salt and pepper

Grind all vegetables very fine, then add mustard, paprika, horse-radish, Tabasco, salt and pepper. Mix with the vinegar, then add olive oil, gradually.

After shrimp have been boiled and peeled, let them soak in sauce for a couple of hours.

Serve cold over shredded lettuce.   – JGF

DANISH-STYLE PÂTÉ

3 lbs. pork liver
1 lb. calf liver
1¾ lbs. fresh pork fat
2 large onions, boiled and
   ground
6 eggs
1½ cups heavy cream

1 cup milk
1 cup cornstarch
3½ tsp. white pepper
2 tsp. allspice
2 tsp. salt
⅔ cup Cognac

Grind livers in large bowl. Grind pork fat in separate bowl. Add onions to pork fat and mix well. Add this to the ground livers.

Mix remaining ingredients together in large bowl; add to liver mixture. Stir until well blended. Spoon mix into 2 3-pound loaf pans; place pans in large pan of water. Bake at 350° for 1½ hours.   – GP

FRIED EGGPLANT FINGERS

2 medium eggplants, cut
   into sticks ½-inch square
   and 2 to 3 inches long
cayenne, garlic powder and
   salt

flour
1 cup milk
2 eggs
fine French bread crumbs

Wash eggplant fingers in cold water and drain very well. Season generously with cayenne, garlic powder, and salt; let stand, seasoned, for 1 to 2 hours. (If you don't have that long to let the eggplant sit, then soak them in cold salted water for at least 30 minutes to draw all bitterness out.)

Mix flour and cayenne, garlic powder, and salt so that flour is well seasoned. Drench eggplant sticks in seasoned flour. Mix milk and egg together. Soak floured eggplant in this mixture for 3 to 5 minutes. Mix eggplant several times while soaking in milk. It is very important that the flour gets completely wet.

Roll in very fine bread crumbs and drop into hot oil (about 360°); fry until golden brown.

Drain well on paper towels.

Serve immediately.

            –PP

OYSTERS PAN ROAST

½ cup butter
½ cup shallots, tops only,
   chopped
pinch thyme
1 bay leaf, crushed

1 cup bread crumbs
4 doz. oysters and their
   liquid
salt and pepper to taste

Sauté shallots in butter until soft. Add oysters with their liquid and seasonings and simmer for 15 minutes. Put into large baking dish or individual ramekins. Sprinkle with bread crumbs. Freshly grated Parmesan cheese may also be sprinkled on top. Put under broiler for about 3 minutes or until topping browns.

Serves 4 to 6.

            –PP

SPRING ROLLS

6 oz. pork, shredded and
marinated with 1½ tsp.
soy sauce and 1 tsp.
cornstarch
4 oz. bamboo shoots, finely
shredded
6 to 8 medium dried black
mushrooms, presoaked
and then shredded
1 lb. cabbage, finely
shredded
2 scallions, finely chopped
1 tsp. salt

3 tbsp. light soy sauce
1 tsp. sesame seed oil
2 tsp. sugar
½ tsp. white pepper
2 tbsp. sherry wine or rice
wine
½ cup soup stock (chicken
broth)
2 tsp. cornstarch, dissolved
in 2 tbsp. water
½ tsp. garlic, minced
2 tbsp. oil
20 spring roll wrappings

Heat wok or heavy skillet; add oil and heat until hot. Add pork and stir-fry for 30 seconds. Remove pork and drain oil.

Reheat wok or skillet, add oil, and toss back pork; add garlic, bamboo shoots, black mushrooms, and cabbage. Shower in sherry. Sprinkle all seasoning along with soup stock and stir for 2 minutes. Add scallions and cornstarch until sauce thickens. Remove mixture and put it in a colander to cool and drain at least 2 hours.

Place about 2 tablespoonsful of filling just below the center of the spring roll wrapping; spread it lengthwise. Fold edge nearest to you over the mixture, then roll up fairly tightly. After wrapping is rolled turn in both edges and continue to roll away from the body. Seal it with beaten egg.

Deep-fry until golden brown. Drain.   – TW

GARLIC SOUFFLÉ

⅓ cup flour
½ cup milk
1 stick butter
salt and pepper to taste

8 eggs
½ cup freshly grated Gruyère
cheese
8 cloves (or less) garlic

To make Bechamel sauce, melt butter, add flour, stir for several minutes over low heat, add milk and whisk until the beater is lightly coated.

Separate eggs. Beat the whites in the machine until firm, but not as firm as for a meringue.

Beat the yolks one at a time into the Bechamel. Fold lightly into the beaten whites. Add Gruyère cheese. Squeeze garlic into the mixture . . . 8 cloves for a garlic lover, less according to taste.

Pour into well-buttered 8-cup mold. Bake 30 minutes at 400°.
Serves 6.   – GP

OYSTERS A LA PROVENCE

24 oysters
¼ cup minced shallots
¼ cup persillade (a mixture
of finely chopped parsley
and garlic)

3 tbsp. sherry wine vinegar
5 tbsp. olive oil
salt and pepper
freshly ground black pepper

Shuck the oysters, leaving them on the half-shell, and place in a shallow baking pan. Season them with a little salt and pepper.

Over each oyster sprinkle approximately ½ teaspoon each of the shallots and the persillade. Follow this with about ⅛ teaspoon of the vinegar for each oyster and ¼ teaspoon of olive oil.

Place about 5 inches under the broiler and cook for 6 minutes or until hot and bubbling. Finish with a generous grind of black pepper on each oyster and serve.

Serves 4 as an appetizer.   – CK

PÂTÉ A LA CUILLÈRE
(A simple mousse of duck or chicken liver)

2 lbs. duck or chicken
  livers
2 whole eggs
2 oz. cognac
2 oz. madeira

5 sticks butter (at room
  temperature)
salt and pepper to taste
buttered parchment paper

In a Cuisinart, puree finely livers, eggs, cognac, madeira, salt, and pepper, turning machine on and off so you won't overheat ingredients (if this should happen, add a little bit of ice). After all ingredients are pureed, incorporate butter in same manner so as not to overheat.

Line a suitable terrine with buttered parchment paper and fill with pureed ingredients. Place terrine in a water bath, and bake approximately 30 minutes at 375°.   – CK

OYSTERS CHELSEY LEE

20 artichoke hearts, sliced
4 cloves garlic, finely
  chopped
2 cups water
½ cup olive oil
4 bay leaves
½ tbsp. thyme
½ tbsp. salt
¼ tsp. white pepper

¼ tsp. red pepper
¼ tsp. black pepper
1 cup bread crumbs
1 cup Romano cheese
chopped parsley
6 hearts of palm, sliced
6 doz. oysters, shucked
  (allow 6 per person)

Place water, olive oil, and seasoning in large saucepan. Add artichokes and garlic and bring to a rolling boil. Stir in bread crumbs and cheese and heat thoroughly. Place aside.

Line oven-proof ramekins with sliced hearts of palm. Add oysters and artichoke sauce. Bake 10 to 15 minutes at 400°. Serve immediately with fresh chopped parsley.   – LLL

CRAB PHYLLIS

4 large mushrooms, finely
  chopped
1 clove garlic, finely
  chopped
3 shallots, finely chopped
1½ sticks butter
½ cup flour
3 cups half-and-half
2 tbsp. chopped fresh
  chives

1 large bay leaf
1 tbsp. Worcestershire sauce
¼ cup white wine
salt and pepper to taste
¾ lb. crabmeat
6 to 8 slices French bread,
  toasted
1½ cups Hollandaise sauce
chopped parsley
lemon slices

Sauté mushrooms, shallots, and garlic in butter until transparent. Remove from heat and mix in flour over low heat; slowly stir in half-and-half. Cook until smooth (about 3 to 4 minutes). Add chives, bay leaf, Worcestershire sauce, wine, and salt and pepper to taste and bring to boil. Simmer 30 minutes. Remove bay leaf. Add crabmeat and cook 3 to 4 minutes. Arrange toasted slices of French bread on heat-proof platter. Spoon hot crabmeat mixture over toast. Cover with Hollandaise sauce; broil until lightly browned, about 1 to 2 minutes. Garnish with parsley and lemon.   – LED

ESCARGOT BOURGUIGNONNE

3 doz. snails
3 cups brown sauce
1 cup red wine
1 tbsp. green onion
½ tbsp. finely chopped
  shallots

¼ tbsp. chopped garlic
3 tbsp. butter
salt and pepper

Combine all ingredients except snails and butter in saucepan; add snails and slowly cook for 8 to 10 minutes. Add butter before serving. Serve in hollowed French bread.
  Serves 6.   – GP

OYSTER PATTIES GRAND-MÈRE

12 patties, 3½ inches in
  diameter; clean centers
  and save tops and inside
  crumbs
¼ lb. butter
1 bunch green onions,
  chopped
½ cup chopped onions
2 toes garlic, chopped
½ tsp. thyme
1 cup plus 2 tbsp. flour
¼ cup oyster liquor

4 doz. oysters
3 cups hot milk
¾ cup finely chopped celery
  heart
¼ cup chopped parsley
¼ tsp. white pepper
⅛ tsp. red pepper
3 egg yolks, beaten
salt to taste
¾ cup chopped patty shell
  crumbs (inside of patty
  shells)

Heat butter and add green onions, onions, garlic, and thyme. Sauté well. Stir in flour and make a roux.

While stirring, add oysters and liquor. Cook until outside edges of oysters begin to get curly. Stir continuously over medium heat. Begin to add hot milk while stirring. Bring almost to boil.

Stir in celery hearts, parsley, salt, and peppers. Return almost to boil. Check taste to be sure flour is cooked.

On slow fire, add beaten egg yolks; *stir well*. Return almost to boil. Then stir in patty shell crumbs to thicken.

Allow mix to cool for 1 hour, then fill patty shells. Place 4 oysters in each shell plus sauce. Place tops on filled patties and bake at 350° for about 20 minutes to heat filling and crisp the filled shells.   – LLL

GRAVLAKS

Rub a 2-pound piece of fresh salmon (boned, not skinned) heavily with sugar and coarse salt. Cover with sprigs of fresh dill and wrap in foil and refrigerate for 48 hours. Weight down with a board or heavy plate; liquid should be drained off from time to time.

After 48 hours remove dill, salt, and sugar (don't wash). Shake off and slice very thin.

Serve with oil-vinegar sauce seasoned with mustard, chopped dill, sugar, salt, and pepper.   – GP

CRABMEAT AU GRATIN

3 green onions, finely
  chopped
2 tbsp. butter
¼ cup milk

½ lb. fresh crabmeat
bread crumbs
grated cheese

Sauté green onions lightly in butter, then make a cream sauce with the milk. To this sauce add the crabmeat, season with salt and pepper, and cook on a slow fire for 5 minutes. Remove from fire and place crabmeat in a pyrex dish. Over it sprinkle bread crumbs, grated cheese, and a little melted butter. Place in 400-degree oven; remove when golden brown.
      – JGF

MORNAY SAUCE

Mix 1 cup cream sauce with ¼ cup grated Swiss cheese.   – CK

TURKEY AND OYSTER POULETTE

1 qt. oysters, drained
½ turkey breast
½ cup dry white wine
¼ lb. butter
3 oz. flour
½ bunch green onions
½ cup sliced fresh
  mushrooms

½ gal. chicken stock
2 bay leaves
3 egg yolks
1 cup half-and-half
salt and pepper to taste
dash of thyme
½ tsp. Lea & Perrins
  Worcestershire sauce

Dice turkey breast and boil with oysters in the chicken stock. Add bay leaves, salt, pepper, thyme, and Lea & Perrins. Let this come to a boil. Skim off the top. In another pan, add the butter, mushrooms, and green onions, sauté for 5 minutes, then add flour. Cook for 3 minutes, then mix with turkey and oyster stock. Cook for 5 minutes, add wine, beaten egg yolks, and half-and-half. Stir well and serve.
Serves 10.
      – LE

CRABMEAT BIARRITZ

shredded lettuce
2 slices of tomato,
   marinated in French
   dressing
2 boiled whole artichokes
1 cup crabmeat, moistened
   with 1 tbsp. mayonnaise

4 tbsp. mayonnaise
2 tbsp. whipping cream
2 tsp. black caviar
1 tsp. capers

Place lettuce on serving plates, and on each place a slice of tomato with an artichoke bottom on top. Heap artichoke bottoms with crabmeat that has been moistened with mayonnaise. Surround this with the artichoke leaves. Cover with a mixture of mayonnaise and whipping cream. Top each with a spoonful of caviar, sprinkle with capers, and serve very cold.

Serves 2.

– LE

CHAIR DE CRABE
A L'OIGNON CROQUANT

1 lb. lump crabmeat
1 cup fresh cream
1 tbsp. port wine
1 tbsp. brandy
1 tbsp. lemon juice

½ tsp. tarragon, fresh if
   possible
1 cup fresh diced tomatoes
finely chopped onions

Note: Scald and remove skins of fresh tomatoes, squeeze juice out, and dice tomato pulp.

Combine cream, port wine, brandy, lemon juice, and tarragon. Reduce by approximately one-half. When thickened, add fresh diced tomatoes, and season to taste. Add lump crabmeat; do not stir. Let simmer approximately 1 minute. Prepare to serve. Sprinkle fresh finely chopped onions on top. Can be served on top of pastry shell, if desired.

Serves 4.

– CK

POÊLE DE GAMBAS
A L'HUILE D'OLIVE

12 to 14 shrimp for main
  course, 6 to 8 shrimp for
  appetizer
shallots, chopped
parsley, chopped
garlic, chopped

1 cup diced fresh tomatoes
stock or white wine
butter
olive oil
arrowroot
egg white

Peel and devein shrimp. Dry very thoroughly. Season with salt and pepper, sprinkle with arrowroot and white of egg, coat with oil, and set aside. In a medium skillet, sauté shrimp in clarified butter or half butter and half oil. Sauté lightly. Remove from pan. Using same pan, sauté shallots, parsley, garlic, and tomatoes for a few minutes. Add stock or wine if necessary. Replace shrimp, bring to boil, and cook for a few minutes. Finish with a little butter; serve.   – CK

FRICASSÉ D'ESCARGOT
AU VIN ROUGE
(Escargot in red wine)

6 large snails per person
3 French shallots, chopped,
  or 1 bunch green onions,
  white part only
½ head garlic, chopped
  very fine

½ bottle red Burgundy
  (Beaujolais preferred)
1 stick butter
2 oz. brandy
salt and pepper

In pot, sauté shallots in ½ stick butter. Add snails and brandy. Cook about 1 minute. Remove snails from pot. Add wine; reduce by about two-thirds. Add snails back to pot. Make persillade with parsley and garlic. Add to sauce. Finish with ½ stick butter. Season to taste. Serve at once.

Serves 6.   – CK

SEVICHE
(Mexican Fish Cocktail)

2 lbs. Halibut fish fillets or
  scallops (or any firm
  white meat fish fillets)
½ cup lime juice
1 large onion, minced
1 clove garlic, minced
4 large tomatoes, peeled,
  seeded, and diced
1 tsp. dried thyme

1 pinch powdered cloves
¼ cup olive oil
1 can chilies serranos or 1
  red hot pepper, minced
1 tbsp. Worcestershire sauce
2 avocados, peeled and
  sliced
12 black olives
1 bay leaf

Cut fish into pieces ½ inch thick and 2 inches long. Place in a shallow dish. Pour in lime juice and bay leaf. Marinate for 2 hours at room temperature, turning frequently. Remove fish from lime juice and mix with remaining ingredients. Marinate 2 hours longer in refrigerator.

Serves 6 as an appetizer.   – WC

LOUISIANA CRABMEAT QUICHE

1 cup fresh sliced
  mushrooms
1 cup lump crabmeat
2 tbsp. butter
2 eggs, beaten

1 cup whipping cream
2 oz. shredded Swiss cheese
¼ tsp. ground nutmeg
salt and pepper to taste
1 9-inch baked pie shell

In saucepan cook mushrooms and sautéed crabmeat in butter until mushrooms are tender. Set aside. In mixing bowl combine eggs, cream, cheese, nutmeg, salt, and pepper. Place crabmeat and mushroom mixture in bottom of pie shell. Pour egg mixture on top. Bake in oven at 350° for 25 to 30 minutes. Let stand for 10 minutes before serving.

      – JLA

OYSTERS ROCKEFELLER

1 stalk celery, chopped fine
4 bunches green onions,
    chopped fine
2 bunches parsley, chopped
    fine
5 oz. Worcestershire sauce

½ oz. Tabasco
6 oz. Herbsaint to taste
17 oz. butter (1 lb. and 1 oz.)
10 oz. bread crumbs
48 oysters

SAUCE:

Sauté everything except Herbsaint and bread crumbs in butter. Then add Herbsaint and bread crumbs to thicken. Open oysters. Place oysters on half-shell. Put about 1½ oz. of sauce on each oyster.
Bake in oven for about 5 minutes at 450°.
Serves 8.

– MR

LA TOURTE
DE CHEVREUIL CHAUDE
(Hot Venison Pâté in Croûte)

16 oz. diced venison
9 oz. venison, ground
14 oz. pork fat
3½ oz. goose liver
2 oz. chopped truffles
½ oz. truffle juice
10 oz. heavy cream
1 oz. salt

½ tbsp. 4 spice blend
3 tbsp. glace of game
3 oz. Cognac
2 oz. Madeira
1 oz. Porto
2 lbs. puff pastry dough (20
    circles, 4½-inch diameter
    and 1/16-inch thick)

Blend all ingredients together in mixing bowl. Roll dough about 1/16-inch thick and cut circles approximately 4½-inch in diameter. Place 3 ounces of pâté mix on each circle and brush with egg wash. Place a circle of dough on top, pressing sides together. Bake in 400° oven approximately 20 minutes and serve with Madeira Sauce.
10 portions.

– LED

CHAMPIGNON FARCI
AU CRABE JERRY

6 large white mushrooms
6 oz. lump crabmeat
2 serving spoons Russian
  dressing
½ tsp. curry powder
1 slice Swiss cheese, cut
  into 6 pieces

1 tsp. fresh chopped parsley
touch of Louisiana hot red
  sauce
1 lemon
1 serving spoon melted
  butter

Remove stem from mushrooms and wash with lemon juice. Place caps in buttered baking dish. Mix crabmeat, Russian dressing, Louisiana hot red sauce, curry powder, and parsley together. Fill mushrooms with mixture. Top with Swiss cheese. Spoon melted butter on top. Bake at 350° for 8 to 10 minutes.   – LED

CRABMEAT AND OYSTERS
AU GRATIN

1 lb. crabmeat
1 qt. oysters
2 tbsp. butter
½ onion, grated
1 tbsp. chopped green
  pepper

2 tbsp. flour
cream
lemon juice
salt
bread crumbs

Cook oysters in their liquor until edges curl; strain, reserving liquor. Sauté onion and green peppers lightly in butter. Add flour, oyster liquid, and enough cream to make a thick sauce. Season with salt and lemon; add oysters and crabmeat. Place in a baking dish, sprinkle with buttered crumbs, and bake until heated.   – LE

CRÊPES GALLANT

1 lb. country ham
2 cups chopped fresh
   mushrooms
2 shallots, finely chopped
1 cup dry sherry

2 bay leaves
¼ cup diced tomatoes
1 cup cream sauce
½ cup grated Swiss cheese
8 crêpes

Dice ham, blanch in water for 10 minutes. Drain. Cook mushrooms and shallots in butter until dry (about 10 minutes). Combine mushrooms, ham, and sherry, simmer and reduce with bay leaves until most of liquid is gone, then add diced tomatoes, cream sauce, and grated Swiss cheese. Roll into thin crêpes, and top with Mornay sauce.
    Serves 4.   – CK

BAKED OYSTERS ITALIAN STYLE

3 doz. fresh oysters
3 tbsp. parsley, finely
   chopped
3½ tbsp. soft bread crumbs

pepper and pinch of salt
olive oil
1 to 2 lemons

Open the oysters with an oyster knife. Arrange them on their half-shells in a fire-proof dish. Sprinkle generously with parsley, lightly with bread crumbs, and finish with salt and plenty of freshly ground pepper. Trickle a little olive oil over each oyster and bake in a slow oven (325°F.) for 10 or 15 minutes. Serve immediately, garnished with lemon wedges.
    Serves 6 to 12.   – GF

SHRIMP REMOULADE

2 cups mayonnaise
½ cup chopped sour
  pickles
1 tsp. prepared mustard

½ cup horseradish
½ tsp. minced parsley
½ tsp. tarragon
dash cayenne

Place mayonnaise in a bowl; add pickles; add other ingredients.
Boil shrimp 5 minutes. Remove shrimp; peel and clean. Dice shrimp into bite size pieces, place on bed of lettuce, and pour on generous amount of Remoulade sauce. – AL

Soups and Salads

BEEF WITH WATERCRESS SOUP

**6 oz. flank steak (cut in 1-
to 1½-inch strips)**
2 bunches watercress

1 qt. chicken broth
1 tbsp. light soy sauce
salt and pepper to taste

MARINADE:

¼ tsp. salt
1 tsp. cornstarch

1 tsp. light soy sauce
1 tsp. oil

Clean watercress thoroughly; discard roots. Cut watercress into 1-inch lengths. Marinate beef 20 to 30 minutes.

In saucepan, bring broth to a boil. Add beef and watercress. Cook until done. Then add soy sauce and salt and pepper to taste. Remove from heat and serve.   – TW

BRENNAN'S OYSTER SOUP

1 cup butter
**2 cups finely chopped
celery**
**1 cup finely chopped green
onion**
1¼ cups flour
**2 tbsp. finely chopped
garlic**
**4 doz. large, freshly
shucked oysters**

**12 cups oyster water (the
oyster liquor plus
sufficient water to make
up 12 cups)**
4 bay leaves
2 tsp. salt
1 tsp. white pepper

Melt the butter over medium heat in a 6-quart heavy saucepan, then sauté the celery and green onions until tender but not browned, stirring frequently. Gradually stir in the flour and cook 5 minutes longer, stirring constantly, over low heat. Add the remaining ingredients and simmer for 20 minutes. Remove the pan from the heat and scoop out the bay leaves with a slotted spoon or a long fork; discard. Serve immediately.

Serves eight.   – MR

STRACCIATELLA
(Egg-Cheese Soup)

3 eggs
4 tbsp. semolina (wheat
   flour)
4 tbsp. grated Parmesan
   cheese (or Romano)

7½ cups meat stock
freshly grated nutmeg and
   salt to taste
1 tsp. chopped parsley

Beat the eggs in a bowl with a good pinch of salt, the semolina, parsley, Parmesan, and nutmeg.

Dilute mixture with ladleful of cold stock.

Bring the remaining stock to a boil, pour in the egg mixture, and stir thoroughly, using wire whisk.

Lower the heat and simmer for 2 minutes, beating constantly. Serve boiling hot, with the beaten eggs just breaking up into strands.

Serves 6.   – GF

LERUTH'S CREAM OF
CAULIFLOWER AND GINGER SOUP

1 head cauliflower
4 tbsp. butter
4 tbsp. green onions
1 tbsp. flour
2 cups cream

⅛ cup ginger, chopped fine
4 slices bacon
nutmeg, salt, and white and
   red pepper to taste

Parboil cauliflower; set aside.

Sauté green onions in butter with salt, pepper, and nutmeg (do not brown). Add flour and cream; bring to boil. Add cauliflower and ginger and simmer until cauliflower is tender. Sauté bacon on the side, drain excess fat and crumble, and garnish soup.

Serves 6.   – LLL

CONFETTI SALAD

1 pkg. extra fine vermicelli
6 oz. French dressing
½ cup crisp sweet pickle
  juice
2 cloves garlic, minced
salt
dash of cayenne pepper

2 tbsp. chopped parsley
1 tbsp. poppy seed
1 tbsp. celery seed
½ tbsp. caraway seed
1 cup finely chopped celery
  hearts
1 bunch green onions,
  chopped

Cook vermicelli in boiling water with salt. Rinse and drain.
Put in large bowl and coat with dressing. Add pickle juice, garlic, salt, cayenne pepper, poppy seed, caraway seed, and celery seed. Marinate for a couple of hours. Before serving add celery, green onions, and parsley. Serve cold.
Serves 8.
                                                              – JLA

SPINACH SALAD
A LA RIVE GAUCHE

2 Cello bags fresh spinach
⅓ cup bacon drippings
2 tbsp. olive oil
¼ cup chopped shallots
¼ cup tarragon vinegar
2 tbsp. Creole or Dijon
  mustard
1 tbsp. sugar

1 tsp. Lea & Perrins
  Worcestershire sauce
1 cup thinly sliced fresh
  mushrooms
⅔ cup chopped crisp bacon
fresh ground pepper and salt
  to taste
4 tbsp. vodka or brandy

Wash spinach well and dry. Remove heavy stems. Sauté shallots in bacon drippings and olive oil. Add all ingredients except vodka or brandy and spinach. Stir and heat. Flambé with vodka or brandy and when flames lower, stir sauce into fresh spinach. Turn pan upside down over spinach for 2 minutes to wilt spinach slightly. Toss well and serve with quartered hard-boiled eggs as garnish.
Serves 4.
                                                              – LLL

MINESTRONE GENOVESE

7 pts. water
1⅓ cups pinto beans
  (frozen)
1 cup fresh string beans
salt to taste
2 stalks celery, diced
1 carrot, sliced
3 zucchini, sliced – if not
  available use squash
  (marrow)
3 large potatoes, peeled
  and diced

1 bunch collard greens or ½
  head of cabbage, sliced
½ cup olive oil
3 large tomatoes or one can
  plum tomatoes
1 cup Romano cheese,
  grated
¼ cup dried basil (if fresh is
  not available)
2 cloves garlic
½ lb. macaroni (any kind)

Bring the water to boil; add salt and olive oil and vegetables. Lower the heat and simmer for 35 minutes. Put the tomatoes, garlic, basil, and cheese in the blender and liquefy. Pour mixture into soup and stir. Take half of the vegetables and put into the blender and liquefy. This is to make the soup thicker. Continue cooking for another 30 minutes. Add the macaroni; cook 8 or 10 minutes. Serve soup. Sprinkle with cheese (Romano).

Serves 6 to 8.

– GF

CHICKEN SALAD THEODORE

4 cups diced poached
  chicken breasts
1¾ cups mayonnaise
½ cup diced fresh apples
½ cup seedless raisins

1 cup slivered blanched
  almonds
8 large leaves of romaine
  lettuce, rinsed, dried, and
  crisped in the refrigerator

Put all the ingredients except the lettuce in a mixing bowl and toss gently but thoroughly with a fork until well mixed. Cover the bowl and chill for about 20 minutes in the refrigerator. To serve, place a lettuce leaf on each plate, then top with ⅛ of the salad mixture. If desired, garnish with several sprigs of fresh parsley and a few tomato wedges.

Serves 8.

– MR

OYSTER AND TRUFFLE SOUP
A LA FRANCIS-RENÉ

This unique oyster soup was developed for Adler's. It is printed on a soup bowl set.

4 tbsp. butter
⅓ cup chopped green
  onions
¼ tsp. thyme
2 tbsp. flour
1 cup cook's milk (⅔ water,
  ⅓ whipping cream)
½ cup oyster liquor or clam
  juice

¾ tsp. salt
⅛ tsp. white pepper
Tabasco to taste
2 tbsp. chopped white or
  black truffle
1 tbsp. chopped parsley
18 small poached oysters

Poach oysters in their juice (barely bring to boil). Strain and save liquor and oysters.

Sauté green onions in butter with thyme. Stir in flour and cook for a minute or two. Add cook's milk and liquor from poached oysters. Add salt, pepper, Tabasco, and truffle. Bring to boil, add oysters, sprinkle with parsley, and serve immediately with tiny croutons that have been cooked in clarified butter.

Serves 4 to 6.   – LLL

RED SNAPPER SOUP

1 pt. tomato sauce
2 pts. fish stock
½ cup diced onion
1 cup diced celery
1 qt. brown sauce

1 cup diced red snapper
1 cup diced green pepper
2 tbsp. butter
sherry wine

Smother onions, celery, and green peppers in butter and add fish stock. Cook for 15 minutes; add red snapper; cook for 10 minutes. Then add tomato sauce and brown sauce, finishing just before serving with sherry wine.
                                                                 – LE

SEAFOOD GUMBO

1¼ cups vegetable oil
1 large white onion, finely
   chopped
2 stalks celery, finely
   chopped
5 to 6 cloves garlic, finely
   chopped
½ green pepper, finely
   chopped
4 sprigs fresh parsley, finely
   chopped
2 8-oz. cans tomato sauce
1 8-oz. can whole
   tomatoes, mashed

3 oz. Lea & Perrins
   Worcestershire sauce
2 cups water
4 lbs. fresh shrimp, peeled
   and deveined
4 hard-shell crabs, boiled
   and broken in half
1½ lbs. fresh okra, cut up
   (or 2 pkgs. frozen cut okra)
2 bay leaves, broken up
1½ tsp. salt
1 tsp. black pepper
½ lb. lump crabmeat

Put the oil in a heavy 6-quart aluminum pot. Add all the chopped vegetables except the okra and simmer over medium heat until the vegetables begin to get soft. Add the tomato sauce and the mashed whole tomatoes and simmer for a few minutes more. Then add the water, shrimp, crabs, okra, bay leaves, salt, pepper, and Lea & Perrins. Stir gently to mix. Cover and cook over low heat until the shrimp and okra are tender. Turn off the heat and leave the gumbo in the pot, covered. When you are ready to serve, turn the heat on low and add the lump crabmeat. Heat just until the gumbo and crabmeat are warmed through. Serve over boiled rice.

Serves 6 to 8.   – MR

SOUPE DE POISSON
(Fish Soup)

3 lbs. fish
1 lb. scallops
1 doz. hard-shell crabs
3 whites of leeks
½ head garlic, crushed
1 medium onion, chopped
6 ripe tomatoes, skinned
  and seeded
  or 3 tbsp. tomato paste

1 tbsp. fennel seed
bay leaf
thyme
1 lb. vermicelli
1 gal. water
1 cup olive oil
3 pinches saffron
Parmesan or Swiss cheese

Boil crabs in large pot.

In large heavy-duty pot, cook vegetables and spices (except saffron) in olive oil for few minutes. Add fish, scallops, and crabs for about 15 minutes.

Remove crabs from pot. Run remaining mixture through food processor. Run through strainer. Replace on fire. Add saffron and crab. Season to taste. Bring to boil. Add vermicelli. Serve with croutons and grated Parmesan or Swiss cheese.

Serves 6.   – CK

ESCARGOT SOUP

16 snails
4 tbsp. butter
4 shallots, minced
6 mushrooms
1 tsp. minced garlic

1½ qt. beef stock
½ cup cream
½ oz. Pernod
1 tbsp. chopped parsley

Mince 8 snails. In a saucepan, melt butter. Add shallots, mushrooms, garlic, and snails. Sauté 4 minutes. Add stock and cream. Cook 15 minutes. Strain and pour back in saucepan, seasoning with salt, white pepper to taste. Add 1 tablespoon chopped parsley and Pernod. Cover and simmer for 10 minutes. Slice the rest of the snails and use as garnish.

Serves 6.   – GP

OYSTER BROTH

½ gal. oysters
1 white onion
2 pieces celery (not whole
   stalk)
½ lb. butter

2 oz. flour
2 bay leaves
½ gal. water
salt and pepper to taste

Chop onion and celery, sauté together in pan with butter (do not brown). Add flour, water, and oysters. Bring to boil. Simmer 10 minutes. Strain and serve with parsley.
Serves 10.

– LE

L'ÉTOILE DE MELON
AU JAMBON FUMÉ

1 cantaloupe melon
3 oz. prosciutto ham, sliced
   thin
1 Boston lettuce (heart)
1 endive, julienned

1 oz. (1 small bunch)
   watercress
½ cup walnut oil
1 tbsp. raspberry vinegar
salt and pepper to taste

First peel the melon and cut in half. Then clean and seed. Take one half of the melon and cut 5 triangles in order to make a star shape.

Each melon triangle should then be wrapped with prosciutto ham slices, but be careful to leave the tip of each triangle exposed for color purposes. Set aside.

Clean and wash heart of Boston lettuce. Set aside. Clean and wash endive. Julienne and set aside. Clean and wash watercress. Set aside.

On a chilled salad plate, arrange heart of Boston lettuce, then arrange watercress around Boston lettuce. Display melon triangles wrapped in prosciutto ham slices around edge of plate in order to make star shape, and place julienne of endive in center of star. Replace in refrigerator to chill until serving time.

Mix together oil, vinegar, salt, and pepper for the dressing and pour over salad just before serving.

– LED

SOUPE GLACÉE A L'AVOCAT
(Avocado Soup)

3 avocados, very ripe
1 lemon
1 celery heart (white part),
  diced
2 tbsp. tomato paste
½ lb. Creole cream cheese

2 to 3 cups chicken broth
1 cup chopped chives or
  green onions
Tabasco sauce to taste
salt and pepper

Remove seed and skin of avocados. Put in bowl and squeeze lemon on them immediately. Place through food processor until smooth. Add tomato paste and cream cheese and mix well. Add salt, pepper, Tabasco, and celery. Dilute with chicken stock. Keep refrigerated until ready to serve. Sprinkle with chopped chives, and serve in a *cold* soup bowl. Serves 6.

– CK

CRÈME D'ASPERGE FRAICHE
(Fresh cream of asparagus soup)

24 fresh thin asparagus
  stalks
1 medium onion, chopped
1 cup flour

bay leaf
thyme
2 qts. chicken stock
1 cup cream

Remove approximately 4 inches from stem of asparagus. Use bottom. Wash thoroughly. Put through food processor, chopping coarsely. Sauté onion with a little butter, very lightly; do not brown. Add asparagus, flour, chicken stock, bay leaf, thyme. Cook for 45 minutes. Strain. Add cream to finish.

– CK

FISH SOUP

2 tbsp. olive oil
½ onion, chopped fine
1 small carrot, chopped
   fine
½ celery stalk, chopped
   fine
4 cloves garlic, chopped
   fine

½ cup chopped parsley
½ bay leaf
¼ tsp. thyme
¾ cup white wine
1½ qts. fish stock
1½ cups tomato puree
20 ounces redfish fillets with
   skin on and scaled

In a large saucepan, sauté the vegetables, parsley, garlic, thyme, and bay leaf in olive oil until tender. Add the white wine, fish stock, and tomato puree and boil. Add the diced redfish. Be sure the skin is on the fillets and they are free of scales. Cook for a few minutes and strain through a food mill. Pass the remainder through the food mill into the liquid. Bring this to a boil and season to taste with salt and pepper.

Note: Saffron can be added as an extra flavor, if desired. Croutons can be served with the soup. — RH

SHRIMP BISQUE

1 lb. shrimp
2 pieces celery
1 onion, diced
4 oz. butter
1 tsp. paprika
1 tbsp. tomato paste
4 oz. flour
1 qt. rich fish stock

1 bay leaf
1 clove
pinch thyme
2 peppercorns
sherry wine
dash brandy
½ cup heavy cream

Sauté shrimp in butter with celery and onion.

Add paprika and tomato paste. Now add flour and cook 5 minutes. Add rich fish stock (hot). Stir until smooth and add bay leaf, clove, thyme, and peppercorns.

Cook 1½ hours and finish with sherry wine, a dash of brandy, and heavy cream. — GP

SEAFOOD SAUCE PIQUANT

The sauce is best if made a day or so in advance without the shrimp. When ready to serve, bring the sauce to a boil and add the shrimp. You can substitute Cajun Magic Seafood Magic for the dry ingredients.

2 tbsp. unsalted butter
2¼ cups chopped onions
1½ cups chopped green
  bell peppers
¾ cup chopped celery
3 cups peeled and chopped
  tomatoes
1 cup canned tomato sauce
2 tbsp. minced jalapeño
  peppers (see Note)
2 bay leaves
5½ tsp. ground red pepper
  (preferably cayenne)
1½ tsp. white pepper
1 tsp. black pepper

1½ tsp. minced garlic
2¼ cups Basic Seafood
  Stock (recipe follows)
1½ tbsp. dark brown sugar
¾ tsp. salt
½ lb. peeled large shrimp
¾ lb. firm-fleshed fish
  fillets, cut into bite-size
  pieces
½ lb. crabmeat (picked over)
2 doz. (about 1 lb.) medium
  to large oysters in their
  liquor
4 cups hot Basic Cooked
  Rice (recipe follows)

Note: Fresh jalapeños are preferred; if you have to use pickled ones, rinse as much vinegar from them as possible.

Melt the butter in a 4-quart saucepan over high heat. Add the onions, bell peppers, and celery; sauté about 2 minutes, stirring occasionally. Add the tomatoes, tomato sauce, jalapeños, bay leaves, ground peppers, and garlic; stir well. Continue cooking about 3 minutes, stirring often and scraping the pan bottom well. Stir in the stock, sugar, and salt and bring to a boil. Reduce heat and simmer until flavors are married, about 20 minutes, stirring often and scraping the pan bottom well. (If mixture scorches, quit stirring and pour mixture into a clean pot, leaving the scorched ingredients in the first pan.)

Add the shrimp to the hot (or reheated) sauce and stir. Turn heat up to high, cover pan, and bring mixture to a boil. Add the fish, crabmeat, and undrained oysters. Remove from heat. Let sit covered for 10 minutes. (Meanwhile, heat the serving plates in a 250-degree oven.) Stir, remove bay leaves, and serve immediately.

To serve, mound ½ cup rice in the center of each heated serving plate; then pour about ½ cup sauce around the rice and arrange about 8 shrimp on top of the sauce.

Serves 8.

Lagniappe: "Piquant" to a Cajun means "it's hot and 'hurts like a sticker in your tongue.' " If you want less "piquant," reduce the jalapeño peppers by half. Sauce Piquant is enjoyed with such gusto in Louisiana that the town of Raceland has a Sauce Piquant Festival every year dedicated to nothing but fish, meat, fowl, and seafood made with variations of this sauce.

BASIC SEAFOOD STOCK

about 2 qts. cold water
1½ to 2 lbs. rinsed shrimp
heads and/or shells or
crab shells (2½ to 3 qts.),
rinsed fish carcasses
(heads and gills
removed), or any
combination of these

1 medium onion, unpeeled
and quartered
1 rib celery
1 large clove garlic,
unpeeled and quartered

Place all ingredients in a large saucepan; bring to a boil over high heat; reduce heat and simmer gently at least 4 hours, replenishing water as needed to keep about 1½ quarts of liquid in the pan. Strain, cool and refrigerate until ready to use. (*Note:* Remember, if you are short on time, that using a stock simmered 20 or 30 minutes is far better than using just water in any recipe.) Makes about 1½ quarts.   – PP

BASIC COOKED RICE

If you make this ahead of time and store it, omit the bell peppers as they tend to sour quickly. Use chicken stock if you are serving the rice with a chicken dish, seafood stock with a seafood dish, beef stock with a beef dish.

2 cups uncooked rice
  (preferably converted)
2½ cups Basic Stock
1½ tbsp. very finely
  chopped onions
1½ tbsp. very finely
  chopped celery
1½ tbsp. very finely
  chopped green bell
  peppers

1½ tbsp. unsalted butter
  (preferred) or margarine,
  melted
½ tsp. salt
⅛ tsp. garlic powder
a pinch each of white
  pepper, ground red pepper
  (preferably cayenne), and
  black pepper

In a 5-inch by 9-inch by 2½-inch loaf pan, combine all ingredients; mix well. Seal pan snugly with aluminum foil. Bake at 350° until rice is tender, about 1 hour 10 minutes. Serve immediately. However, you can count on the rice staying hot for 45 minutes and warm for 2 hours. To reheat leftover rice, either use a double boiler or warm the rice in a skillet with unsalted butter.

Makes 6 cups.
—PP

OYSTER CHOWDER

1 bell pepper
1 onion
2 stalks celery
1 clove garlic
1½ qts. oyster water
roux
¼ tsp. thyme

1 bay leaf
1 cup diced oysters
  (blanched)
1 cup diced potatoes
¼ pt. whipping cream
salt and pepper

Finely dice the pepper, onion, celery, and garlic and cook in water and a little oyster water until completely tender and dry.

Add oyster water and thicken with roux, 1 tablespoon at a time, until chowder is desired thickness. Add bay leaf and thyme and cook until there is no flour taste from the roux.

Add diced oysters, potatoes, and cream and salt and pepper to taste.
—RH

MIXED GREEN SALAD
WITH HOT CHICKEN LIVERS

½ lb. chicken livers
2 shallots
brandy
salad greens
½ cup Balsamic Red Wine
  Vinegar

1½ cups walnut oil
1 tbsp. finely chopped
  French shallots
1 tbsp. Dijon mustard
salt and pepper

Wash and tear the salad greens. Drain and chill them. Make a vinaigrette with vinegar, oil, chopped shallots, mustard, salt, and pepper.

Clean chicken livers. Cut them into bite-size pieces and put them in a strainer to drain out the excess liquid.

Chop 2 shallots and sauté the livers with the shallots in butter over high heat. Be sure not to overcook the livers. When the livers are almost ready, flame them with a touch of brandy. When the flames subside, spoon the livers over the salad.

Toss the greens in a bowl with the vinaigrette prior to topping them with the livers. Garnish the salad with marigold or nasturtiums and cracked black peppercorns.

Note: Duck livers can be substituted for chicken livers.

Serves 6.

– RH

SOUPE AU CHOU-FLEUR

1 cauliflower
1½ oz. double cream
2 tsp. cumin
2 egg yolks

salt and pepper
parsley
croutons

Blanch the cauliflower in a pot of boiling water for 30 minutes. Remove from the water and drain. Plunge into 3½ pints of boiling water, seasoned with salt, pepper, and the cumin. Cook for a further 30 minutes. Pass this soup through a vegetable mill. Blend the cream with the egg yolks and add to the soup just before serving.

Serve with croutons and parsley.

– LED

POTAGE CRÈME D'ASPERGES
(Cream of Asparagus Soup)

¼ lb. butter
1½ cups chopped
  asparagus pieces (fresh)
1 small onion, chopped
½ tbsp. chopped garlic
¼ lb. all-purpose flour
3 cups chicken stock (or
  asparagus water)

juice of ½ lemon
salt and white pepper to
  taste
1 cup heavy cream (whipping
  cream)

Melt butter in a soup pot. Add asparagus, onion, and garlic and cook (do not brown) for 5 minutes.

Add flour and cook, stirring occasionally, for 10 minutes.

Pour in stock, lemon juice, salt, and pepper, blend well, and simmer 15 to 20 minutes.

Add cream, then return to near boiling.

Garnish each soup cup (or bowl) with a spoonful of freshly whipped cream and fresh chopped parsley.

Serves 4. — GP

LEEK SOUP

1 lb. leeks
1 qt. chicken stock
½ onion
2 oz. butter
2 oz. flour

1 bay leaf
1 clove
pinch thyme
1 cup heavy cream
salt and pepper

Take leeks and separate the green part from the white part. Combine the greens with chicken stock and simmer for 1½ hours.

Strain off greens. Slice white part of leeks about ⅛-inch thick. Also dice up onion. Sauté both in butter and flour. Cook about 2 minutes. Now add hot stock and stir until smooth.

Add bay leaf, clove, pinch of thyme.

Simmer 1½ hours and add salt and pepper to taste.

Finish with heavy cream. — GP

TURTLE SOUP

3 lbs. turtle meat
5 qts. water
2 bay leaves
2 tsp. Italian seasoning
½ cup chopped white onion
½ cup finely chopped green pepper
½ cup finely chopped celery
1½ cups finely chopped parsley
1 lemon, thinly sliced

1 tsp. paprika
½ cup tomato paste
1 tsp. caramel color (or Kitchen Bouquet)
¼ cup Worcestershire sauce
1 cup sherry
1 cup flour
¾ cup butter
salt
1 tsp. black pepper
2 cups finely chopped hard-boiled eggs

In a large saucepan or kettle combine the turtle meat, water, bay leaves, Italian seasoning, and 1 tablespoon salt. Bring to a boil over high heat, then lower the heat slightly and cook until the turtle meat is quite tender. Add more water while cooking as necessary to maintain about 3 quarts of liquid at all times. Strain and reserve the 3 quarts of stock. Cut the turtle meat into small cubes and set aside.

Add all chopped vegetables, lemon slices, paprika, tomato paste, caramel color, Worcestershire sauce, and sherry to stock in a large saucepan. Cook over low heat for 20 minutes or until vegetables are very tender.

In a separate pan, add flour to melted butter, stirring to a smooth consistency. Add this roux to stock while stirring, along with turtle meat, salt, pepper, and eggs. Simmer for 15 minutes and serve at once.

Makes 8 servings.

– MR

LENORMAND CRAWFISH BISQUE
A LA SAINT MARTINVILLE

Marin Joseph Lenormand was one of the first settlers of St. Martinville. The great-granddaughter of M. J. Lenormand was Darcey Lenormand Leruth, who was the great-great-grandmother of Laurence and Lee Leruth, Warren Leruth's sons who are the chefs at LeRuth's Restaurant in Gretna, La.

30 LBS. FRESH CRAWFISH
(alive and kicking) serves
10 to 12

Wash really well. Steam crawfish for 5 minutes in a Cajun bouquet (onion, garlic, bay leaves, hot red pepper, thyme, etc.). Cool. Peel crawfish tails; retain fat from heads. Save large claws. Clean heads to be stuffed and added to final bisque. Always remove eyes. Crawfish tail meat should be 2½ to 3 lbs. net.

STUFFING FOR HEADS

Take about one third of the crawfish tails (meat only) and grind with ⅛-inch plate. Set aside.

½ lb. butter
6 branches celery, chopped
5 toes garlic, chopped
1 bunch green onion,
  chopped

1 large onion, chopped
¾ of all the crawfish fat
  saved from heads
salt, black pepper, and red
  pepper to taste

Sauté seasonings in butter really well. Add crawfish and simmer to reduce by half, then cool. Make a paste with 4 eggs, 1 cup milk, and enough bread crumbs to make a paste. Add cooked seasonings and ground crawfish tails and crawfish fat to the paste. Stuff cleaned heads with stuffing. Then dip heads in egg wash (1 egg and ¼ cup milk) and roll in flour. Place in greased baking pan and bake at 450° till browned. Set aside, as the stuffed heads will be added later to the bisque.

BISQUE

½ cup salad oil
1¼ cups flour
2 large onions, chopped
4 toes garlic, chopped
remainder of crawfish fat
from heads (this is
important for flavor)

salt, red and black pepper to
taste
remainder of crawfish tails
from first step
stuffed heads and large
claws

Make a brown roux. Add onions and garlic just before the roux is complete. Then add the fat from crawfish heads and 8 cups water. Simmer for 30 minutes with cover. Add balance of tails, stuffed heads, and claws and return to boil. Serve.

Serves 10 to 12.

– WL

WAR WON-TON SOUP

40 Won Ton wrappings
6 oz. small shrimp
8 oz. pork (lean or roast)
3 oz. water chestnuts,
minced

1 egg white
8 cups chicken stock

SEASONING:

¾ tsp. salt
¼ tsp. white pepper
¼ tsp. garlic powder

1 tbsp. sesame seed oil
1 tbsp. light soy sauce
1 tbsp. cornstarch

Shell and devein shrimp; cut shrimp into small pieces. Mince pork until very fine.

Mix shrimp, pork, water chestnuts, egg white, and seasoning well. Wrap final product into Won Ton wrappings and fry until golden and crispy.

Bring soup stock to a boil; add meat and vegetables desired. Place the Won Ton in individual soup bowls and pour hot soup over them. Top with green onion.

– TW

LERUTH'S "BACK-OF-THE-HOUSE" GUMBO

This rich gumbo is served five or six times a year to the cooking staff at 4:30 P.M. in LeRuth's kitchen. It is served as an entrée dish with rice.

½ lb. smoked slab bacon, diced
½ cup salad oil
4 branches celery, chopped
2 large onions, chopped
1 bunch green onions, chopped
4 toes garlic, chopped
1 small bell pepper, chopped
1½ tsp. thyme
2 fresh bay leaves
3 tbsp. tomato paste

¾ lb. fresh okra, chopped
2 lbs. headless shrimp (26 to 30 count) boiled in 1½ qts. water (shrimp stock)
brown roux (1 cup salad oil and 2½ cups flour)
3 tbsp. chopped parsley
salt and pepper to taste
1 lb. fresh lump crabmeat
Tabasco sauce

To make brown roux, mix together 1 cup salad oil and 2½ cups flour. Brown in 425-degree oven for 1 hour. Stir every 15 minutes. Cool and store in plastic cup. Refrigerate leftover for other needs.

Cook bacon and remove cooled bacon. Sauté okra well in bacon drippings until there are no signs of sliminess. Remove okra from pot. Heat salad oil and sauté all chopped seasonings and herbs really well. Add tomato paste and sauté a minute or two. Add shrimp stock, cooked bacon, and okra. Bring to boil and thicken with brown roux to desired consistency. Cover and simmer for about 1 hour. Add peeled shrimp, parsley and lump crabmeat. Adjust salt and pepper and add a little Tabasco. Serve with freshly steamed rice.

Serves 6 to 8.

– WL

HOT AND SOUR SOUP

¼ lb. pork
4 dried Chinese black
  mushrooms
1 tsp. dried mo-er
  mushrooms
14 tiger lily buds
¼ cup bamboo shoots
1 square fresh bean curd

2 tbsp. plus 1 tsp.
  cornstarch
1 tsp. soy sauce
1 egg, beaten
5 cups soup stock
1 small green onion, finely
  chopped
1 tsp. sesame seed oil

SEASONING:

1½ tbsp. light soy sauce
2½ tbsp. red wine vinegar
½ tsp. black pepper

salt to taste
1 tsp. chili oil or 1 tsp. red
  hot pepper flakes

Cut pork into matchstick-sized shreds. Marinate with 1 teaspoon of soy sauce and 1 teaspoon of cornstarch.

Soak Chinese mushrooms and lily buds in 1 cup of hot water for 20 minutes. Then rinse, drain, and shred mushrooms. Cut tiger lily buds into 1-inch lengths. The bean curd is to be cut into shreds.

Heat soup stock until boiling and add pork and mix with chopsticks. While soup is boiling, add the mushrooms, lily buds, bamboo shoots, bean curd, and green onion.

Add the seasoning and boil for 2 more minutes, stirring a few times.

To thicken, add remaining cornstarch mixed with 3 teaspoons water. Pour in beaten egg. Sprinkle in sesame seed oil. — TW

FRUIT SALAD DRESSING

½ cup honey
1 cup sugar
2 tsp. paprika
2 tsp. dry mustard
½ tsp. salt

1 tsp. celery seed
1 tbsp. lemon juice
½ cup white vinegar
1½ cups salad oil

Add oil slowly to other ingredients and beat well. — WL

BOUILLABAISSE

⅓ cup olive oil
1 onion, finely sliced
3 cloves garlic, chopped
½ bay leaf
¼ tsp. thyme
⅛ tsp. powdered anise
1 tomato, peeled, seeds removed, and crushed
1½ qts. white wine

1¼ qts. fish stock
16 shrimp (cooked if frozen), peeled
12 oysters
¼ lb. crabmeat or gumbo crabs
8 fish fillets (trout, redfish, etc.)
¼ tsp. powdered saffron

Heat ⅓ cup of olive oil in very large skillet and add 1 finely sliced onion. Sauté onion slices for a few minutes on medium fire until transparent. Then add garlic, bay leaf, thyme, anise, tomato, wine, and stock.

Simmer uncovered until onions are tender (about 15 to 20 minutes). Then add shrimp, oysters, crabmeat, and fish fillets.

Continue to simmer until the fish fillets are tender. Do not overcook the fish fillets! Add saffron. Serve the bouillabaisse immediately, very hot, in large soup plates with toasted garlic bread rounds and rouille in separate plates. Add some rouille to enhance the flavor of the bouillabaisse.

GARLIC BREAD ROUNDS:

Cut some French bread into ¼-inch rounds (about 6 pieces per person), baste with olive oil and finely chopped garlic, and toast on a tray under broiler until light brown.

ROUILLE:

Make a regular mayonnaise using 3 egg yolks (at room temperature) and 1 pint olive oil. Add 1 heaping teaspoon chopped garlic and ¾ teaspoon cayenne pepper.

Serves 4 to 6.

– RH

THOUSAND ISLAND DRESSING

1 cup mayonnaise
½ cup catsup
¾ cup sweet pickle relish

½ tsp. Lea & Perrins
Worcestershire sauce
2 chopped hard-boiled eggs

Mix well and refrigerate.

– WL

"CINCINNATI" CHILI (1955)

This chili recipe was served in the dining room for management employees of Proctor and Gamble in Ivorydale, Ohio.

15 lbs. lean ground
hamburger (¼-inch plate)
3 lbs. white suet (¼-inch
plate)
3 lbs. chopped onion
½ lb. chopped bell pepper
¾ cup salt
½ cup sugar

1 tbsp. black pepper
½ tsp. cayenne pepper
½ cup chili powder
2 tbsp. ground cumin
2 #10 cans tomato puree
1 gal. beef stock
4 #10 cans red kidney beans

Sauté meat, suet, and seasonings. Add spices, puree, and stock and simmer for 1½ hours with cover. Add beans and thicken to desired consistency with flour or cracker meal. Adjust salt and pepper.

Usually served with chopped raw onions and shredded Cheddar cheese on the side.

Serves about 100.

TEXAS CHILI POWDER

76 ozs. ground dried chili
peppers
13 ozs. ground cumin
4 ozs. garlic powder
2 ozs. onion powder

3 ozs. ground oregano
½ oz. cayenne pepper
1½ ozs. black pepper
½ oz. ground coriander

Blend well. Makes 100 ounces.

– WL

TURTLE SOUP

2 lbs. turtle meat
2 large onions, chopped
1 cup celery, chopped
1 clove garlic, finely
chopped
4 medium-sized bay leaves
1 cup tomato sauce
3 tbsp. flour

3 tbsp. Wesson oil
1 wine glass of sherry
1 tbsp. Worcestershire sauce
½ lemon, sliced
3 hard-cooked eggs
parsley
salt and pepper to taste

Prepare turtle meat, season with salt and pepper, and fry in oil until brown. Remove from fat and add flour, browning slowly until golden. Add onions, celery, and garlic and cook until tender. Return the turtle meat to the pot, add the tomato sauce and 1 cup of water and cook about 30 minutes. Add lemon, bay leaves and 2 quarts of water and simmer for 1 hour, or until soup has reduced to desired thickness. Add parsley, sherry, and Worcestershire sauce. Place slices of hard-cooked eggs (sprinkled with paprika) in soup plates before serving.
Serves 6. – LE

BAHAMIAN CHOWDER

1 tbsp. chopped parsley
and stems
1 medium carrot
2 green onions, sliced
1 small green bell pepper
1 small stalk of celery
1 small onion
1 large bay leaf
1 small garlic toe
1 medium tomato, peeled
and sliced
2 tbsp. olive oil

1 tbsp. flour
2 tbsp. tomato paste
½ cup dry white wine
1½ qts. good fish stock
4 oz. peeled shrimp
4 oz. fish (redfish, catfish,
etc.)
⅓ tsp. thyme leaves
cayenne pepper, salt, and
ground black pepper to
taste

Bring all ingredients to boil and simmer for 10 minutes.
Serves 6 to 8. – WC

BIBB LETTUCE AND MUSHROOM SALAD WITH VERMOUTH DRESSING

2 heads Boston bibb
  lettuce
1 cup sliced fresh
  mushrooms

⅓ cup salad oil
2 tbsp. dry vermouth
¼ tsp. salt

Break cleaned bibb lettuce to desired size. Arrange sliced fresh mushrooms over lettuce. Pour over dressing and gently toss.

Leruth created this recipe for Les Amis du Vin because they wanted to have wine with salad without having the acidity from vinegar or lemon spoil the flavor of a delicate wine.

Serves 4.

– WL

SWEET & SOUR CELERY SEED DRESSING

3 tbsp. catsup
2 tbsp. white vinegar
1 tbsp. sugar
¼ tsp. salt
¼ cup light corn syrup

2 tsp. steak sauce
2 tbsp. water
1 tsp. onion juice
¼ tsp. whole celery seeds
3 tbsp. corn oil

Mix well and refrigerate.

– WL

COLE SLAW DRESSING

1 egg
½ cup white vinegar
⅔ cup sugar
2 tbsp. yellow mustard

1 tsp. salt
2 tbsp. finely chopped onion
1 cup corn oil
¼ tsp. Tabasco

Place ingredients in blender and mix 1 minute on medium speed. Optional – add ½ teaspoon whole celery seeds after mixing.

– WL

FILÉ GUMBO

½ lb. margarine
1 rib celery, chopped
4 sprigs parsley, finely
  chopped
1 onion, finely chopped
½ cup flour
1 gal. shellfish stock
½ lb. smoked ham, diced
6 crabs, in shells

½ lb. Creole hot sausage,
  cut in bite-size pieces
½ lb. smoked sausage, cut
  in bite-size pieces
½ lb. shrimp, cleaned and
  shelled (reserve shells for
  stock)
salt and pepper
2 tbsp. filé powder

Place margarine at bottom of a large soup or seafood pot; add celery, parsley and onions. Sauté and then simmer for 15 to 20 minutes over low heat. Add flour and stir constantly for 15 more minutes. Add stock and heat over medium flame for 20 minutes. Stir in ham, crabs, and pieces of sausage, and cook for 30 minutes. Bring to a boil and keep stirring to avoid mixture sticking. When pot returns to boil, add shrimp, salt, pepper and filé powder and allow to return to the boiling point again. Remove from heat and check seasoning, adding more if needed.
Serves 10 to 12.

– AL

POTATO SALAD

1 lb. Idaho potatoes
3 hard-boiled eggs
1 rib celery
4 sprigs parsley, chopped
½ cup mayonnaise

2 tbsp. prepared yellow
  mustard
1 onion, diced
¼ cup cooking oil
salt and pepper to taste

Peel and dice potatoes and boil until tender, approximately ½ hour. Cool potatoes for ½ to 1 hour. Chop eggs, celery, and parsley. Place potatoes in mixing bowl. Add eggs and seasonings (celery and parsley). Stir in mayonnaise and mustard, onion, oil, salt, and pepper. Mix all ingredients until well blended.
Serves 4.

– AL

TURTLE SOUP

4 lbs. turtle meat
1 cup butter
3 cups chopped white
  onion
1 cup flour
½ cup tomato puree
10 cups turtle stock
1 cup sherry
½ cup Worcestershire
  sauce

1 green pepper, finely
  chopped
1 tbsp. salt
1 tsp. black pepper
¼ cup paprika
3 hard-boiled eggs, finely
  chopped
1 cup finely chopped parsley
1 lemon, thinly sliced

COURTBOUILLON FOR COOKING TURTLE MEAT:

4 qts. water
2 bay leaves

2 tsp. cayenne
2 tbsp. salt

In a large saucepan or kettle combine the turtle meat and the ingredients for the courtbouillon. Bring to a boil over high heat, then lower the heat slightly and cook until the turtle meat is quite tender. Add more water during cooking as necessary to maintain about 3 quarts of liquid at all times. Strain and reserve the stock. Cut the turtle into small cubes.

Melt the butter in a heavy kettle over medium heat. Add the onion and sauté until glazed and transparent. Gradually stir in the flour, mixing thoroughly, and continue cooking and stirring until the flour is browned. Add the tomato puree and cook 5 minutes longer, then add the turtle stock, sherry, Worcestershire sauce, green pepper, salt, pepper, and paprika. Stir to mix thoroughly and cook over low heat for 25 minutes more. Then add the turtle meat and chopped egg. Simmer for another 15 minutes. Remove the pan from the heat and stir in the parsley and lemon slices. Serve at once.

Serves 8.

– MR

SALAD DRESSING A LA PROVENCE

1 oz. garlic
3 oz. anchovies
3 oz. prepared mustard
4 eggs
2 tbsp. oregano

½ cup wine vinegar
½ cup lemon juice
salt and pepper
4 cups salad oil

Blend together garlic and anchovies, then add mustard, eggs, and oregano. Mix well, then add vinegar, lemon juice, and salt and pepper. Slowly add salad oil.

– CK

ZUPPA DI FAGIOLI
(Bean Soup)

1½ cups dried white beans
4 potatoes, peeled
2 carrots, chopped
2 onions, chopped
2 tbsp. tomato paste

½ lb. bacon ring or salt pork
¼ cup olive oil
salt, ground pepper, dash
   olive oil
12 slices of bread, toasted

Soak the beans overnight. The following morning, in a large enameled cast iron casserole put the bacon ring or salt pork, onions, and oil. Sauté until the onions are golden. Add beans, whole potatoes, carrots, tomato paste, and water. Bring to a boil, reduce the heat and simmer gently for about 3 hours. The salt should be added. Remove the potatoes and two-thirds of the beans with a slotted spoon and put through a food mill back into the pot. Before removing the soup from the stove, test it for seasoning, grind in some pepper, and add dash of olive oil. Serve the soup from the pot together with slices of toast.
Serves 6.

– GF

BUTTERMILK DRESSING

1 cup mayonnaise
1 cup buttermilk
½ tsp. onion salt
½ tsp. garlic salt
1 tsp. coarsely ground
   black pepper

1 tsp. M.S.G.
½ tsp. parsley flakes
2 tbsp. finely chopped
   onions

Stir well and refrigerate.   – WL

ITALIAN DRESSING

3 to 4 garlic toes, chopped
¼ tsp. oregano
pinch red pepper flakes
¼ cup white vinegar

½ cup plus 2 tbsp. corn oil
1½ tsp. salt
1½ tsp. sugar
3 tbsp. water

Place ingredients in bottle and shake well. Make one day in advance
(refrigerate).
For Italian Gorgonzola Dressing add 2 ounces crumbled Gorgonzola
cheese to above recipe.   – WL

AVOCADO DRESSING

1 mashed ripe avocado
1½ cups mayonnaise
1 lemon, juice only
1 toe garlic, chopped

1 tsp. salt
¼ tsp. crushed black pepper
½ tsp. anchovy paste
¼ cup whipping cream

Mix well and refrigerate.   – WL

EGGPLANT SOUP

4 tbsp. butter
3 cups diced onions
3 cups diced celery
3 cups diced potatoes
4 medium eggplants, diced
pinch thyme

pinch sweet basil
1 level tsp. curry (very
   important not to add more
   than called for)
2 qts. chicken stock
1 qt. whipping cream

In a 3-quart saucepan, sauté onions, celery, eggplants and potatoes in butter. Add curry, thyme, and sweet basil. Cook until potatoes are done and ingredients begin to stick to bottom of pan. Add chicken stock and continue cooking until the mixture begins to thicken. This will take about 45 minutes on a quick simmer. Remove from heat and with a wire whisk stir in cream. Serve immediately.

If you reheat this soup, reheat in a double boiler.
Serves 8.

– PP

OYSTER AND ARTICHOKE SOUP

½ gal. oysters and oyster
   water
1 white onion, chopped
1 lb. butter
2 stalks celery, chopped
3 small cans artichoke
   hearts

1 gal. water
2 bay leaves
8 oz. flour
1 tbsp. chicken base
dash of salt and pepper
dash of thyme

Sauté onions and celery in butter for 5 minutes. Add flour and cook for 5 minutes. Add oysters and water, artichoke hearts, salt, pepper, thyme, and chicken base, and cook for 45 minutes. Skim off top of soup.
Serves 20.

– LE

CRABMEAT SALAD

2 cups crabmeat, fresh-
   cooked or canned
3 tbsp. finely chopped
   green pepper

1 cup celery, minced
½ cup shallots, minced
½ tbsp. minced fresh parsley
½ cup mayonnaise

Combine crabmeat and all seasonings (pepper, celery, shallots, and parsley). Season to taste and chill. Drain and add enough mayonnaise to moisten. This recipe may be used for shrimp and tuna.

Serve in tomato, avocado, or lettuce cups; top with strip of pimento. Garnish with wedge of lemon.

Serves 4 to 6.
         – AL

SOUP DE POISSON
A LA PROVENÇALE

½ cup olive oil
2 shallots, chopped
4 leeks (white part only),
   chopped
1 medium onion, chopped
2 branches fresh parsley
6 ripe tomatoes (cut into
   eighths)
6 large garlic cloves,
   smashed

4 bay leaves
1 tsp. thyme
1 tbsp. fresh fennel
peel of ½ orange
1 tsp. crushed pepper
1½ gals. water
3 ¾-lb. scraps of fish
2 squid
6 fresh crabs, chopped
5 medium potatoes, sliced

Cook shallots, leeks, onion, and parsley in olive oil until transparent. Add tomatoes and continue cooking over medium-high flame. Add garlic, bay leaves, thyme, fennel, orange peel, and pepper. Reduce for 10 minutes over medium-high flame. Add water, fish, squid, crabs, and potatoes. Cook for 1 hour over medium flame.

Serves 20.
         – CK

SOUPE DE CRABE SAFFRANE

INGREDIENTS FOR THE STOCK:

1 onion
2 stalks celery
2 whites of leek
1 carrot
4 cloves garlic
2 stems parsley
3 oz. olive oil

3 crab shells, cleaned and
   cut into pieces
1 lb. fish bones
2 qts. water
1 qt. whipping cream
1 dash bouquet garni

INGREDIENTS FOR THE SOUP:

1 generous pinch saffron
3 tomatoes
1 bunch green onions
1 carrot
2 stalks celery

1 sprig fennel
2 lbs. lump crabmeat
salt and pepper
cayenne pepper

PREPARING THE STOCK:

Wash vegetables, garlic, and parsley; dice and briefly sauté in olive oil in large sauté pan. Stir in shells and bones and cover. Heat for 5 minutes. Pour this into deep pan with water, cream, and bouquet garni and stir together. Partially cover and cook over high heat for 20 minutes. Carefully strain finished stock. Place aside 1½ quarts for the soup. The rest may be frozen for later use.

PREPARING THE VEGETABLES FOR THE SOUP:

Remove skins and seeds from tomatoes, dice, and squeeze off the juice. Place aside. Wash, then make a very fine julienne of the green onions, carrot, celery, and fennel. Place with tomatoes.

PREPARING THE SOUP:

Bring 1½ quarts of stock to boil, add saffron and boil for 5 minutes. Add vegetable preparation and crabmeat. Add salt, pepper, and cayenne to taste. Boil for 3 minutes (do not overcook).   — CK

CREOLE SEAFOOD GUMBO

3 whole crabs
1 lb. large shrimp
1 whole bell pepper
2 stalks celery
1 medium whole white
   onion
3 oz. shortening
6 oz. flour
⅓ tbsp. pepper

⅓ tbsp. thyme
1 tbsp. salt
1 tbsp. Lea and Perrins
   Worcestershire sauce
2 bay leaves
a dash of cayenne
½ pt. canned tomatoes
1 can okra

Peel shrimp and boil the hulls in ½ gallon of water. Remove shell from crab and clean away "deadmen" on sides and sandbag under mouth. Clean and chop your vegetables.

Using ingredients above, make a roux by heating 3 oz. shortening. When hot, add 6 oz. flour and stir. When roux becomes dark brown, add vegetables and stir constantly as you cook them a few minutes to reduce moisture. Then add the raw shrimp, the crabmeat, which should be fried in butter first, and your seasonings. Strain liquor from the hulls of the shrimp and add to roux mixture. Add the tomatoes and bring to a boil. Reduce heat and simmer for 2½ hours. Then add okra, but cut the hard ends off the okra first. Since the okra is already cooked before canning, there is no need to bake it first. It should be cut up fine before you add it to the gumbo. Cook another half hour or until the gumbo is thickened to the consistency you like it. Freeze if desired.
Serves 20.   — LE

GREEN GODDESS DRESSING

1 cup mayonnaise
  (homemade)
1 cup sour cream
½ cup whipping cream
5 sprigs parsley, chopped
3 tops green onions,
  chopped

2 toes garlic, chopped
1 tbsp. anchovy paste
1 tsp. salt
½ tsp. white pepper

Combine all ingredients.
Few people know that Leruth developed Green Goddess under the Seven Seas Label.   – WL

FRENCH DRESSING BELLE RIVES

⅔ cup peanut oil
⅔ cup olive oil
3 tbsp. wine vinegar

2 tsp. salt
1 tsp. white pepper
1 tsp. oregano

Blend together. Can be made in advance.   – WL

CHINESE SALAD DRESSING

3 oz. red wine vinegar
½ oz. vodka
2 tbsp. light soy sauce
3 tbsp. peanut oil
1½ tsp. sesame seed oil
1½ tbsp. sesame paste
½ tbsp. peanut butter

1 tsp. Worcestershire sauce
1 egg yolk
½ tsp. black pepper
¼ tsp. salt
3 tbsp. sugar
1½ tsp. powdered mustard

Mix together until blended well.   – TW

CREAM OF FRESH CELERY SOUP

¼ lb. butter
1 cup or more chopped
  celery with leaves
1 small chopped onion
1 tbsp. chopped garlic

¼ lb. all-purpose flour
2 cups beef broth
1 cup water
salt and pepper to taste
1 cup heavy cream

Melt butter in soup pot. Add celery, onion, and garlic and cook for 5 minutes (do not brown). Add flour; cook for 10 minutes. Pour in broth, water, salt and pepper; blend well, then simmer 15 minutes. Add cream, then return to boiling. Simmer 10 minutes. Serve with fresh chopped parsley and a fresh grating of nutmeg.
  Serves 4.   – GP

RUSSIAN DRESSING

⅔ cup mayonnaise
½ cup chili sauce
1½ tbsp. chopped green
  pepper
1 tbsp. chopped pimento

1 tbsp. chopped onion
1 tbsp. sugar
1 tbsp. vinegar
¼ tsp. Lea & Perrins
  Worcestershire sauce

Mix well and refrigerate.   – WL

TARTAR SAUCE

1 cup mayonnaise
½ cup chopped dill pickle
¼ cup chopped onion

2 tbsp. chopped parsley
Tabasco to taste

Mix well and refrigerate.   – WL

BOUILLABAISSE

4 medium carrots, sliced
2 onions, sliced
6 pieces celery, sliced
2 leeks (white parts only),
  sliced
2 fennel roots, if available
2 tbsp. tomato paste
1 cup brandy
2 cups white wine
3 tomatoes, peeled and
  seeded
½ tsp. finely chopped
  garlic

pinch presoaked saffron
fish broth
1 lb. shrimp
1 lb. fish fillets, skinned
6 freshly shucked oysters
meat from 6 medium lobster
  tails
mussels in shell, if available
butter
chopped parsley
lump crabmeat

Sauté sliced carrots, onions, celery, leeks (white parts only), and fennel roots in butter until glazy looking.

Add tomato paste, sauté, and flame with brandy. Extinguish flame with white wine.

Add tomatoes, garlic and saffron.

Add 3 quarts of fish broth. Cook until vegetables are done.

Separately sauté in butter shrimp, fish fillets cut in 1-inch pieces, oysters, lobster meat, and mussels.

Fill up pot with prepared fish broth. Cook until fish is done. Reduce heat; cook for 10 minutes. Correct seasoning and wine to taste. Top with fresh lump crabmeat and chopped parsley. Serve garlic croutons with soup.

Serves 6.   – GP

LA SOUPE DE COURGETTE GLACE SAZERAC
(Chilled Zucchini Soup Sazerac
Restaurant Style)

4 cups chopped zucchini
2 tbsp. olive oil
2 tbsp. butter
3 tbsp. fresh chives or
  green onion tops
2½ cups chicken stock
2 tbsp. curry powder

1 cup whipping cream
2 tbsp. chopped onions
2 oz. fresh orange juice
2 tbsp. diced mango
1 tbsp. chopped mint leaves
1 tbsp. julienne orange rind

Heat olive oil and butter in large saucepan. Add zucchini and diced onions. Cook on medium heat covered for approximately 8 minutes, stirring occasionally until zucchini is soft. Add curry powder, diced mango, orange juice, and chicken stock. Simmer for 10 minutes and remove from heat to cool. Put soup in blender and add 1 cup whipping cream, mint and chives. Blend until smooth.

Serve well chilled with julienne of orange rind on top for garnish.
Serves 6.   – LED

ANTIPASTO SALAD

1 head iceberg lettuce
½ cup sliced mushrooms
½ cup sliced celery
½ cup garbanzo beans
½ cup artichoke hearts
¼ cup sliced green peppers
6 cherry tomatoes

½ cup onion rings
6 ripe black olives
3 oz. salami, julienned
3 oz. Provolone or Swiss
  cheese, julienned
chopped parsley

Trim, core, rinse, and drain lettuce. Chill to crisp. Cut lettuce into rafts about 1 inch thick. Arrange lettuce in bowl with other ingredients. Toss with Italian dressing.
Serves 6.   – JLA

SEAFOOD FILÉ GUMBO

¾ cup margarine
2 cups chopped onions (in ½-inch pieces)
2 cups chopped green bell pepper (in ½-inch pieces)
2 cups chopped celery (in ½-inch pieces)
3 tbsp. gumbo filé (may be called filé powder)
1½ tsp. ground red pepper, preferably cayenne
½ tsp. white pepper
½ tsp. black pepper
1 tsp. salt
1 tsp. minced fresh garlic
1 bay leaf, crumbled

½ tsp. dried thyme
½ tsp. dried oregano
1½ tsp. sweet paprika
1 tbsp. Tabasco
1¼ cups crushed tomatoes in tomato puree
5 cups seafood stock (see recipe below)
1 doz. oysters, optional
1½ cups crabmeat
1 lb. shrimp with shells and heads (size 21 to 25 per pound), or if shrimp with heads are not available, use 9 oz. peeled shrimp
cooked rice

SEAFOOD STOCK

2 qts. cold tap water
shells and shrimp heads from the shrimp called for in this recipe
2 fish carcasses, heads and gills removed (each fish approximately 3 to 5 lbs.)

1 medium onion, quartered
1 medium fresh tomato, quartered
1 rib celery

First, make seafood stock. Wash the shrimp heads, shells, and fish carcasses in cold water. Place all ingredients in a 3-quart saucepan. Bring liquid to a boil. Reduce heat to maintain a simmer, and simmer uncovered for 6 to 8 hours, replenishing water as necessary to keep 3½ quarts of stock. Strain. Cool and refrigerate until ready to use.

In a small bowl, mix together thoroughly the red pepper, white pepper, black pepper, salt, garlic, bay leaf, thyme, oregano, and paprika. Reserve.

In a 4-quart or larger heavy soup pot, melt the margarine over medium heat. Add the onions, bell pepper, and celery. Turn heat to high. Stir in the gumbo filé, mixed seasoning, and Tabasco sauce. Cook 6 minutes, stirring constantly. Stir in the tomatoes, and continue cooking over medium heat, stirring constantly, for 5 minutes. (During this time the mixture will begin sticking to the bottom of the pan; as it does so, continually scrape the pan bottom well with a spoon. The scrapings not only add to the gumbo's taste, but also decrease the gumbo filé's ability to thicken). Add the seafood stock and return heat to high. Bring mixture to a boil, uncovered. Allow the gumbo to simmer an additional 45 to 60 minutes, uncovered, stirring occasionally. Add the seafood, cover the pot, and turn the fire off. Leave the pot covered 6 to 10 minutes until the seafood is just poached. Serve immediately.

As a main course, allow for each person 6 tablespoons of cooked rice in a bowl, topped with about 1 cup of gumbo. For an appetizer, serve each person 2 tablespoons of cooked rice in a cup topped with approximately ½ cup of gumbo.

Note: You can substitute fish pieces for any or all of the seafood in this recipe. If the gumbo is made in advance, do not add the seafood. When ready to serve, bring the gumbo to a rapid boil, lower the heat so that the gumbo simmers, and add the seafood. Immediately cover the pot, turn off the heat, and let pot stand covered for 6 to 10 minutes. In this way you avoid overcooking the seafood.

When making the gumbo, be sure to use margarine instead of butter. This is because the margarine has more oil, and the oil seems to conduct more heat. The extra heat intensity plus the additional oil itself develop the gumbo filé to a more desirable taste, texture, and color – which is the good part! The bad part is that upon reaching a temperature above 140°, the oil separates out and rises to the surface. Some people prefer to skim the oil before serving.

Serves 4 as a main course, 8 as an appetizer.   – PP

OYSTER STEW

1½ qts. milk   1½ sticks butter
1 pt. oysters   chopped parsley

Melt butter; add milk and oysters. Bring to a boil. Add chopped parsley for garnish. Serve immediately.   – JGF

CRAWFISH SALAD

⅓ cup finely chopped
  celery
¼ cup minced parsley
2 tbsp. finely chopped
  pimento
½ tsp. white pepper

¼ tsp. salt
¼ cup mayonnaise
4 cups boiled and peeled
  crawfish
crisp salad greens

Mix first 6 ingredients together thoroughly. Add crawfish and mix well; chill. Mold in mounds and serve on bed of greens. Garnish with slices of cucumber and radish roses. Sprinkle lightly with paprika.

4 servings.
– MR

PASTA SALAD WITH MAYONNAISE

1 lb. Rotelle pasta (3
  colors)
1 medium Vidalia onion
  (purple onion can be
  substituted)
4 stalks celery
2 tbsp. capers

3 anchovy fillets
mayonnaise
⅓ cup reconstituted English
  mustard
½ tsp. mashed green
  peppercorns
1 package spinach leaves

Cook the pasta, rinse it twice, drain and chill it. Dice the celery and onion and put it in a large bowl. Chop the anchovies and add them to the bowl. Add the green peppercorns, capers, and the pasta. Toss it.

Add as much mayonnaise as you want in your salad. Season it with salt. Add the mustard until there is a slight hot taste. Chill this while you wash your spinach.

Place the spinach greens on the plates and spoon the salad on top. Serve with hot bread.

Serves 4.
– RH

CREAM OF CAULIFLOWER AND SALSIFY SOUP

1 medium head of
  cauliflower, cooked and
  mashed
3 tbsp. butter
3 tbsp. chopped green
  onion
1 tbsp. flour
2 cups cook's milk (⅔
  water, ⅓ whipping cream)

salt and white pepper to
  taste
tiny pinch of nutmeg
¾ cup sliced salsify (oyster
  root – imported from
  Belgium)
shredded Swiss cheese and
  bacon bits for garnish

Sauté green onions; add flour. Then add cook's milk, salt, pepper, and nutmeg and bring to boil. Add cauliflower and salsify and simmer 10 minutes. Sprinkle shredded Swiss cheese and bacon bits on top when serving.

Serves 4 to 6.

– WL

OYSTER SOUP

8 oz. butter
8 oz. flour
1 gal. oysters, drained
  (reserve liquor)
½ gal. clam broth
1 cup green onions, finely
  chopped

1 tsp. garlic, finely chopped
1 cup celery, finely chopped
½ cup parsley, finely
  chopped
2 bay leaves
1 tsp. Lea & Perrins sauce
salt and pepper

To reserve oyster liquor, add enough clam broth to make one gallon of liquid, then bring to boil in separate pot and keep warm. Gently sauté in a large pot green onion, celery, and garlic in butter for 3 minutes. Add flour and sauté 3 more minutes. Add to the pot the hot oyster liquor, bay leaves, Lea & Perrins sauce and whip for 2 minutes. Bring to boil, then reduce to a simmer. Simmer for 30 minutes, then add drained oysters and simmer 15 minutes more. Add salt and pepper to taste. Sprinkle chopped parsley on each serving.

Serves 12-15.

– AL

CORN AND OYSTER SOUP

3 stalks celery
1 medium onion
½ head garlic
4 jalapeño peppers, with
    seeds
2 red bell peppers (or 1 can
    pimentos)
2 green bell peppers

½ cup chopped parsley
1 cup flour
¾ cup oil
½ gal. chicken stock (or
    water)
½ qt. heavy cream
2 10-oz. pkgs. frozen corn
36 oysters

Dice all vegetables; sauté in oil. Add flour; do not brown. Add chicken stock and corn. Cook for approximately 15 minutes. Add cream, and cook another 5 minutes. Just before serving, add oysters, just enough to curl, but not cook.

Serve at once.

Serves about 12.

        – CK

MUSSEL SOUP

2½ lbs. fresh mussels
1 cup white wine
1 cup water
1 tbsp. chopped shallots

4 oz. roux
2 cups cream
salt and pepper

Steam the mussels in the white wine, water, shallots, salt, and pepper until they open. Strain them and reserve the liquid. Remove the mussels from the shells and set aside.

Bring the liquid to a boil in a saucepan. Add the cream and the roux. Boil this to make sure the roux has thickened as much as it can. Strain through a fine strainer to remove any lumps and return it to the saucepan. Boil sauce and if it is too thick, thin it with water. Season it with salt and white pepper, and when you are ready to serve add the mussels to the soup.

Serves 6.

        – RH

U.S. ARMY BEAN SOUP
(Aboard the S.S. *Gen. Washington*)

While in the army on his way to Korea, Pvt. Leruth was cooking aboard a troop transport that carried 5,000 men to Japan and on to Korea. This recipe is approximately one-thousandth of what he cooked at that time in 1952.

4½ cups ham stock
¼ cup chopped onions
1 cup dry white beans
   (soaked in water
   overnight)
2 tbsp. bacon drippings

⅓ cup tomatoes
salt and black pepper to
   taste
⅓ carrot, shredded, for
   garnish
2 tbsp. chopped ham

Place first four ingredients in pot and bring to boil. Cover and simmer 3 to 4 hours till beans are soft and mushy. Mash beans well. Add tomatoes and other ingredients and simmer for 40 minutes. Thicken slightly if needed.

Serves 4.

– WL

BEEF AND WATERCRESS SOUP

6 oz. beef
1 bunch watercress
6 cups chicken stock
salt and pepper to taste

½ tsp. salt
1 egg white
2 tsp. oil
2 tsp. cornstarch

Place the sliced beef in a bowl and sprinkle over ½ teaspoon salt. Add egg white, oil, and cornstarch. Stir until the mixture is smooth. Let the coating sit in the refrigerator for 30 minutes.

Bring 6 cups chicken stock to a boil in a small saucepan and then adjust the heat to a slow simmer. Add beef and stir with chopsticks or wooden spoon. Then scatter in watercress. Add salt and pepper to taste and serve.

– TW

TURTLE SOUP

1 lb. turtle meat
1 medium-size white onion
2 tbsp. flour
2 qts. water
½ can tomato sauce

¼ tsp. paprika (for color)
1 lemon
salt and pepper
2 hard-boiled eggs, minced
sherry

Sauté turtle meat until brown. Add onions and flour and cook until flour is brown. Add 2 quarts water, tomato sauce, and peeling from lemon. Let cook for 1 hour and remove lemon peel. Squeeze lemon into soup. Simmer slowly, add hard-boiled eggs. Sherry should be added just before serving, if desired. Garnish with a slice of lemon or parsley.

– JGF

MARGIE'S OYSTER SOUP (1951)

This soup has been served on numerous holidays in our home. I learned it from my mother-in-law, the late Marie Margarite Huet Rizzuto, lovingly known as "Margie" to all of us. Her Christmas oyster patties will never be duplicated by any chef – they were finest ever! Enjoy her oyster magic.

1 stick butter
2 bunches chopped shallots
  (green onion)
1 medium onion, chopped
1 toe garlic, chopped
1 celery heart, finely
  chopped
¾ cup flour
4 doz. salty oysters,
  poached (save liquor)

2 qts. oyster liquor and
  water
1 cup whipping cream
½ bunch chopped flat
  parsley
salt and white and red
  pepper to taste

Oysters should be freshly shucked and unwashed.
Sauté shallots, onion, garlic, and celery till tender. Stir in flour to make smooth paste. Add oyster liquor, cream, and water. Bring barely to boil. Add parsley and poached oysters.
Serves 10.

– WL

SOUPE DE MIRLITON
(Mirliton Soup)

5 mirlitons
½ lb. bacon
1 onion
3 stalks celery
4 cloves garlic
2 jalapeño peppers
1 bay leaf

1 tbsp. chicken base
1 tsp. curry powder
1 cup cream
2 qts. water
salt and pepper to taste
rice

Remove skins and core from mirlitons. Dice bacon to medium size pieces, sauté till crisp. Remove bacon pieces and save.

Dice onion, celery, garlic, and mirlitons, sauté the vegetables briefly in bacon fat until limp; do not brown. Add water, jalapeño peppers, bay leaf, and chicken base. Let simmer approximately 45 minutes. Add cream and curry just before serving.

Place a little rice in bottom of soup bowl. Pour hot soup over rice and place a couple of crisp bacon pieces on top. — CK

ABILENE CHILI (1958)

This recipe comes from a leading restaurant in West Texas where chili is taken very seriously.

30 lbs. ground chuck and
   cow round (1-inch plate)
2 qts. chopped onion
1 oz. garlic powder
½ cup salt
1 lb. Morton's chili powder

1 gal. water
1 gal. tomato juice
½ oz. cayenne pepper
equal parts of flour, cracker
   meal, and corn masa
   (about 1¼ lbs. total)

Brown meat with onions and seasonings. Add water and tomato juice and simmer 2½ hours with cover. Then thicken with flour, cracker meal, and corn masa mix to desired thickness. Boiled pinto beans are usually served on the side.

Serves about 55. — WL

GODCHAUX SALAD

1 head iceberg lettuce,
  cubed
2 large tomatoes, cubed
1 lb. backfin lump
  crabmeat
30 to 35 large shrimp,
  boiled and peeled

2 hard-boiled eggs
8 anchovies
5 oz. salad oil
5 oz. red wine vinegar
4 oz. Creole mustard

In a large salad bowl combine lettuce, tomatoes, crabmeat, and shrimp. To make dressing, in a small bowl combine oil, vinegar, and mustard. Mix well, pour over salad, and toss. Divide salad onto 4 chilled plates and garnish each with ½ sieved hard-boiled egg and 2 anchovies. Serves 4 as entrée. — JGF

CREOLE CHICKEN SALAD

⅓ cup plain yogurt
⅓ cup mayonnaise
⅓ cup Brennan's Special
  Sauce
4 cups chicken breasts,
  skinned, boned, cooked,
  and diced

1 cup chopped apple
1 cup walnuts, coarsely
  chopped
½ cup raisins

In a large bowl, blend together the yogurt, mayonnaise, and Special Sauce. Add the chicken to the dressing and combine thoroughly. Stir in the apples, walnuts, and raisins. Cover the bowl and refrigerate for 1 hour. Serves 6. — MR

COLD PASTA WITH VINAIGRETTE

1 lb. Rotelle pasta
1 small Vidalia onion
   (purple can be
   substituted)
2 stalks diced celery
½ lb. blanched snow peas
2 florets broccoli, broken
   in small bites

2 florets cauliflower, broken
   in small bites
1 diced red bell pepper
1 diced green bell pepper
1 jalapeño, optional, diced
   very small

Cook the pasta, rinse it twice, drain and chill. Mix together in a bowl all of the above ingredients.

Then add:

1½ oz. Balsamic vinegar
1 tsp. Dijon mustard
4 oz. walnut oil

Toss the mixture well and season it with salt. Then season it with white and black pepper until you can taste the pepper.
Serve on a bed of lettuce greens with hot bread on the side.   – RH

CHICKEN ASPARAGUS SOUP

2 chicken breasts
¾ cup sliced fresh
   mushrooms
5 cups chicken stock
1½ cups half-inch long
   asparagus

salt and white pepper to
   taste
1 tsp. light soy sauce
½ tsp. sesame seed oil
2 egg whites, thoroughly
   whipped

Bring chicken stock to boil. Add in thinly sliced chicken breast, stirring until separated.
Place asparagus into stock and simmer for 10 minutes. Add mushrooms, seasonings, oil, and soy sauce. Whip 2 egg whites and pour into soup slowly while constantly stirring. Serve immediately.   – TW

COLD TOMATO BASIL SAUCE

4 medium tomatoes,
  peeled and seeded
1 medium onion, chopped
2 small cloves garlic,
  chopped
3 tbsp. chopped fresh basil

3 tbsp. chopped fresh
  parsley
2 tbsp. olive oil
salt and finely ground black
  pepper

Chop tomatoes coarsely. Mix onion, garlic, basil, and parsley with olive oil, salt, and pepper. Taste for seasoning and refrigerate.

Serve with cold roasted beef or veal or cold poached redfish.   – GP

TURTLE SOUP

3 lb. turtle meat (diced)
1 cup cooking oil
2 cups brown roux
2 onions, chopped
2 ribs celery, chopped
2 green peppers, chopped
4 toes garlic, finely
  chopped
¾ cup parsley, finely
  chopped
1 gal. beef stock (hot)
1 qt. tomato puree

4 green onions, chopped
2 lemons, sliced
1 tsp. thyme
4 bay leaves
1 tsp. black pepper
2 tsp. salt
½ tsp. cayenne
½ tsp. allspice
½ tsp. basil
1 tsp. cloves (ground)
8 hard-boiled eggs, chopped
1 cup dry Spanish sherry

Sauté turtle meat in vegetable oil until brown, then set aside. Heat roux over low heat in soup pot. Add onions, green onions, green pepper, celery, parsley, and garlic. Stir constantly for 5 minutes. Then add all other ingredients, except eggs, turtle meat and sherry. Stir for several minutes and simmer for 1 hour. Stir occasionally. After the soup has simmered for 1 hour add the turtle meat and eggs and simmer ½ hour longer. If soup starts to get too thick, add more beef stock. Before serving, add the sherry and serve immediately.

Serves 10-12.   – AL

POT AU FEU

4 lbs. lean brisket
2 medium onions
2 bay leaves
3 carrots
garlic toast
1 small cabbage

¼ lb. parsley
1 celery root or 3 pieces
  celery
2 leeks, green only
12 ½-inch marrow bones
salt and pepper to taste

Simmer meat for 1½ hours in ½ gallon water. Skim regularly until ¾ done to create stock for soup. Add salt, pepper, bay leaves, greens from leeks, and stems from parsley. Cut onions in half (don't peel), brown and add to stock. (Option: short ribs, beef shoulder or lean stew meat).

Cut vegetables in one inch pieces, wash and layer in heavy pot. Strain beef broth on top, put brisket on vegetables, and simmer until vegetables and meat are done. Five minutes before serving blanch marrow bones (do not lose marrow from bones).

Slice beef and serve in soup bowl on top of vegetables.

Garnish with marrow bones, chopped parsley, and garlic toast.

Serves 6.   – GP

SHRIMP BISQUE

2 lbs. peeled shrimp
½ gal. chicken stock
1 pt. half-and-half
2 oz. white wine
1 small white onion
1 small piece of celery

1 small piece of green onion
dash of white pepper
salt to taste
½ lb. butter
3 oz. flour
dash of thyme

Finely chop all seasonings (white onion, celery, green onion). Sauté in butter. Add flour and cook for 5 minutes on slow heat. Add chicken stock. Chop shrimp finely and add to the chicken stock. Add salt, pepper, thyme, and white wine. Cook for half an hour on low heat. Heat half-and-half in a separate saucepan, then stir in with rest of ingredients. Turn fire off immediately. Serve.

Serves 10.   – LE

CREOLE ONION SOUP

8 oz. butter
8 oz. flour
1 gal. brown stock (hot)
12 medium onions (sliced
   thinly with the grain)
2½ cups red wine
1 tbsp. Lea & Perrins sauce

16 slices toasted French
   bread
1 tsp. caramel coloring
1 lb. freshly grated Parmesan
   cheese
salt and pepper to taste

Sauté onions in butter over medium heat until they brown lightly. Add flour and cook several more minutes. Add hot brown stock, wine, Lea & Perrins sauce, caramel coloring, and salt and pepper to taste. Blend with wire whip for several minutes and simmer over medium heat for 45 minutes. Serve in bowls topped with toasted French bread and Parmesan cheese.

Serves 16. — AL

OYSTER STEW

1 qt. whipping cream
1 qt. oysters and liquor
¼ cup parsley, finely
   chopped
½ cup green onion, thinly
   sliced

1 stick unsalted or lightly
   salted butter (diced)
salt
cayenne pepper
paprika

Drain oysters and reserve liquor. In heavy 4-quart pot, heat cream and oyster liquor to a boil. Add oysters and bring to boiling point again. When edges of oysters curl, remove from heat. Stir in diced butter and add parsley and green onion. Add salt and cayenne pepper to taste. (Be careful with salt.) Ladle into soup bowls and sprinkle with paprika. Serve immediately.

Serves 8. — AL

Sauces

SAUCE FOR OYSTERS BIENVILLE

¼ lb. margarine
1 fish fillet (3 to 4 ounces
  trout preferred), skin
  removed
¼ lb. fresh shrimp, peeled
  and deveined
¼ lb. fresh lump crabmeat
6 egg whites, unbeaten

¼ cup white wine
1 tsp. yellow food coloring
salt and pepper to taste
½ cup homemade bread
  crumbs
½ cup grated Parmesan
  cheese

Heat margarine in a large pot, add fish, shrimp, and crabmeat. Sauté for 20 minutes. Add egg whites and stir. Add wine, continue stirring and let simmer for 10 minutes. Add food coloring, salt, and pepper and stir for another 10 minutes. (Remember to stay with pot; don't leave!) Let cool and serve over oysters. Combine bread crumbs and cheese. Top with sprinkling of bread crumb mixture.

Serves 6.

–AL

BIENVILLE SAUCE

6 oz. flour
6 oz. butter
½ gal. fish stock
½ lb. trout fillets, skinned
  and chopped
½ lb. very small shrimp
½ lb. lump crabmeat

6 egg yolks, whipped
1 cup Chablis
1 tbsp. egg shade or yellow
  coloring
1 cup heavy cream
salt and pepper to taste

Heat butter in heavy pot. Add flour and cook slowly for 3 minutes (do not brown roux). Add fish stock and whip vigorously for 1 minute using a wire whip, then simmer for ½ hour. Stir occasionally. Next, add trout, shrimp, and crabmeat. Whip constantly for 4 minutes and remove from fire. Add egg yolks, mix with cream, and beat vigorously for 4 minutes. Add Chablis and beat 1 more minute. Add egg shade or yellow coloring until desired color is obtained (it should be light yellow). Refrigerate at least ½ hour.

– AL

ROQUEFORT DRESSING

1 cup mayonnaise
2 tbsp. sour cream
2 tbsp. buttermilk
¼ tsp. Lea and Perrins
    Worcestershire sauce

¼ tsp. white pepper
⅛ tsp. M.S.G.
½ tsp. salt
2 to 3 oz. Roquefort cheese,
    crumbled

Mix well and refrigerate.

– WL

AMERICAINE SAUCE

1 lb. raw shrimp heads
¼ cup oil
½ medium-size white
    onion, diced fine
½ carrot, diced fine
3 shallots (French), diced
    fine
4 cloves garlic, diced fine
½ cup tomato puree
3 cups fish stock

1 cup white wine
2 oz. brandy
whipping cream
¼ tsp. salt
½ tsp. dried tarragon (fresh
    if available)
2 bay leaves
a few parsley stems
a pinch of cayenne pepper
¼ tsp. thyme

Heat oil to smoking point, add shrimp heads, and sauté under high heat until very red. Add diced vegetables and cook until tender. Add liquids (tomato puree, fish stock, white wine, and brandy) and seasonings and cook for 15 minutes, skimming occasionally. Strain through a fine strainer.

Add roux to the liquid to thicken it. Mixture must be boiled for roux to thicken completely. When desired consistency is reached, strain again and pat butter on top to prevent skin from forming.

To serve, bring sauce to a boil, add whipping cream to desired consistency, and adjust seasonings to taste with salt, brandy and cayenne pepper. Garnish with peeled, cooked shrimp.

– RH

EGGS HUSSARDE

16 large eggs
1 qt. water

½ cup dry white wine
½ tsp. salt

MARCHAND DE VIN SAUCE:

1½ lbs. butter
3 tbsp. finely chopped
  garlic
¾ cup finely chopped white
  onion
½ cup finely chopped
  boiled ham
¾ cup finely chopped green
  onion
1 cup finely chopped
  mushrooms

5 tbsp. flour
1 tsp. salt
½ tsp. black pepper
1 tsp. Worcestershire sauce
1½ cups beef stock
½ cup dry red wine
8 slices Canadian bacon or
  ham
8 slices tomato
8 slices Holland rusk or
  toast

HOLLANDAISE SAUCE:

8 large egg yolks
4 tbsp. lemon juice
2 lbs. hot melted butter

1 tsp. salt
about ¼ tsp. cayenne

To prepare the Marchand de Vin sauce, melt the butter in a heavy saucepan over low heat. Add the chopped vegetables and cook until they are slightly soft. Sprinkle in the flour, salt, and pepper and stir to mix. Cook for about 4 minutes, then add the Worcestershire sauce, beef stock, and wine. Mix thoroughly and simmer over low heat, stirring very frequently, until the sauce is very thick and a rich brown color, about 1 hour. Place the pan of sauce in a warm oven or over the pilot on the surface of the stove to keep it warm while you prepare the other ingredients.

Grill the ham and tomato slices and, if necessary, prepare the toast. Set aside to keep warm as for the sauce.

To prepare the Hollandaise sauce, put the egg yolks and lemon juice in a mixing bowl. Place the bowl over or near the pilot on top of the stove. Beat briefly with a whisk, then slowly pour in the hot melted butter, beating briskly and constantly while you pour. When the sauce begins to thicken, sprinkle in the salt and pepper. Continue to beat while adding the rest of the butter. Beat until the sauce reaches an attractive thick consistency. When the sauce is finished, leave the bowl over the pilot to keep warm, or place it in a basin of warm water.

To poach the eggs, bring the water, wine, and salt to a boil in a large skillet or sauté pan. Keeping the water at a continuous low rolling boil, crack the eggs one by one into it. Cook until the egg whites are firm, about 2 minutes. Lift the poached eggs out of the water with a skimmer or slotted spoon, allowing the water to drain back into the pan. Place them on a heated platter while you assemble the dishes.

To assemble the dishes, first place a slice of toast on each warmed plate, then top with a slice of grilled ham. Ladle about ⅓ cup Marchand de Vin sauce over the ham. Carefully place 2 poached eggs side by side on the sauce, then top with about ½ cup Hollandaise sauce. Garnish each portion with a slice of grilled tomato placed to one side, and serve.

Serves 8. – MR

COCKTAIL SAUCE

½ cup catsup
½ cup chili sauce
3 to 4 tbsp. horseradish
½ tsp. Lea & Perrins
 Worcestershire sauce

¼ tsp. Tabasco
1 lime, juice only
1 lemon, juice only
1 tbsp. olive oil

Mix well and refrigerate. – WL

RASPBERRY SAUCE

2 10-oz. packages frozen
   raspberries (with juice) or
3 pints fresh raspberries
1 cup sugar
½ cup Kirschwasser (cherry
   brandy)

¼ cup white wine
¼ cup port wine
¼ cup cornstarch

Combine all ingredients except cornstarch in a saucepan. Cook over medium heat until boiling. Dissolve cornstarch in a little water or wine. Whisk this into sauce and simmer 10 to 15 minutes. Strain through a sieve and cool until ready to use.

Note: Fresh strawberries may be substituted. Also water can be substituted for wine, depending on desired taste.   – GP

MIAMI MUSTARD SAUCE
(For boiled seafoods – especially good with crab claws)

2 oz. Coleman's dry
   mustard
¼ cup white wine

2 cups mayonnaise
½ cup whipping cream
½ tsp. Tabasco

Mix dry mustard with white wine and let stand for ½ hour. Then add mayonnaise, cream, and Tabasco.   – WL

SWEET & SOUR DIPPING SAUCE
(especially good with French-fried mushrooms, zucchini, onion rings, pork chops or ribs)

1 10-oz. jar red currant jelly

1 8-oz. jar yellow mustard

Heat jelly to about 150° to melt. Add mustard, stir well. Ready to use.   – WL

SAUCE AU POIVRE VERT
(Green Peppercorn Sauce)

3 tbsp. carrot
2 tbsp. onion
1 tbsp. celery
bay leaves
leaf thyme
bottled green peppercorns

1 cup white wine
1 cup wine vinegar
2 cups demi-glace
1 cup heavy cream
liquid from green
peppercorns (to taste)

Put in a saucepan the carrot, onion, celery, bay leaves, and thyme. Add wine and vinegar, and reduce by half. Add demi-glace, cream, and liquid from green peppercorns. Reduce to desired consistency. Then strain the sauce; add whole peppercorns and salt to taste.
Makes 3 cups.   – GP

VERSAILLES VINAIGRETTE
DRESSING

1 tbsp. finely diced celery
1 tbsp. finely diced green
  peppers
1 tbsp. finely diced dill
  pickles
1 tbsp. finely diced white
  onions

1 tbsp. finely diced
  pimentos
1 tsp. minced garlic
salt and pepper to taste
1 tbsp. Dijon mustard
3 cups desired salad oil
1 cup wine vinegar

Combine first 5 ingredients, then add rest of ingredients. Chill and serve over crisp greens.
Makes about 5 cups.   – GP

DEMI-GLACE

5 lbs. veal bones
5 lbs. chicken bones
1 onion
2 carrots
3 stalks celery

a few sprigs parsley
2 cups tomato puree
thyme
bay leaf

Brown the veal bones and boil for 8 hours.

In a separate pot, boil the chicken bones, vegetables and seasonings. Simmer for about 4 hours.

Strain both pots and mix them. Chill mixture in order to remove the fat from the top.

Bring mixture to a boil and add the tomato puree. Reduce this and skim it constantly. When reduced by half, strain again through a fine mesh strainer. Bring back to a slow boil. Reduce the stock until it is thick and coats a spoon with a nice glaze. This final reduction must be skimmed whenever film comes to the top. Strain through a fine mesh strainer and put into container to store.   – RH

HOLLANDAISE SAUCE

1 lb. butter
8 egg yolks
1 oz. tarragon vinegar
1 oz. water

1 pinch salt
1 pinch pepper
1 dash Tabasco sauce
2 tbsp. crushed ice

Melt butter in saucepan. Place egg yolks, vinegar, water, salt, pepper, and Tabasco in the top of a double boiler. Beat well. Place egg mixture over boiling water and continue to beat while slowly adding melted butter to egg mixture. Be sure butter is added slowly and thoroughly mixed so as not to allow sauce to break. Continue to heat and beat until thick. Remove from fire, add crushed ice and stir.   – LE

BÉARNAISE SAUCE

4 egg yolks
juice of one lemon
2 cups melted butter
salt and pepper

1 tbsp. capers
¼ cup chopped parsley
1 tbsp. tarragon vinegar

In top half of double boiler, beat egg yolks and lemon juice. Cook slowly in double boiler over very low heat, never allowing the water in bottom pan to come to a boil. Slowly add melted butter, stirring constantly with wooden spoon or wire whip. Add salt, pepper, capers, parsley, and vinegar. Makes 2 cups.   – PP

DIABLE SAUCE

1 tbsp. butter
2 tbsp. sliced green onions
1 tbsp. minced shallots
½ cup white wine

1½ cups brown sauce
degreased pan juices
green peppercorns to taste

Sauté onions and shallots lightly, until clear. Add white wine and pan juices with green peppercorns to your taste; reduce by one half. Add brown sauce and reduce by one quarter. Salt to taste.

To serve, place golden brown hens on plates, sprinkle with chopped parsley. Serve Diable sauce in a sauce boat separately.

Serves 6.   – GP

CREOLE MUSTARD SAUCE

4 minced shallots
1 tbsp. green peppercorns
12 oz. softened unsalted
   butter
4 oz. champagne vinegar
6 oz. whipped cream

1 tbsp. Creole mustard
salt and white pepper to
   taste
2 oz. Beurre Marnier (soft
   butter and flour blended
   together)

In heavy saucepan add vinegar, green pepper, and shallots. Cook over high heat to reduce this to 1 ounce, or just before scorching point. Add cream and mustard, bring to a boil and cook 2 minutes. Add small pieces of beurre, whipping very quickly to blend. When mixture has formed a very light sauce, add all the softened butter at one time, mixing quickly so butter is incorporated in sauce without breaking. Strain sauce through fine china cap, pressing on shallots firmly to extract all juices. Cover and keep sauce warm.

This sauce cannot be boiled for it will break due to the butter content. The sauce should be served warm. — LED

FISH FUMET

Quantities for making 4 quarts.

4 lbs. trimmings and bones
   of sole or whiting
½ lb. sliced blanched
   onions

2 oz. parsley stems
½ bottle white wine
juice of 1 lemon

Butter the bottom of a thick deep saucepan; put in the onions and the parsley. Upon these lay the fish remains. Add the juice of a lemon, cover the saucepan, put it on the fire, and allow the fish to exude its essence. Shake the pan at intervals. Moisten with the white wine. Then with the lid off, reduce the liquid to about half.

Now add 4 quarts of cold water, bring to a boil, skim, and then cook for 20 minutes only on a moderate fire. Strain and reserve. — RH

PESTO ALLA GENOVESE

2 oz. fresh basil leaves
1/4 cup pine nuts or walnuts
2 cloves garlic
large pinch of salt

1/4 cup olive oil
1/3 cup grated Parmesan or
   Romano cheese
a little parsley can be added
   to enhance the green
   color

Chop the basil, parsley, nuts, garlic, and salt in a food processor until reduced to a thick paste. Add oil and cheese; process until the sauce is the consistency of thick cream. Keep the sauce covered until required and use fresh.   – GF

NEW ORLEANS RAVIGOTE

MAKE MAYONNAISE:

2 egg yolks
1 whole egg
1/2 tbsp. salt
1/4 tsp. white pepper

1/4 tsp. red pepper
1 pt. chilled oil
1 1/2 tbsp. vinegar

(Use chilled bowl, very important)

Chop following ingredients fine:

1/4 cup green bell peppers
1/4 cup red bell peppers
3/4 cup pimento
3/4 cup green onions

1/4 cup chopped anchovy
   fillets
16 oz. jumbo lump crabmeat

For garnish use tomato, lettuce, black olives, and parsley chopped.

Stir in oil with eggs to make mayonnaise. Add salt, white and red pepper, and vinegar. Stir in green and red bell peppers, pimento, green onions, and chopped anchovy fillets. Gently mix in jumbo lump crabmeat and chill. Garnish with lettuce, tomatoes, black olives, and parsley.   – LLL

FISH VELOUTÉ

1 qt. fish fumet   **3½ oz. white roux**

Dissolve the roux in the cold fish fumet and put the saucepan containing this mixture on an open fire, stirring the sauce with a whisk. Add salt, white pepper, and a pinch of nutmeg. Bring to a boil and reduce heat until flour taste has left the velouté, about 10 minutes. Strain and pat with butter to keep from forming a skin.   – RH

CHOCOLATE SAUCE

2 squares German's sweet   **¼ pt. cream**
**   chocolate**   **½ cup sugar**
2 squares bitter chocolate

Cook all ingredients in double boiler until thick, using only half of cream to start with. Add the balance of cream to achieve pouring consistency.
Serves 5.   – LE

REMOULADE SAUCE

¾ cup Creole mustard   **½ cup chopped celery**
2 tbsp. paprika   **2 tbsp. chopped parsley**
1 cup corn oil   **½ tsp. sugar (optional)**
¼ cup chopped onion   **Tabasco to taste**

Mix well and refrigerate.   – WL

FOND OR FUMET DE POISSON
(Fish Stock)

1 tsp. olive oil (optional)
1 large carrot, peeled
1 large onion
6 fresh mushrooms and
  stems (optional)
1 white of leek
4 lbs. whole fish, cut in
  pieces

1 bouquet garni
6 stems parsley
5 black peppercorns (fresh
  green peppercorns
  preferred)
1 clove
2 gals. cold water
2 chicken bouillon cubes

Dice vegetables into approximately ¼-inch pieces. Combine oil and vegetables in an approximately 4-gallon pot. Sauté vegetables about 2 minutes, cover, add fish and bones. Cook for 5 minutes, covered. Add water and bouillon, parsley stems, clove, peppercorns, and bouquet garni. Cook 45 minutes slowly. Skim top when needed. Strain through very fine strainer. Must be completely cooled to refrigerate.

Note: Use for poaching, sauces, and soups. – CK

MARINADE FOR 5 LBS. HEADLESS
BOILED SHRIMP
(Shells On)

1½ cups corn oil
1 cup coarsely cut celery
½ cup thinly sliced carrots
¼ cup chopped onion
  (optional)
2 tsp. leaf thyme

4 bay leaves
1 tsp. freshly ground pepper
⅓ cup chopped parsley
4 to 5 thinly sliced lemons
Tabasco to taste
½ cup wine vinegar

Mix ingredients together. Marinate shrimp 6 hours or more in refrigerator. – WL

BIENVILLE SAUCE

¼ cup olive oil
½ cup chopped onion
1 cup chopped green onion
1 cup chopped celery
2 cups chopped
   mushrooms
2 tsp. chopped garlic
2 cups small shrimp (150-
   200 count)
1 tsp. thyme

1 bay leaf
1 tsp. parsley
Tabasco sauce to taste
¼ cup white wine
1 tbsp. lemon juice
1 cup heavy cream
roux
1½ cups bread crumbs
salt and pepper to taste

Sauté in olive oil: onion, green onion, celery, and mushrooms until onions are just clear. Add garlic and shrimp. Simmer 5 minutes. Add spices, white wine, lemon juice, and cream. Bring to a boil. Add roux until mixture is very thick and cook until roux taste has dissipated. Stir in bread crumbs and parsley. Add salt and pepper to taste.

Spoon over raw oysters in shell, dot each oyster with a drop or two of Tabasco sauce, then bake in 350° oven until bubbly.   – GP

BÉARNAISE SAUCE

½ cup red or white wine
2 tbsp. tarragon vinegar
1 tbsp. minced shallots
2 crushed peppercorns

1 tbsp. chopped parsley
1 tbsp. chopped tarragon
3 egg yolks
¾ cup clarified butter

Cook first 6 ingredients over direct heat until reduced by one half. Strain and let cool. Then whisking constantly over hot water, add egg yolks and cook until mixture begins to thicken. Remove from heat still whisking constantly. Add clarified butter a little at a time. After all butter is added, correct seasoning, and finish with 1 tablespoon chopped parsley and tarragon. Serve in a sauce boat separately.

Serves 6 (1½ cups).   – GP

SAUCE MAISON

¼ lb. butter
1 tbsp. Worcestershire
sauce

¾ cup jus (from meat)
pinch chopped parsley

Melt butter until golden brown. Add Worcestershire sauce and jus and cook one minute. Add parsley and serve with meat.　　　　　－ MR

Seafood

SEAFOOD PÂTÉ

1 lb. cleaned, deboned, raw
  fresh fish (especially
  scallops, redfish, and
  trout)
1 cup crushed ice
2 whole eggs
6 egg yolks
1 lb. heavy whipping cream

salt and white pepper
1 tsp. grated nutmeg
2 large tbsp. fresh tarragon
  (or basil, or herbs as
  available)
buttered paper (to line
  terrine)

Grind in a food processor (in this order): the fish with the ice, eggs and yolks (one at a time), the cream (slowly), salt and white pepper to taste, nutmeg, and herb or herbs. Line a terrine with buttered paper, bake in bain marie at 300° for 45 minutes.

May be served hot or cold. (When served cold, use Aioli or Coulis de Tomates; when hot, use hot Beurre Blanc.) — CK

LE COULIS DE TOMATES FROID
(To accompany cold seafood and vegetable terrine)

6 ripe tomatoes
1 qt. hot water

½ cup olive oil
3 limes

Wash tomatoes, drop into hot water and quickly remove (this facilitates removal of the skins). Peel skins and discard. Cut each peeled tomato in half, squeeze out juice and seeds. Save pulp, throw away juice and seeds. Place tomato pulp in food processor, add olive oil and juice of limes. Pour blended result through strainer and refrigerate until ready to serve. — CK

HOT BEURRE BLANC

2 oz. finely chopped
 shallots
½ cup white vinegar

1 cup white wine
½ cup whipping cream
½ lb. butter

In 10-inch sauté pan heat shallots, vinegar, and wine. Reduce by half. Add cream and again reduce by half. Slowly stir in butter, whipping to creamy consistency.

Pour small amount of the sauce onto each plate. Place slice of hot seafood or vegetable pâté in sauce and pour additional sauce over pâté.
– CK

AIOLI
(For use over cold seafood or cold vegetables or as a dip)

4 cloves garlic
2 egg yolks
1 cup salad oil

1 cup olive oil
½ lemon

Clean garlic cloves, chop, and crush (with dash of salt) into a paste. In a bowl, whip paste with egg yolks to smooth consistency. Then *slowly* add both oils while continuing to whip, until a mayonnaise-like texture is achieved. Blend in lemon juice and salt and pepper to taste. Refrigerate until ready to serve.
– CK

COLD TROUT MOUSSE WITH
WATERCRESS COLOR

2 lbs. fresh trout fillets
2 qts. whipping cream
2 egg whites
salt, pepper, cayenne
  pepper, nutmeg

2 bunches watercress
  (washed) with stems
Garnishes (any of these):
  shrimp, oysters, crawfish,
  basil, tarragon, etc.

Chop 2 pounds of trout in a food processor. The fish must be very fresh. Force the fish through a food mill to remove the nerves. Place the fish back in the food processor and add salt, pepper, cayenne, and a pinch of nutmeg. Puree the fish until smooth, add egg whites and puree for about 4 more seconds. Scrape the bowl and add 1 pint of whipping cream. Puree this for about 5 seconds. Scrape the bowl and add 1 more pint of cream. Puree until the cream is blended (about 5 to 10 seconds). Do not overblend because the mousse will lose its texture and fall apart when cooked.

Place this in a mixing bowl over ice and beat in the other quart of cream a little at a time.

Cook a sample and adjust the seasoning. Overseason the mousse slightly because when it is cold the seasonings will be dulled. Keep this over ice and separate into 2 bowls.

Chop watercress in a food processor and squeeze it dry. Reserve the liquid, place it in a small saucepan and heat slowly. When a film rises to the top, (just before it boils) pour it through a cloth strainer. The residue that stays in the towel is the color that is used. Scrape it from the towel and mix it into one of the bowls of mousse. Before placing the mousse in a mold to cook, you must put your garnish in it.

Use seasonal and fresh ingredients such as crawfish, oysters, shrimp, or fresh basil, thyme, and tarragon. These should be stirred in the mousse so the colors will be contrasting, such as pink shrimp in the green mousse or greenish-gray oysters in the white mousse.

Butter a pâté mold generously and alternate the layers of mousse in the mold. Place a buttered parchment paper on top and cook in a little water in a roasting pan in a 325-degree oven for 1 to 2 hours until it is very warm in the center.

Cool, slice, and serve with your favorite kind of seasoned mayonnaise.   – RH

SCAMPI

2 lbs. large raw shrimp
½ cup butter
1 tsp. salt
6 cloves garlic

¼ cup chopped parsley
3 tbsp. lemon juice
1 tbsp. paprika
6 lemon wedges

Preheat oven to 400°F.

Remove shells from shrimp, leaving shell on tail only. Devein shrimp and wash under running water; drain on paper towels.

Melt butter in baking dish in oven, then add salt, garlic, 1 tablespoon parsley, and mix well. Arrange shrimp in single layer in baking dish. Bake uncovered for 5 minutes. Turn shrimp, sprinkle with lemon juice and paprika; add remaining parsley. Bake 8 to 10 minutes until tender (DO NOT OVERCOOK).

Arrange shrimp on heated serving platter; pour garlic butter over all. Garnish with lemon wedges.

Serves 6 to 8.   – GF

OYSTERS EN BROCHETTE

½ lb. bacon
3 doz. oysters, drained
2 cups flour

1 tsp. salt
1 tsp. pepper
vegetable oil for frying

Cut bacon strips in half and cook lightly. Alternating two oysters with two pieces of bacon, place on 6 skewers. Oysters and bacon are placed close together. Season the flour with salt and pepper. Combine eggs and milk in a shallow bowl. Dip skewers in egg wash, then in seasoned flour. Fry in a 3-quart deep fryer at 360° for 4 minutes. Remove skewers.

EGG WASH

3 eggs, beaten   1½ cups milk

Serves 6.   – AL

REDFISH AU POIVRE VERT

2 10-oz. redfish fillets
½ pt. whipping cream
¼ tsp. green peppercorns

½ cup white wine
pinch salt

Poach the fillets in fish stock or sauté them in a buttered pan. Drain the fillets and keep warm.

Put ¼ teaspoon of green peppercorns in a sauté pan and add the wine. Cook until the wine is almost dry and add the cream. Reduce the cream until thick and season with salt and more green peppercorns if necessary.

Spoon the sauce over the fillet of redfish and serve immediately.
Serves 2.   – RH

SHRIMP CREOLE

1½ lbs. large shrimp
1 clove garlic
2 medium pieces of celery, chopped
1 medium white onion, chopped

1 medium green pepper
1 pt. tomato puree
1 pt. water
1 pinch each sugar, thyme
salt and pepper to taste

Clean shrimp. Put enough butter in a pan to cover the bottom. Add onion, garlic, celery, and green pepper. When the vegetables are half cooked, add the shrimp. When these are half cooked, add tomato puree and water. (Add more or less water depending on how thick the puree is; each manufacturer's puree is different.) Add sugar, thyme, salt and pepper to taste. Cook until shrimp are finished, about 15 minutes, depending upon size. The creole should have a nice thick consistency. Serve over rice.   – LE

TROUT CHAPON

1 lb. trout
white asparagus
white wine courtbouillon
2 cups fish sauce

1 lb. fresh tiny shrimp
sliced mushrooms
green onions, chopped
pinch thyme

Take trout and slice in 2-ounce pieces. Wrap each slice around a white asparagus spear and hold with a toothpick.

Poach each spear in a white wine courtbouillon for 7 minutes.

Make a sauce out of fish sauce, shrimp, sliced fresh mushrooms, chopped green onion, and a pinch of thyme.

Remove spears from poaching liquor and remove toothpick.

Serve shrimp sauce over.

– GP

CRAWFISH BISQUE

8 lbs. crawfish
½ lb. shallots
2 tbsp. minced parsley
3 cloves garlic
salt, pepper and cayenne
    pepper
bread

2 tbsp. flour
2 tbsp. lard
6 cups water from boiled
    crawfish
1 minced onion
juice of crawfish heads
salt and pepper

Be sure the crawfish are alive. Rinse them well and boil them. Save water and press juice and meat from heads into separate dish. Clean heads and save until later. Cook meat from tails in skillet in a little lard; season with minced shallots, parsley, and garlic. Soften a little bread in some water and add to mixture. Season with salt and pepper; cook until thoroughly done. Use mixture to stuff the heads that were saved.

To make the soup brown flour in lard, add the onion and the juice with 6 cups of water. Cook for 1 hour, add the stuffed heads, and serve hot.

Serves 8.

– JGF

GRATIN OF OYSTERS AND MUSHROOMS

2 cups freshly shucked
  oysters
1 stick butter
1 green pepper, shredded
2 shallots, thinly sliced
1 lb. small whole
  mushrooms
4 tbsp. flour
1 to 1½ cups heavy cream

1 cup thin cream
2 tbsp. grated Parmesan
  cheese
⅓ cup dry white wine
salt and pepper
nutmeg
paprika
bread crumbs

Gently sauté pepper and shallots in 4 tablespoons butter. After 2 or 3 minutes, add mushrooms and salt and pepper to taste, and cook these slowly for 4 minutes more.

In the top of a double boiler melt remaining 4 tablespoons butter and stir in flour. Add slowly, stirring constantly, heavy cream, thin cream, grated Parmesan, and a pinch of nutmeg and paprika. Cook the sauce, stirring it, for 6 minutes or until it is thick. Add to the sauce the sautéed vegetables and freshly shucked oysters. Add white wine, pour the mixture into a baking dish, and sprinkle it with bread crumbs. Brown the crumbs quickly under the broiler and serve the dish immediately.   – LE

CRABMEAT EN COQUILLES

1 lb. crab flakes
½ cup cream sauce
1 egg, beaten
2 tbsp. minced parsley
½ tbsp. lemon juice

Worcestershire sauce
2 tbsp. catsup
salt, pepper
1 tbsp. horseradish
buttered bread crumbs

Combine crabmeat and other ingredients lightly together. Fill shells, or ramekins, sprinkle with crumbs, and bake in 350-degree oven until they are brown, 10 to 12 minutes.   – LE

POMPANO MEUNIÈRE

2 1½- or 2-lb. pompano,
  cut lengthwise
½ lb. butter
juice of 1 lemon

oil for broiling
½ tbsp. chopped parsley
salt and pepper

Put a small amount of oil on pompano before broiling.

In a separate pan melt and continuously whip butter until brown and frothy; add lemon juice and pour over pompano.

Garnish with chopped parsley.

Serves 4.   – JGF

BROKEN SHRIMP JAMBALAYA

1½ lbs. broken shrimp
  (cooked)
1 cup peanut oil
4 onions, chopped
5 toes garlic
2 bunches shallots
1 bell pepper, chopped

2 tbsp. paprika
salt, red pepper, and black
  pepper
¼ lb. sliced smoked sausage
3 cups rice
5 cups water or shrimp stock

Heat oil, add onions, garlic, shallots, bell pepper, smoked sausage, paprika, salt, and pepper and sauté well. Add shrimp pieces, rice, and shrimp stock. Bring to boil, cover, and over very low heat steam for 20 to 25 minutes. Stir with fork and replace cover.

Serves 6.   – WL

FRIED MARINATED FRESHWATER CATFISH

(Marinate the fish the day before frying.)
6 1-pound whole freshwater catfish, gutted, skinned, and heads removed (have butcher prepare); if already dressed, each fish should weigh 8 to 9 oz.

MARINADE:

3 cups water
1 cup finely chopped
  onions
3 tbsp. Tabasco sauce

1 tbsp. salt
1 tsp. dried thyme leaves
2 bay leaves

SEASONING MIX
(or substitute Louisiana Cajun Magic Seafood Magic)

2 tsp. salt
2 tsp. ground red pepper
  (preferably cayenne)
2 tsp. sweet paprika
1¾ tsp. granulated garlic
  (preferred) or garlic
  powder
1¾ tsp. black pepper
1 tsp. granulated onion
  (preferred) or onion
  powder

1 tsp. dried oregano leaves
1 tsp. dried thyme leaves
1 cup corn flour (available at
  many health food stores)
1 cup cornmeal
pork lard or cooking oil for
  pan frying

Cut out a 1½-inch strip across the center of the body on both sides (down to the bone but not through it) of each catfish; reserve the fish and fish strips.

In a large bowl combine the ingredients for the marinade, stirring until salt is dissolved.

Lay the fish and fish strips in a single layer in a pan; pour the marinade over the top. Cover pan and refrigerate 8 to 16 hours (turn fish over every few hours if not totally submerged in the marinade).

$$0 \quad \times \quad 0 \quad 8 \quad 4 \quad \triangle$$

ᠪᠢᠴᠢᠭ᠌ ᠂ ᠂ ᠂

ᠳᠤᠷᠠᠯᠠᠯ

ᠤᠳᠠᠭᠠᠨ

ᠮᠣᠩᠭᠣᠯ

→

ᠪᠢᠴᠢᠭ᠌

ᠳᠤᠷᠠᠯᠠᠯ

ᠤᠳᠠᠭᠠᠨ

ᠮᠣᠩᠭᠣᠯ

Combine the seasoning mix ingredients in a small bowl, mixing well. Drain the fish and sprinkle some of the mix on the fish and fish strips, patting it in with your hands (use about ¾ to 1 teaspoon mix on each fish). Combine the remaining mix with the corn flour and cornmeal in a pan (a 13-inch by 9-inch pan works well), mixing till thoroughly blended. Set aside.

In a large skillet heat about ½ inch of oil to 350° (use just enough oil to come up the sides of the fish but not cover the top). Just before frying each fish, dredge it in the seasoned corn flour mixture, pressing the mixture firmly into the fish with your fingers; shake off excess. Fry the fish in the hot oil until cooked through and golden brown and crispy, about 1½ to 2 minutes per side. (Adjust heat as needed to maintain the oil's temperature at about 350°). Drain on paper towels and serve immediately.

Serves 6.   – PP

CRAWFISH ETOUFFÉE

½ cup oil
¾ cup flour
1½ cups chopped celery, puree half in blender
1½ cups chopped onions, puree half in blender
1½ cups chopped bell pepper, puree half in blender

2 lbs. crawfish tails
1 qt. crawfish stock (reserved from boiling crawfish) or water

Make roux by heating oil till very hot. Add flour all at once and blend well with wire whisk, stirring constantly.

When roux has reached a deep golden brown color, remove from heat and stir in pureed vegetables, crawfish tails and chopped vegetables. Stir until vegetables begin to wilt. Return to low heat; slowly add 1 quart of crawfish stock or water and bring to simmer. Season to taste with salt and cayenne pepper.

Serves 6.   – PP

COD FISH CAKES

1 lb. can of cod fish flakes
½ cup shallots, minced
1 tsp. minced fresh parsley
1½ lbs. Irish potatoes
3 eggs

¼ tsp. salt or to taste
½ tsp. pepper or to taste
flour
¼ cup finely chopped bell
pepper

Boil and mash potatoes. Combine all ingredients except flour in large bowl. Form into flat cakes. Roll cakes in flour. Fry in large frying pan in vegetable oil that has been preheated to a medium temperature. Brown fish cakes on one side then turn and brown on other side. Place cooked cakes on paper towels to drain excess oil. – AL

CRAWFISH ETOUFFÉE

3 lbs. crawfish tails
1 cup crawfish fat
2 cups fish stock (hot)
2 medium onions, chopped
2 ribs celery, chopped
6 tbsp. brown roux
1 green pepper, chopped
3 toes garlic, chopped
½ cup parsley, finely
    chopped

½ cup green onions, finely
    chopped
1 cup tomato puree
1 tbsp. lemon juice
½ tsp. cayenne pepper
¼ tsp. thyme
1 tbsp. Lea & Perrins
    Worcestershire sauce
½ cup dry sherry (optional)
salt and pepper to taste

Warm roux over low heat for 3 minutes. Add onions, celery, green pepper, and garlic and sauté slowly for 5 minutes. Then slowly whisk in the hot fish stock and bring to a boil. When sauce reaches boil, reduce heat to a simmer and add tomato puree, lemon juice, cayenne, thyme, and Lea & Perrins sauce. Simmer uncovered for ½ hour. Then strain sauce into another pot. Add crawfish tails and crawfish fat to pot and simmer covered for 15 minutes. Stir in chopped parsley and green onions, sherry, and salt and pepper to taste. Serve over steamed rice.
    Serves 6. – AL

FILLET OF SOLE WITH OYSTER

Poach 6 oysters until edges begin to curl. Strain the oysters, reserve the liquid and add enough fish fumet to cover the fillet. Hold the oysters on the side.

Poach the fillet, drain it, and put it on a dish. Reduce the poaching liquid, add some velouté and cream and season to taste with salt, pepper, and red pepper. Add the oysters, heat again, and spoon sauce over the fish.   – RH

SHRIMP CREOLE

¼ cup flour
¼ cup bacon grease
1½ cups chopped onions
1 cup chopped green
  onions
1 cup chopped celery
1 cup chopped bell pepper
4 cloves garlic
2 or 3 bay leaves
1 tsp. thyme
1 tsp. Worcestershire sauce
1 tbsp. lemon juice
4 lbs. peeled, deveined raw
  shrimp

½ cup chopped fresh parsley
1 6-oz. can tomato paste
1 16-oz. can whole tomatoes
  with liquid
1 8-oz. can tomato sauce
1 cup water
5 tsp. salt
1 tsp. pepper
½ tsp. red pepper or Tabasco
  sauce to taste
2 to 3 cups cooked rice
1 tsp. sugar

In a large heavy iron pot make a dark roux of flour and bacon grease. Add onions, green onions, celery, bell pepper, and garlic. Sauté until golden brown. Add tomato paste, whole tomatoes, and tomato sauce. Let simmer for 15 minutes. Add water, salt, pepper, red pepper or Tabasco, bay leaves, thyme, sugar, Worcestershire sauce, and lemon juice. Simmer for about 1 hour, stirring occasionally. Add shrimp and cook for about 10 to 20 minutes or until shrimp are tender. Add parsley. Serve on rice.

Serves about 10.   – AL

TROUT VÉRONIQUE

1 fillet of fresh sea trout
   (from 1½- to 2-lb fish)
1 cup white wine
1 lemon

8 seedless white grapes,
   split
½ cup very rich Hollandaise
   sauce

Place white wine and the juice of the lemon, as well as lemon rind, in a shallow pan. Put on moderate heat and place fillet of trout in pan. Poach trout for approximately 7 or 8 minutes, or until fish is white and flaky. Remove fish from liquid and place on a heatproof dinner plate. Drain well. Place split grapes on top of trout, then ladle Hollandaise sauce on trout and grapes so that fish is completely covered. Place under broiler until Hollandaise just begins to brown. Remove from heat; garnish with parsley. Serve with broiled new potatoes in jackets.　– LE

RED SNAPPER CHEVILLOT

12 8-oz red snapper fillets
4 bell peppers
1 stalk celery
4 small white onions
4 cans artichoke hearts
2 whole lemons
¾ lb. butter

2 eggs
2 pts. milk
1 lb. all-purpose flour
1 lb. shortening
salt and pepper
dash of Lea & Perrins
   Worcestershire sauce

Finely chop onions, bell pepper, and celery and sauté in ½ pound of butter. Add salt and pepper, juice of 2 lemons and a dash of Worcestershire sauce, cook for 15 minutes on slow fire. In another pan, place drained artichokes, add ¼ pound butter and sauté 5 minutes.

Prepare egg wash with 2 beaten eggs added to 2 pints of milk. Place fish in the egg wash, then in flour. In sauté pan, place the shortening. Sauté fish on slow heat until brown on both sides. Place the sauce over the fish with artichokes on the side.

Serves 12.　– LE

GRENOUILLE ST. MICHAEL

2 doz. frog legs
½ lb. crawfish tails, peeled
  and deveined
1 tbsp. chopped green
  onions
1 tbsp. fresh chopped dill
1 tbsp. chopped shallots
1 bay leaf
1 tbsp. Creole mustard
2 oz. brandy (or cognac)
1 cup fresh sliced
  mushrooms

1 cup julienne of leeks
1 cup julienne of artichoke
  bottoms
1 cup milk
1 cup whipping cream
1 cup flour
1 cup white wine
⅓ cup olive oil
¾ lb. butter (¼ lb. to be
  used for roux)

Place frog legs in milk with salt and pepper to soak for 30 minutes, or more if desired. Remove from milk and dredge with flour.

In a large pan, heat the oil with ¼ lb. butter until very hot. Add frog legs to skillet and sauté over high heat for about 2 minutes, then lower heat and continue to cook for 5 minutes, turning once until cooked. They should be golden brown in color.

Place frog legs on large platter and keep warm in 160-degree oven.

Pour off all oil and add another ¼ lb. butter to pan to heat. Add crawfish tails and bay leaf, then sauté for 1 minute. Add brandy, then shallots, leeks, green onions, artichoke bottoms, and mushrooms. Continue to cook for 2 minutes. Add white wine to pan and cook for 3 to 4 minutes; add cream. Bring mixture to a boil and thicken with roux, stirring constantly to make a smooth sauce.

Correct seasonings, if needed, add dill, and stir in Creole mustard. Serve over frog legs with steamed rice or boiled potatoes and green vegetable.

Serves 4.   – LED

CRABMEAT DRESSING

2 lbs. crabmeat
2 loaves stale French bread
6 eggs
¼ cup fresh parsley
1 large onion

1 cup celery
½ lb. margarine
1 tsp. thyme
salt and pepper to taste

Melt margarine in large skillet, add seasonings; simmer 20 minutes. Add crabmeat and cook 20 minutes, stirring constantly. Wet stale bread in large baking pan; add whole eggs and mix thoroughly. Add crabmeat from skillet to the mixture, stir well together. Add thyme, salt and pepper. Place pan containing mixture into 350-degree oven. Stir well every half hour. Bake 2 hours. Cool in refrigerator. Dressing is now ready for use (for example, stuffing crab shells, shrimp, or lobster). After stuffing, top with bread crumbs and melted margarine and brown under broiler.

– AL

SALT AND PEPPER SHRIMP

1 lb. medium to large
  shrimp, in shell
4 green onions (cut into 2-
  inch lengths)
½ tsp. minced garlic
¾ tsp. salt

½ tsp. white pepper (or
  ground szechuan
  peppercorns)
1½ tsp. light soy sauce
2 tbsp. cornstarch
1½ tsp. dry sherry

Trim feet from shrimp. Make shallow cut about ⅛ inch deep into back of shell and devein. Pat shrimp dry thoroughly with towel. Mix salt, pepper, and 1½ teaspoons sherry with shrimp to marinate (15 to 30 minutes in refrigerator).

Coat shrimp with cornstarch. Shake off excess cornstarch.

Heat 1 cup of oil in wok to approximately 375 to 400°. Add shrimp, stir to separate until crisp (about 80 percent done). Remove shrimp and drain oil from wok.

Reheat wok; when hot, add 1 tablespoon oil. Add garlic and stir. Return shrimp, then green onions; sprinkle with sherry and soy sauce. Stir-fry well (approximately 1 minute).

Remove to serving plate and serve hot. Peel before eating.

Serves 6.   – TW

TROUT MARGUERY

3 2½-lb. trout tenderloins
4 oz. margarine, melted (or
  butter, if preferred)
salt and pepper to taste
3 cups Hollandaise sauce
½ cup bread crumbs

½ cup grated cheese, mild
  Cheddar suggested
1 lemon, thinly sliced
½ clove garlic, minced
6 sprigs parsley, finely
  chopped

Preheat broiler. Arrange trout in baking pan that has been greased with margarine. Brush fish with remaining margarine and season with salt and pepper. Place in broiler for 10 minutes. Remove from broiler and place on heatproof serving platter. Top with Hollandaise and sprinkle with bread crumbs and cheese. Return to broiler for 5 minutes. Garnish with sliced lemon, garlic, and parsley.

Serves 6.   – AL

FILLET OF CATFISH WITH CREOLE MUSTARD

6 catfish fillets, skin
  removed
1 cup olive oil
¼ cup minced shallots
¼ cup fresh herbs (thyme,
  basil, rosemary, and
  optional mint)
1 tbsp. crushed black
  peppercorns

2 cups white wine
3 tomatoes, peeled, seeded,
  and diced
¼ lb. butter
2 tbsp. Creole mustard
salt and pepper

Between plastic wrap, flatten catfish fillets with a light cleaver. Place them in a pan coated with ¼ cup of the olive oil. Sprinkle the fish with the fresh herbs, peppercorns, and half of the shallots. Add remaining olive oil and 1 cup of white wine. Cover and refrigerate for 2 to 3 hours.

Fold chilled fillets in thirds with herbs inside. Place in one layer in a skillet, sprinkle with remaining shallots, the butter, and the remaining cup of wine. Bring to a simmer, cover, and cook on low for 7 minutes.

Remove catfish from pan and keep warm. Strain the liquid and reduce by two-thirds over high heat. Add the tomatoes; cook for 2 minutes. Reduce heat to low and stir in Creole mustard but do not boil. Adjust seasonings. Pour sauce over catfish; garnish with diced green onion.

– CK

TROUT MEUNIÈRE AMANDINE

4 6- to 8-oz. fillets of
  speckled trout
½ lb. butter
juice of 1 lemon
oil for frying

4 oz. sliced toasted almonds
½ tbsp. chopped parsley
salt and pepper
flour
milk

Dip salted and peppered fillets in milk, then roll in flour. Fry in hot oil in shallow pan until golden on both sides. In a separate pan melt and continuously whip butter until brown and frothy. Add sliced almonds and lemon juice and pour over trout. Garnish with chopped parsley.

Serves 4.

– JGF

LETTUCE BLOSSOM

1 head lettuce
1 lb. fresh shrimp, shelled
    and deveined, chicken, or
    squab
4 to 6 stalks celery hearts
4 stalks scallions or green
    onions (cut into 1-inch
    strips)
1 small carrot
8 to 12 water chestnuts
4 to 6 reconstituted black
    mushrooms
1 tsp. finely chopped fresh
    ginger

2 cloves garlic
3½ tbsp. chicken broth
1 tsp. cornstarch
2 tbsp. peanut oil
1 tbsp. sherry wine
¾ tsp. salt
½ tsp. sugar
1 tsp. oyster sauce
1 tsp. light soy sauce
1 tsp. vinegar
¼ tsp. white pepper
Hoisin sauce

Soak black mushrooms in warm water for at least 30 minutes. Clean and separate lettuce, cut to palm size, and refrigerate. Finely mince black mushrooms, celery, carrots, and water chestnuts to same size. Finely chop shrimp or chicken or squab. Mince garlic and ginger together.

Heat wok and add 2 cups peanut oil; heat until hot. Add meat and stir gently to separate. When meat is 80 percent done, remove and drain oil. Reheat wok and add 2 tablespoons peanut oil; add ginger and garlic; stir. Add finely chopped vegetables, stir 10 to 15 seconds (over medium-high to high heat). Toss in meat; shower with wine and then vinegar and stir. Mix all other seasonings with liquefied cornstarch (cornstarch mixed with chicken broth to a paste consistency) and add when liquid at the bottom of the wok comes to a boil. Mix well and remove to a serving dish. Serve in the chilled lettuce leaves and top with Hoisin sauce and scallions. Roll and eat with the hands.　　　　　　　　　　　　　　– TW

SEA TROUT GOLDEN ISLAND

8 6-oz. sea trout fillets
1 onion, finely minced
3 tomatoes, finely sliced
3 lemons, peeled and sliced
¼ cup olive oil
1 tsp. salt
½ tsp. white pepper

½ tsp. curry powder
¼ tsp. turmeric (optional)
½ tsp. paprika
½ tsp. thyme leaves
2 tbsp. Dijon mustard
¼ cup lemon juice
⅔ cup olive oil

Grease a baking dish with ¼ cup olive oil. Lay down the vegetables and then the fillets over the vegetables.

To make sauce, mix seasonings together, then add mustard and lemon juice. Whisk lightly with ⅔ cup olive oil. Cover fish with sauce. Bake the fish fillets for 15 to 20 minutes at 375°. Garnish with sliced lemons, chopped parsley and serve with boiled potatoes or rice.   – JLA

CASSOULETTE JEAN BATISTE REBOUL

3 lbs. fresh mushrooms
4 oz. garlic
2 oz. shallots or white of
   green onion
3 cups dry white wine

1 or 2 bay leaves
pinch of thyme
salt and pepper
3 to 4 doz. raw fresh oysters

Sauté chopped fresh mushrooms in butter, add garlic and shallots, chopped fine. Then add white wine, and reduce with bay leaves and thyme. Add salt and pepper to taste.

Cover fresh oysters in a casserole dish with mushroom sauce. Cook in 450-degree oven until oysters are done. Cover with Hollandaise sauce and lightly brown under broiler.   – CK

QUN MING SHRIMP

12 oz. medium shrimp,
  peeled and deveined
⅓ cup imported straw
  mushrooms
1 bunch rice noodles (heat
  oil to 400° and deep-fry
  noodles until they float
  and expand)
4 egg whites, well beaten
peanut oil
¾ tsp. salt

½ tsp. sugar
dash of white pepper
1½ tsp. sesame seed oil
1 tbsp. cornstarch, dissolved
  in 4 tbsp. water
¼ tsp. mixture of ginger and
  garlic, coarsely chopped
½ cup chicken stock
⅓ cup milk
rice wine or sherry

MARINADE:

¼ tsp. salt
1 egg white, well beaten

1 tbsp. cornstarch
1 tsp. peanut oil

Slice the shrimp three-quarters of the way through along the outside curve; remove the vein. Put them in a large mixing bowl and sprinkle in 1 teaspoon of salt. Mix well and put shrimp in a colander and spray with cold water. Shake them in colander and roll them dry in a kitchen towel. Put them in a mixing bowl; add the ¼ teaspoon salt, egg white, cornstarch and oil and mix well. Cover and let them marinate under refrigeration for at least half an hour.

Heat a wok or heavy skillet to 275°. Add 3 cups of peanut oil, scatter in the shrimp, and stir quickly to separate them. Toss in straw mushrooms and then turn them rapidly until shrimp are 80 percent cooked. Gently pour 4 well-beaten egg whites around wok in a circular motion; swirl 2 to 3 times until egg white is fluffy. Drain them immediately by pouring all contents and oil into a strainer set over a pot.

Reheat wok and add 2 tablespoons of oil over high temperature, swirl, and then toss in the garlic and ginger, pressing them in the hot oil. Shower in rice wine or sherry. Pour in chicken stock and the remainder of seasonings (salt, sugar, pepper, and sesame seed oil). Pour milk and dissolved cornstarch into the wok or pan and stir vigorously until smooth and glazy. Add the shrimp and straw mushrooms, give them a few fast folds, and pour into a serving platter. Dress the edges of the platter with the crushed rice noodles and serve.   – TW

SHRIMP CREOLE

½ cup vegetable oil
1 cup coarsely chopped
  green peppers
2 cups coarsely chopped
  onion
1 cup coarsely chopped
  celery
2 tbsp. minced garlic
2 cups whole tomatoes

1 tbsp. paprika
¼ tsp. cayenne
1 tsp. salt
1 tsp. white pepper
3 cups water
1 bay leaf
2 tbsp. cornstarch
3 lbs. raw shrimp, peeled
  and deveined

Heat vegetable oil and sauté first 4 ingredients until tender, add tomatoes, and cook 3 to 4 more minutes. Stir in paprika, cayenne, salt, pepper, water, and bay leaf. Simmer 15 minutes. Add shrimp and continue to cook an additional 15 minutes. Thicken with cornstarch mixed in cold water. Serve with hot fluffy rice.   – MR

CREVETTES GEORGE PANETIER

32 medium shrimp
  (approx.)
mirepoix – (½ carrot,
  celery, small onion,
  chopped finely)
pinch of cayenne
pinch of thyme

2 oz. cognac
2 oz. dry sherry
4 oz. fish stock
6 oz. heavy cream
1 tbsp. lobster base
1 tbsp. tomato puree
3 tbsp. butter

Sauté shrimp (in shell) in butter and mirepoix. Add cayenne and thyme; flame with cognac. Add sherry and fish stock. Remove shrimp from pan. Peel and devein. Reduce liquid in the pan, then add cream, lobster base, and tomato puree. Strain into another pan, return shrimp and finish cooking. Remove shrimp to a plate, whip butter into the sauce, and pour over shrimp.
Serves 4.   – CK

LOBSTER WITH BLACK BEAN SAUCE

1 1½-lb. live Maine lobster
6 oz. pork
6 scallions, cut in 2½-inch
  lengths
1 egg, beaten
3 tbsp. cornstarch
¾ cup chicken stock
5 to 6 cups peanut oil
6 slices ginger
3 cloves garlic, coarsely
  chopped

1 tbsp. fermented black
  beans, rinsed and coarsely
  chopped
1 tsp. light soy sauce
½ tsp. dark soy sauce
½ tsp. sesame seed oil
¾ tsp. sugar
salt and pepper to taste

Split the lobster in half lengthwise. Remove and discard the stomach sac (a pouch about 1 inch long that is in the head) but keep intact the greenish tomalley and any roe. Apply the beaten egg with a brush to both halves of the lobster. Follow with a light coat of cornstarch and set aside. Chop the pork until its formation is loose and fluffy. Place it on the platter with the ginger, scallions, garlic, and fermented black beans. Dissolve 1 tablespoon cornstarch in ¾ cup of water. Gather all the seasonings within reaching distance.

Heat a wok or heavy skillet over high temperature until hot. Pour in 5 to 6 cups of peanut oil and heat to 325°. Gently place both halves of lobster into wok. Swirl a few times until lobster is 80 percent cooked. Set lobster aside and drain oil. Reheat wok with 2 tablespoons of oil. Add pork and stir vigorously in poking and pressing motions to break up the lumps; keep stirring until the meat has lost all pinkness. Toss in garlic, ginger, scallions (white parts only but reserve green parts), and fermented black beans; shower in rice wine prior to adding the two halves of lobster. Pour ¾ cup of chicken stock and steam-cook until lobster is completely cooked (about 3 to 5 minutes).

Remove lobster and place both halves on a serving platter (facing up). Add both light and dark soy sauce, sugar, salt, and pepper. Give the dissolved cornstarch a big stir and pour it into the sauce. Add the sesame seed oil and scallions (green parts only). Stir in a circular motion until the sauce thickens. Scoop the aromatic finished product onto the lobster and serve.   – TW

SHRIMP (OR CRAWFISH) AND ANDOUILLE SMOKED SAUSAGE STUFFED MIRLITON PIROGUE WITH TASSO AND OYSTER HOLLANDAISE

3 large mirlitons
(chayotes)
½ cup milk
1 egg, beaten
½ cup all-purpose flour
½ cup dry, very fine bread
  crumbs
3 tbsp. unsalted butter

1 cup (about ¼ lb.) chopped
  andouille smoked sausage
  (preferred) or any other
  good pure smoked pork
  sausage such as Polish
  sausage (Kielbasa)
1 lb. peeled large shrimp or
  crawfish tails

SEASONING MIX (or substitute Seafood Magic)

1 tbsp. salt
1 tsp. white pepper
1 tsp. dry mustard
¾ tsp. granulated garlic
  powder
½ tsp granulated onion
  powder
½ tsp. ground red pepper
  (preferably cayenne)

½ tsp. black pepper
½ tsp. dried sweet basil
  leaves
vegetable oil for deep frying
Tasso and Oyster
  Hollandaise sauce (recipe
  follows)

Boil the mirlitons just until fork tender. Cool, then cut each in half lengthwise; peel and remove seed (eat or save to put in a salad). Carefully scoop pulp out with a spoon, leaving about a ¼-inch-thick shell. Coarsely chop the pulp and reserve for the stuffing.

In a pan (loaf, cake, and pie pans work well) combine the milk and egg until well blended. Place the flour in a separate pan and the bread crumbs in another. Combine the seasoning mix ingredients in a small bowl; mix well. Add 2 teaspoons of the mix to the flour and 2 teaspoons to the bread crumbs, mixing each well. Season both sides of the mirliton halves by sprinkling with 2½ teaspoons of the seasoning mix.

Heat 1 inch of oil in a large skillet (or use a deep fryer) to 350°. Meanwhile, dredge the mirlitons in the flour, shaking off excess; coat well with the egg wash, then, just before frying, dredge lightly in the bread crumbs. Fry the mirliton halves in the hot oil until golden brown, about 1 to 2 minutes per side. Drain on paper towels and keep warm with the serving plates in a 200-degree oven.

Make the Tasso and Oyster Hollandaise sauce and set aside in a warm place.

In a large skillet, melt the butter over high heat. Add the andouille and reserved mirliton pulp; sauté until browned, about 5 minutes, stirring occasionally and scraping the pan bottom well. Add the shrimp and remaining seasoning mix. Continue cooking just until shrimp are plump and cooked, about 3 minutes, stirring frequently. Pour in the reserved 2 tablespoons oyster liquor from the Hollandaise and cook 1 minute more, stirring constantly. Serve immediately.

To serve, place 1 mirliton half on each warmed serving plate. Using a slotted spoon, spoon about ⅔ cup slightly drained shrimp mixture on top. Then arrange about 6 shrimp (or several crawfish) that are in the stuffing over the top, and pour a generous ⅓ cup Hollandaise sauce over it. (The leftover Hollandaise is great to dunk bread in with this meal.)   – PP

TASSO AND OYSTER HOLLANDAISE SAUCE

1 doz. medium to large oysters in their liquor (about 10 oz.)
1 lb. unsalted butter
4 tbsp. margarine
4 egg yolks
2 tsp. white wine

2 tsp. lemon juice
½ tsp. Tabasco sauce
½ tsp. Worcestershire sauce
3 tbsp. finely chopped tasso (preferred) or other smoked ham (preferably Cure 81)

Place the oysters and their liquor in a small saucepan over high heat; cook until plump and edges curl, about 2 minutes, stirring once or twice. Remove from heat, drain oysters (reserve 2 tablespoons liquid to make the shrimp and andouille stuffing), and cool. Then slice each oyster across into as many thin slices as possible.

Melt the butter and margarine in a 1-quart saucepan over low heat. Raise heat and bring to a rapid boil, then immediately remove from heat and cool 5 minutes. Skim froth from the top and discard. Pour butter mixture into a large glass measuring cup and set aside.

Meanwhile, in a medium-sized stainless steel mixing bowl or in the top of a double boiler, combine the remaining ingredients, except for the oysters. Mix together with a metal whisk until blended.

Place over (not touching) a pan of slow simmering (not boiling) water. Vigorously whisk the egg mixture, picking up the bowl frequently to let the steam escape, and making sure the egg bowl doesn't touch the hot water; whip until the egg mixture is very light and creamy and has a sheen, about 5 minutes. (This amount of beating is important so that the cooked eggs will better be able to hold the butter.) Remove bowl from over hot water. Gradually ladle about ¼ cup of the butter mixture (use the top butterfat, not the butter solids on the bottom) into the egg mixture while vigorously whipping the sauce; make sure the butter you add is mixed into the sauce well before adding more. Continue gradually adding the surface butterfat until you've added about 1 cup. So that you can get to the butter solids, ladle out and reserve about ½ cup surface butterfat in a separate container. (The butter solids add more flavor and also thin the sauce.) Gradually ladle all but ½ cup of the bottom solids into the sauce, whisking well. (Use any remaining bottom solids in another recipe). Then gradually whisk in enough of the reserved top butterfat to produce a fairly thick sauce (the butterfat thickens the sauce, so you may not need to use it all.) Stir in the oysters. Keep the sauce in a warm place (such as on top of the stove) until ready to serve. Makes 3 cups.

Serves 6. – PP

SOLE AU SAUTERNE

Poach the sole in a buttered dish with ½ pint of sauterne. Strain the fillet and reduce the cooking liquid by half. Add velouté to thicken and finish the sauce with ½ ounce of best butter. Season to taste with salt, pepper, and red pepper.

Cover the sole with this sauce and glaze; garnish each side of the dish with a heap of julienne of filleted sole, seasoned, dredged, tossed in clarified butter and sautéed at the last moment in order to have it very crisp. – RH

SEA TROUT FEUILLETÉ

5 oz. fillet of trout
1½ oz. crawfish tails
1½ oz. lump crabmeat
1 serving spoon lobster
  sauce
½ tsp. chopped shallots
2 serving spoons cooking
  oil
½ serving spoon butter

3 oz. puff pastry (pâte
  feuilletée)
salt and pepper
1 egg yolk
½ tsp. chopped red pimento
½ tsp. fresh chopped parsley
1 serving spoon flour
1 soup spoon butter
1 dash brandy

Preheat the skillet; add the cooking oil. Flour the fillet of fish. Sauté the fish lightly. Remove from skillet and allow to cool.

Preheat saucepan. Add butter and shallots. Then add crawfish, lump crabmeat, and lobster sauce. Cook over slow fire 8 to 10 minutes. Add remaining ingredients (except the pastry and egg yolk). Remove from fire and allow the filling to cool.

With rolling pin, roll the dough thin, to twice the size of the fillet of fish. Place filling on top of the fillet of fish. Place fish on dough, fold dough over fish, and seal like a turnover. Brush with egg yolk. Place in baking pan and bake at 325° for 16 to 20 minutes.   – LED

GRATIN DE ST. JACQUES A LA
JULIENNE DE LÉGUMES
(Scallops with Julienne of Vegetables)

1 lb. scallops
1 large carrot
1 large leek
½ stick butter

4 cups white wine
1 pt. cream
juice of 1 lemon
salt and pepper

Julienne vegetables. Sauté lightly in butter. Add white wine. Simmer for 3 to 5 minutes. Set aside. Reduce cream, add lemon juice, and season to taste. Arrange scallops in casserole. Spoon cream over scallops. Add julienne. Cook in hot oven approximately 10 minutes. Brown under broiler. Serve immediately.

Serves 6.   – CK

REDFISH WITH CRAWFISH AND SCALLOPS

6 6-oz. fillets of redfish
½ lb. sea scallops
½ lb. peeled crawfish
1 bay leaf
1 qt. crawfish stock
1 cup white wine
½ tsp. salt
¼ tsp. white pepper
¼ bunch green onions,
  chopped

4 large fresh mushrooms,
  sliced
¼ lb. butter
¼ lb. all-purpose flour
1 cup half-and-half
1 tsp. thyme
1 pt. milk
2 eggs
2 lbs. all-purpose flour
5 oz. shortening

In sauté pan, place butter, chopped green onions, sliced mushrooms. Cook for 5 minutes. Add scallops and crawfish; cook for 5 more minutes. Add flour and mix well. Then add crawfish stock, bay leaf, salt, pepper, half-and-half, and white wine. Cook for 15 minutes.

In another sauté pan, place shortening. Mix milk and eggs to make egg wash. Place redfish fillets in egg wash, dust in flour, then place in sauté pan. Brown on both sides over medium heat. Take out of pan and place the crawfish and scallops over the fish and serve. Suggest boiled parslied potatoes be served with this dish.

Serves 6.   — LE

SOFT-SHELL CRABS

6 medium-size soft-shell
  crabs, cleaned
1 cup flour
egg wash

1 cup commercial fish fry
  mixture
oil for frying

Roll crabs in flour, then in egg wash (1 beaten egg added to 1 pint milk), then in fish fry. Heat oil in frying pan and brown crabs evenly, allowing 10 minutes on each side (20 minutes in all.)

Serves 3.   — AL

FILLET OF SOLE FLORENTINE

Poach the fillet of sole in fish fumet and butter. Spread a layer of shredded spinach, stewed in butter, on the bottom of the dish; place the sole on it and cover it with Mornay sauce. Sprinkle with a little grated cheese and brown the top.

MORNAY SAUCE

4 parts Bechamel sauce   **1 part fish fumet**

Reduce by one quarter, add 2 ounces each of grated Gruyère and Parmesan cheese. Add 2 ounces of butter a little at a time and whisk until very smooth.   – RH

TROUT MARGUERY

4 trout fillets
1 doz. shrimp, boiled and finely chopped

1 doz. medium-size mushrooms, sautéed and finely chopped

Take 4 good-sized trout fillets and fold. Place the folded fish in a pan to which you add 1 tablespoon of oil and a glass of water. Bake in a hot oven for 15 minutes.

HOLLANDAISE SAUCE

½ lb. melted butter
3 egg yolks
juice of strained lemon

salt and cayenne pepper to taste

Place egg yolks in a double boiler; gradually add melted butter, stirring very slowly so that it doesn't curdle until thick. Then add shrimp and mushrooms. Add salt, cayenne pepper, and lemon juice to taste.
Dress the fish and pour sauce over it for serving.   – JGF

FROG'S LEGS

6 frog's legs, separated at
joint
1 cup flour
egg wash

1 cup commercial fish fry
mixture
oil for frying

Roll frog's legs in flour, dip in egg wash (1 beaten egg added to 1 pint milk), then in fish fry. Heat oil in frying pan. Add frog's legs and brown evenly for 10 minutes on each side (20 minutes in all), being sure to move them around.
Serves 3.

– AL

TERRINE OF LOUISIANA CATFISH
WITH LUMP CRABMEAT

2 lbs. catfish, roughly
chopped
1 egg
1 qt. heavy cream
½ tsp. cayenne pepper
¼ tsp. nutmeg

1 cup carrots, cut into fine
dice
1 cup zucchini, cut into fine
dice
½ cup water
½ stick butter

In a chilled food processor puree the catfish with the egg and spices. Add the cream slowly and puree until smooth. Set the mixture aside in the refrigerator.

Bring the water and butter to a simmer in a small pot. Add the carrots and zucchini; simmer until the water is gone. Cool slightly and fold the vegetables and the crabmeat into the catfish puree.

Line a terrine with buttered parchment paper. Fill it with the catfish puree and cover with buttered paper. Place the terrine in a water bath and bake in a 300-degree oven for 45 minutes or until a knife inserted in the pâté comes out clean.

Terrine can be served hot or cold. A simple sauce can be made by whisking 2 tablespoons of vinegar with a little salt and pepper and gently stirring in 1 cup of cream. Sauce can be heated to serve with hot terrine and ½ cup of diced tomato can serve as a garnish in the sauce.   – CK

OYSTERS EN BROCHETTE

2 doz. raw oysters
12 strips bacon cut in half
4 8-inch skewers
1 egg
¾ cup milk

flour
salt and pepper to taste
oil for deep frying
lemon wedges

Fry bacon until not quite crisp. Alternate 6 oysters and 6 half-strips of bacon (folded) on each skewer. Make a batter with egg and milk and season well with salt and pepper. Dip each skewer in batter, roll in flour and deep fry until golden. Serve on toast points with lemon wedge.

Serves 4 as appetizer or 2 as main course. – JGF

CALAMARI ALLA RIVIERA
(Baked Stuffed Squid)

12 medium-size squid
2 tbsp. chopped fresh
  parsley
3 cloves garlic
2 tbsp. bread crumbs

½ cup olive oil
½ cup dry white wine
rosemary sprig
salt and pepper to taste

Cut out the eyes and mouth of the squid. Remove the ink sac and internal bone. Cut off the tough point of the tentacles. Rub off the skin and wash under running water until white. Cut off the heads and tentacles (leaving the body) and chop them with the parsley, garlic, and rosemary, mixed with the bread crumbs. Season with salt, pepper and 3 tablespoons of the oil. Mix together well and stuff the squid. Sew the tops closed (or use toothpicks) and lay the squid in a large skillet containing the remaining hot oil. Sauté the squid, turning until golden brown. Add the wine and when it has partially evaporated, cover the skillet, reduce the heat, and cook the squid slowly for about 25 minutes or until the squid is tender and the sauce has thickened. Remove from the heat. Place the stuffed squid in a hot oven-proof dish and garnish with lemon wedges.

Serves 6. – GF

FILLET OF DRUM IN LIME BUTTER

4 6-oz. drum fillets
16 oysters
6 oz. small peeled shrimp
1 cup white wine
1 lb. unsalted butter
2 cups flour
salt and pepper
½ cup lime juice

1 pinch saffron threads
1 cup julienne carrots
1 cup julienne celery
1 cup julienne artichoke
  bottoms
½ cup chopped dry shallots
½ cup olive oil

Poach oysters and shrimp in ¼ cup white wine and ¼ cup water; reserve liquid. Blanch all vegetables in 2 cups of lightly salted water until crisp; reserve liquid. Set oysters, shrimp, and vegetables aside.

Put 2 tablespoons butter in saucepan, add chopped shallots, and sauté briefly (do not brown). Add ¾ cup white wine and bring to boil. Reduce volume to ⅓ cup. Add liquid from seafood, ½ cup liquid from vegetables, lime juice, and saffron. Bring to a boil again and reduce broth by one half.

Add olive oil and 1 tablespoon butter to a sauté pan large enough to hold all fish fillets and heat to approximately 350°. Salt and pepper fish fillets to taste. Dredge in flour. Sauté until golden brown. Do not overcook. Place fish in serving platter.

Pour off oil in sauté pan, reserving 1 tablespoon; add poached oysters, shrimp, and vegetables. Sauté quickly and arrange on top of fish.

As the broth continues to boil, whip softened butter a little bit at a time into the reduced liquid, until it will coat the back of a spoon.

Adjust seasoning and pour half of the sauce over the fish fillets and the rest in a sauce boat.

Serve immediately with parsley, potatoes, and green salad.   – LED

BRAISED TROUT DEMOISELLE
DE MER

4 5-oz. trout fillets
4 1½-oz. lobster tails

butter
white wine (champagne)

Roll fillets around lobster tail and place in buttered 8-inch by 8-inch baking dish. Brush with butter, pour white wine over fillets, cover with foil, and bake 20 to 25 minutes at 450°.   – WL

FROG LEGS ST. MICHAEL
(in Bordelaise sauce)

8 frog legs
1 cup Progresso bread
**   crumbs**
1 cup flour

1 cup milk
1 egg
½ cup butter

BORDELAISE SAUCE

¼ cup minced garlic
1½ cups butter
⅛ cup brandy
1 bunch parsley, chopped
**   very fine**

½ oz. Lea & Perrins
**   Worcestershire sauce**
salt and pepper to taste

Dip frog legs in flour, egg and milk batter, and in bread crumbs. In 9-inch skillet over medium heat, melt butter and sauté frog legs for about 5 minutes. Remove frog legs from skillet.

To make Bordelaise sauce, sauté garlic and parsley in butter until wilted, 1 to 2 minutes. Add Worcestershire sauce, flame with brandy, and add salt and pepper to taste.

Arrange frog legs on serving dish, add Bordelaise sauce, and pop in oven about 2 minutes, then serve.   – MR

CRABMEAT YVONNE

2 lbs. fresh backfin lump
  crabmeat
6 fresh artichoke bottoms,
  boiled and sliced
1 lb. fresh mushrooms,
  sliced

½ cup clarified butter
salt and white pepper to
  taste
finely chopped parsley
lemon wedges

In a large skillet sauté the mushrooms, then add the artichoke bottoms and crabmeat. Sauté gently until heated thoroughly. Season with salt and white pepper. Garnish with finely chopped parsley. Serve over toast points and with a lemon wedge.
Serves 6.   – JGF

CRABMEAT FAR HORIZONS

1 cup light cream
pinch of salt
¼ tsp. Coleman's prepared
  mustard
12 capers
5 oz. fresh white crabmeat

1½ tsp. butter, melted
1½ tbsp. Hollandaise sauce
  or 1 egg yolk
Progresso Italian bread
  crumbs

Combine first five ingredients in a thick aluminum pan and bring to a short boil. Add melted butter.

When mixture starts to thicken, add Hollandaise sauce or in the summertime, when Hollandaise has a tendency to break down faster than usual, substitute an egg yolk. Fold lightly without using spoons or stirrers. This is to avoid breaking the crabmeat lumps. When consistency is right, fill a shell or serving dish with contents. Sprinkle this with Progresso Italian bread crumbs and then sprinkle with small lumps of butter.

Place coquille into 350-degree oven for approximately 5 minutes, or place under broiler until color appears.   – LE

STUFFED EGGPLANT

1 lb. cooked eggplant meat
  (2 medium eggplants)
3/8 lb. medium cream sauce
  (use 1/4 can Pet milk plus
  1/2 pt. water plus 1 large
  spoon of roux)
1/4 lb. claw meat
1/4 lb. special white
  crabmeat

1/2 lb. cooked whole shrimp
1 cup chopped green onion
  (approximately 1/2 bunch)
1/2 tbsp. black pepper
1 tbsp. salt
roughly 1 large spoon
  chopped parsley
2 1/2 oz. bread crumbs
butter

Combine all ingredients except bread crumbs and butter thoroughly, being careful not to over mix.

Place 7 ounces of mixture on cooked eggplant skin and sprinkle with bread crumbs. Ladle butter on and broil until it starts to brown.

Bake in 350-degree oven until bubbling and top with butter before serving.

Serves 6.   – RH

MUSSELS AU MIREPOIX

4 doz. mussels
1/3 lb. celery
1/3 lb. carrots
1/3 lb. onions

2 cups fish sauce
1/2 cup white wine
pinch garlic
shallots

Take mussels, clean with cold water, and remove beard. Grind celery, carrots, onions.

Place in a pot with fish sauce, white wine, pinch garlic, and shallots. Place mussels on top and steam over hot fire with a cover on.

Mussels are done when completely opened.

Place 1 dozen mussels in each soup bowl and pour juices over each bowl.

Serve with garlic toast.   – GP

BROILED REDFISH WITH CRABMEAT

4 fillets of redfish
1 pt. lump crabmeat
½ stick butter

salt and pepper
lemon

Broil fillets of redfish; put butter in pan. Sauté lump crabmeat very lightly until hot. Place crabmeat on top of fish. Place slice of lemon alongside. Serve immediately. – JGF

BUTTERFLY SHRIMP

1 lb. medium to large
shrimp

BATTER:

¾ cup flour
¾ cup cornstarch
¾ tsp. baking powder
½ tsp. salt

¾ cup water
2 tbsp. oil
1 egg yolk

MARINADE:

1 tsp. ginger juice
1 tsp. sherry
¼ tsp. salt

1 tsp. sesame seed oil
dash of white pepper

Shell and devein shrimp, leaving tails on. Split the shrimp along the outer curve, not all the way through. Marinate shrimp in the marinade for 15 minutes. Make batter by measuring out all dry ingredients. Add the liquid ones and stir until the mixture is a smooth, thick batter.

Heat oil in wok to 350°. Holding shrimp by its tail, dip into batter to coat evenly; slip it into oil. Repeat rapidly with the rest of the shrimp and deep-fry for 3 minutes. Turn shrimp constantly with a gentle motion. Remove shrimp with chopsticks when golden brown. – TW

REDFISH HERBSAINT

1 oz. Herbsaint (may
  substitute Pernod or
  Anisette)
1 oz. white wine
½ tsp. shallots, chopped
  fine
1 tsp. carrots, julienne
  (matchstick cut)
1 tsp. celery, julienne
  (matchstick cut)
1 tsp. leek (white part),
  julienne (matchstick cut)

1 mushroom cap, stem
  removed
4 oz. redfish fillet (may
  substitute bass or
  pompano)
2 oz. cream
salt to taste
white pepper to taste
juice of ½ lemon
2 oz. lump crabmeat
1 oz. butter
½ oz. Herbsaint

In a sauté pan, combine the Herbsaint, white wine, shallots, carrots, celery, leeks, and mushroom cap. Add the redfish fillet and poach on low heat for approximately 8 to 10 minutes (until the flesh is firm but not dry.) Remove the fish from the pan and set on a dinner plate. Hold warm.

Increase the heat and reduce the poaching liquid by half. Add the cream and reduce by half again. Season to taste with salt, white pepper, and lemon juice. Reduce to a simmer and add the crabmeat. Toss until it is heated through. Finish the sauce by swirling in the butter and splashing in a small amount of Herbsaint. Serve the sauce immediately over the warm fish.

Serves 1.   – GP

SHRIMP ETOUFFÉE

1½ lbs. small shrimp
1½ cups chopped green
  onions
¼ cup cooking oil
1 cup flour
¼ tsp. thyme

3 bay leaves
4 toes garlic, chopped
1 pinch cayenne pepper
3 cups fish or shrimp stock
2 oz. Pernod or Herbsaint
salt to taste

In a thick, 2-quart pot, heat oil, add flour, stir till very brown, add seasoning and green onions, stir for 30 seconds, add shrimp and stock. Cook for 30 minutes on medium heat. Add Pernod and remove from heat. Allow to sit while the Pernod flavors the dish, about 20 minutes.
Serves 6. – GP

REDFISH KOTTWITZ

5 tbsp. butter
8 fillets redfish
1 cup artichoke bottoms,
  cut into large pieces

1¼ cups sliced mushrooms
1 tsp. salt
¼ tsp. pepper

LEMON BUTTER SAUCE

½ cup brown sauce (rich
  beef stock and flour
  cooked together to a
  medium-thick
  consistency)

2 tbsp. lemon juice
1½ lbs. melted butter

Melt the butter in a large heavy skillet and sauté the trout, artichoke bottoms, and mushrooms over medium heat for about 7 to 8 minutes, until the fish is cooked through. Sprinkle in the salt and pepper while sautéeing. Remove the fish and vegetables to heated plates while you prepare the sauce. If possible, set the plates in a warm (175°) oven. To make the lemon butter sauce, combine the ingredients listed and heat over a low flame, mixing with a whisk to get a smooth, even texture. To serve, ladle about ⅓ cup sauce over each portion.
Serves 8. – MR

SHRIMP TOAST

1 lb. medium shrimp
2 bacon slices
3 water chestnuts, minced
1 tbsp. chopped scallion,
  white part only

2 tsp. cornstarch
1 egg white
8 thin slices of stale white
  bread

SEASONING:

¾ tsp. salt
1 tsp. fresh ginger juice
½ tsp. sesame seed oil

¼ tsp. white pepper
1 tbsp. rice wine or sherry

Shell and devein shrimp, dry, and mince very fine. Steam bacon and dice. Mix all ingredients (except bread) and seasoning together. Mix thoroughly to form a thick paste.

Trim crusts and cut bread into 4 equal parts. Spread the shrimp paste on bread and press lightly.

Heat oil to 350°; gently put bread shrimp-side down on pan. Fry until both sides are golden brown.   – TW

STUFFED EGGPLANT

1 eggplant
4 tsp. butter
½ cup chopped green
  onions
¼ cup chopped parsley
salt and pepper to taste

½ lb. fresh lump crabmeat
1 doz. medium shrimp,
  boiled and peeled
bread crumbs
grated Swiss or Parmesan
  cheese

Take a good-size eggplant, cut it lengthwise and cook in oven. When cooked, scrape the pulp from the skin; save the skin. Put butter in pan, add chopped green onions and parsley, and brown. Season with salt and pepper and let cook for a few minutes until soft. Add the pulp, the crabmeat and shrimp (previously boiled) and cook for a few minutes. Dress the stuffing on the eggplant peel, put on bread crumbs and grated cheese, bake for a few minutes until brown, and serve.

Serves 2.   – JGF

STUFFED LOBSTER TOULOUSE

4 large or 8 small Florida
   lobsters (or 8 African or
   Danish rock lobster tails)
1 cup butter
¾ cup chopped white onion
¾ cup chopped green onion
½ cup chopped celery
2 tbsp. finely chopped
   garlic
½ cup chopped parsley
¾ cup chopped mushrooms

⅓ cup chopped lobster
⅓ cup chopped shrimp
⅓ cup chopped crabmeat
2 cups water, more if
   necessary
¾ cup dry white wine
1 tsp. thyme
2½ tsp. salt
1 tsp. black pepper
2½ cups flour
2 tbsp. Worcestershire sauce

Boil the lobsters in the shell for 10 to 12 minutes, then drain and split. Set aside in a warm oven while you prepare the stuffing. To prepare the stuffing, melt the butter in a large saucepan, then add the chopped vegetables. Simmer until the vegetables are soft. Add the chopped shellfish, water, wine, and thyme. Mix thoroughly and cook for a few minutes, then gradually stir in the flour, blending to keep the sauce smooth. Add the salt, pepper, and Worcestershire sauce and mix. Cook for a few minutes, then taste and add more water, salt, or pepper if necessary. Cook until the mixture is semi-moist. Fill the empty part of each lobster half with about ½ cup stuffing. Preheat the broiler, then place the stuffed lobster halves on a shallow broiling or baking pan and place under the broiler about 5 to 6 inches from the heat. Broil until the tops brown, about 6 to 8 minutes. Serve 1 or 2 stuffed lobster halves per portion, depending on size.

Serves 8.   – MR

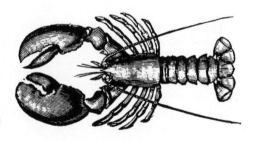

POMPANO PAPILLOTE

**3 2-lb. pompano, cleaned,
  skinned, and boned
3 tbsp. olive oil
1 cup chopped green
  onions
5 cloves
salt and pepper**

**6 tbsp. butter
juice of 3 lemons
3 egg yolks
½ can mushrooms
¼ can truffles
few shrimp**

Preheat oven to 400°F.

Bind each tenderloin of pompano. Put in a frying pan with olive oil, chopped green onions, cloves, salt and pepper. Bake in hot oven for 10 minutes.

When cooked, dress your fillets in individual greased sheets of paper. Melt butter in pan in which fish was cooked.

Add the lemon juice, egg yolks, mushrooms, truffles, and a few shrimp (mince the mushrooms, truffles and shrimp very fine).

Stew on low fire, stirring until thickened and serve over fillet. Close paper and heat in oven 5 minutes and serve hot.

Serves 6.   – JGF

OSTRICHE ALL' ITALIANA
(Baked Oysters Italian Style)

**3 doz. fresh oysters
3 tbsp. finely chopped
  parsley
3 cloves garlic, chopped
3 tbsp. Parmesan cheese**

**3½ tbsp. soft bread crumbs
2 lemons
olive oil
freshly ground pepper**

Open the oysters with an oyster knife. Arrange them on their half-shells in a fire-proof dish. Sprinkle generously with parsley and the garlic, lightly with bread crumbs and cheese, and finish with plenty of freshly ground pepper. Trickle a little olive oil over each oyster and bake in a slow oven (325°) for 10 or 15 minutes.

Serve immediately, garnished with lemon wedge.

Serves 6.   – GF

REDFISH AU SAUTERNE

redfish fillet
French shallots, chopped
sauterne

heavy cream
salt and pepper
cayenne pepper

Garnishes:

¼ cup julienne of fennel
¼ cup julienne of
  mushrooms

¼ cup boiled shrimp
¼ cup blanched oysters
¼ cup diced tomatoes

    In a small frypan place a redfish fillet with some chopped French shallots. Half-fill the pan with sauterne, cover, and cook in a low oven at 350° for about 12 minutes, until the fish is just cooked. Remove the fillet and keep warm.

    Reduce the remaining liquid until just before it becomes dry. Add heavy cream and reduce again until it thickens. Add your garnishes to the sauce, season with salt, pepper, and cayenne, and spoon over the fillet.

    Serve immediately.

    – RH

GAMBERI ALLA GRATICOLA
(Grilled Shrimp)

16 large shrimp, shelled
  and deveined
½ cup cognac
16 thin slices fatty ham
16 sage leaves or bay leaves

2 tbsp. bread crumbs
½ tsp. salt
½ tsp. pepper
2 tsp. lemon juice

    Wash shrimp and marinate in cognac 1 hour. Drain and wrap each shrimp in slice of ham. Place shrimp on skewers alternately with sage or bay leaves. Place in broiler and cook until ham fat begins to sizzle. Roll skewers in bread crumbs, sprinkle with salt and pepper. Return to broiler until golden brown in color. Sprinkle with lemon juice and serve very hot.

    Serves 2.

    – GF

TROUT MEUNIÈRE

3 2½-lb. trout tenderloins,
  halved
2½ cups peanut oil
1 cup flour
½ cup margarine
½ cup white wine

1 lemon, sliced
½ clove garlic, finely
  chopped
6 sprigs parsley, finely
  chopped
salt and pepper to taste

Preheat oil in frying pan to 350°. Test temperature by dropping a small amount of water in the oil to see if it pops. Dredge trout evenly in flour and fry, 2 pieces at a time, over medium flame for a total of 10 to 15 minutes, or 5 to 7 minutes on each side. After all 6 pieces are fried, place on a platter to keep warm. Heat the margarine with the wine and pour over the trout. Garnish with lemon slices, garlic and parsley. Add salt and pepper to taste.

Serves 6.

– AL

CRAWFISH VERSAILLES

2 tbsp. fresh butter
2 tbsp. sliced green onions
1 tbsp. minced dry shallots
2 tbsp. minced garlic
½ cup white wine
juice of ¼ lemon
1¾ cups medium bechamel
  sauce

1½ tbsp. fresh dill (1 tbsp.
  dried)
1½ lbs. fresh boiled crawfish
  tails
salt to taste
pinch cayenne pepper

Sauté onions, garlic, and shallots in butter for 2 minutes without browning. Add white wine and lemon juice, reduce by one half. Add bechamel sauce and dill and reduce by another third. Add crawfish tails and simmer 10 minutes. Salt to taste and add a pinch of cayenne pepper.

To serve, put in ramekins or small sea shells, sprinkle with freshly grated Parmesan cheese and bake in 350-degree oven until cheese is golden. Garnish with a boiled crawfish and serve.

Serves 6.

– GP

REDFISH STEAK WITH LUMP CRABMEAT JAIME

8 fillets of redfish
pepper and salt for
  sprinkling

melted butter for basting

RED WINE AND MUSHROOM SAUCE:

3 qts. beef stock
1 cup chopped carrots
1 cup chopped white
  onions
1 cup chopped celery
2 cloves garlic, chopped
1 tsp. leaf thyme
2 bay leaves
3 cups dry red wine
about 4 tsp. salt, more if
  desired

about 1 tsp. black pepper
8 fresh ripe tomatoes, cut up
  (or 4 cups canned
  tomatoes)
3 tbsp. Worcestershire sauce
1½ lbs. butter
3 cups flour
1¾ cups sliced mushrooms
1½ lbs. lump crabmeat

Preheat the broiler and prepare the pan and fish fillets for broiling. Set aside. To prepare the red wine sauce, combine all the ingredients except the butter, flour, mushrooms, and crabmeat in a large kettle and cook over medium-high heat for about 4 to 6 minutes, or until heated through. Add the butter and cook, stirring, until the butter is completely melted and evenly blended in. Then gradually stir in the flour and cook over medium high heat until thoroughly blended. Add the mushrooms and cook for several minutes longer, then remove the kettle from the heat. Stir well and ladle about 1½ quarts of the sauce into a saucepan. (Reserve any remaining sauce for later use; let cool, then refrigerate.) Add the crabmeat and cook over very low heat for about 5 minutes. Remove the pan from the heat and set aside while you broil the redfish fillets. Then place each fillet on a warmed dinner plate and top each with about ⅓ cup of the red wine sauce and lump crabmeat. Serve immediately.

Serves 8.

         – MR

SOGLIOLA ALLA VENEZIANA
(Sole Venetian-style)

2 lbs. fillet of sole or
    flounder
1 cup flour
½ cup olive oil
1 large onion, chopped
½ cup wine vinegar

1 tbsp. fine granulated sugar
1 tbsp. white seedless
    raisins
1 tbsp. pine nuts (or
    almonds), chopped
salt and pepper to taste

Dust fish with flour. Heat oil in skillet and brown fish gently on both sides over moderate flame. Remove fish and keep hot. In same oil sauté onion 5 minutes. Combine vinegar, sugar, and rest of ingredients and add to the onion. Cook 5 minutes longer. Carefully add fish, cover, and simmer 2 minutes or until fish is very hot. Serve at once with sauce.
    Serves 4.   – GF

MIKE ROUSSEL'S OYSTER LOAF

1 medium-size loaf French
    bread or ½ loaf, sliced
    across
1 tbsp. butter
1 tbsp. mayonnaise
½ tbsp. finely chopped
    garlic
¼ cup chopped lettuce
several drops Tabasco

½ tomato, sliced
1 sliced dill pickle, cut into
    several slivers
1 doz. deep-fried oysters
    (see note below for frying
    directions)
about 4 to 5 very thin slices
    fresh lemon

Note: To fry the oysters, drain them well, then roll in cornmeal seasoned with salt, pepper, and cayenne, or use seasoned flour if you prefer. Fry in vegetable oil in a deep fryer heated to 375° for about 3 minutes per batch, or until golden brown and crisp, then drain on paper towels for a few minutes.

Butter both the inner sides of the French bread, then put the remaining ingredients on the bottom half in the order given above. Cover with the top piece of French bread, then place in a 400-degree oven until crisp, about 3 to 5 minutes.   – MR

CRABMEAT AMBASSADOR

60 pieces Louisiana crab
  fingers
2 oz. butter
2 garlic cloves, chopped
1 medium onion, chopped

½ bunch parsley
2 tsp. Creole mustard
1½ oz. Courvoisier cognac
salt and pepper to taste

In skillet melt butter; add onions, garlic, mustard, and parsley. Sauté lightly but do not brown. Add crab claws and simmer for a few minutes until claws are well covered. Correct taste with salt and pepper. Pour cognac over, then flame. Serve piping hot.

Serves 6.   – JLA

SQUID AU BRETONNE

2 squid, cleaned
4 tbsp. oil
4 oz. plus 1 tbsp. butter
2 fresh shallots, finely
  chopped
1 clove garlic, crushed
1 oz. brandy
7 oz. white wine
½ cup fish stock
½ cup chopped fresh
  tarragon

2 tomatoes, peeled, seeded
  and chopped
pinch chopped parsley
salt and cayenne pepper to
  taste
1 tbsp. beurre manie (equal
  parts flour and butter,
  blended together)

Heat oil and 1 tablespoon butter in sauté pan until very hot. Add squid and fry quickly on all sides until flesh is set. Drain off fat and sprinkle the squid with the chopped shallots and garlic. Add brandy and flame. Then add the white wine, fish stock, tomatoes, fresh tarragon, parsley, and a touch of cayenne pepper. Cover with lid and cook gently for 8 to 10 minutes.

Whip beurre manie into hot sauce and cook 2 to 3 minutes. Adjust seasoning and add 4 ounces butter cut in small pieces; sprinkle with chopped parsley.   – LED

SHRIMP KEW

12 oz. medium or large
  shrimp
½ cup celery
½ cup straw mushrooms
½ cup baby corn, cut in
  halves

¼ cup sliced carrots
½ cup snow peas
½ tsp. chopped garlic
½ tsp. ginger
2 tbsp. rice wine or sherry
¼ cup water chestnuts

MARINADE:

1½ tsp. cornstarch
½ egg white, beaten

pinch of salt and white
  pepper

GRAVY:

Mix together:
½ tsp. salt
½ tsp. sugar
1 tsp. oyster sauce
1 tbsp. light soy sauce
½ tsp. sesame seed oil

1 tsp. oil
dash of white pepper
1½ tsp. cornstarch dissolved
  in ½ cup chicken stock

Mix together ingredients for the marinade. Marinate shrimp in refrigerator for 30 minutes.

Heat 2 cups oil in wok, scatter in the shrimp and toss them rapidly until 80 percent cooked. Drain the shrimp and oil immediately into a strainer that is set over a pot.

Reheat wok and add 3 tablespoons oil. Toss in the ginger and garlic, shower in all the vegetables, stir-fry for 90 seconds, and add shrimp back to wok. Sprinkle rice wine or sherry and stir for another 30 seconds. Add gravy mix until sauce thickens.   – TW

TROUT MOUSSE FLORENTINE WITH SHRIMP SAUCE

2 lbs. fresh trout fillets
4 to 5 egg whites
1½ tsp. salt

⅓ tsp. white pepper
1 tsp. nutmeg
5 cups heavy cream

Cut trout fillets in small pieces and run through a food chopper until very fine, all the while adding egg whites, salt, pepper, and nutmeg. When mixed and chopped fine, add heavy cream about a cup at a time allowing for a thorough blend between additions.

Butter inside of a ring mold lightly; fill the bottom third of the mold with mousse compactly. With a pastry bag, pipe a circle of spinach (see recipe below) around the mold, keeping within the center of the mousse. Now finish filling the mold with mousse and pack tightly again, keeping the spinach in the center. Now place mold in a pan of hot water (water should come three-quarters of the way up the mold) and bake in a 350-degree oven for 25 to 30 minutes. A toothpick inserted in the center will come out clean when done. Allow mold to sit 5 to 6 minutes before unmolding.

FLORENTINE GARNISH
(Creamed spinach in center of mousse)

2 tbsp. butter
2 tbsp. flour
½ cup minced white onion
1 tsp. finely chopped garlic
1 tsp. frozen chopped
   spinach (thawed)

½ cup finely chopped
   shallots
½ cup heavy cream
salt and pepper to taste

Melt butter, add flour, and cook roux slowly about 15 minutes. Add onion, garlic, shallots, and chopped spinach and mix thoroughly. Now add cream little by little, then add salt and pepper to taste, and cook on stovetop on low to medium heat, stirring occasionally, about 30 minutes or until excess moisture and flour taste diminishes. Cool before adding to mousse.

SHRIMP SAUCE

¼ lb. fresh butter
8 tbsp. flour
1 cup sliced green onions
2 shallots, chopped fine
2 garlic cloves, chopped
  fine
2 bay leaves

1 tbsp. leaf thyme
2 tbsp. paprika
2 lbs. medium-size peeled
  and deveined shrimp
1½ cups heavy cream
salt and pepper to taste
½ cup white wine

Melt butter, add flour and cook roux slowly, about 15 minutes. Add green onions, shallots, garlic, bay leaves, leaf thyme, paprika, and shrimp. Cook approximately 5 to 6 minutes. Add white wine and cream slowly, allowing sauce to thicken as you go. Add salt and pepper to taste, simmer 10 minutes, and serve as directed.

To serve, invert mold on platter to free mousse, then fill center of mousse with shrimp and sauce, also coating mousse with sauce. Sprinkle with chopped parsley and serve, carved at tableside; pass extra sauce.

Serves 6 to 8. — GP

SHRIMP AND GRAPEFRUIT

fresh shrimp, peeled and
  butterflied
fresh grapefruit
French shallots
whipping cream

butter
salt and cracked black
  pepper
lemon juice

Cut the grapefruit meat into segments, making sure there are no membrane or seeds remaining. Reserve any juice and keep together.

Take a few shallots, finely chopped, and slowly sauté in butter until clear. Add the shrimp and sauté until firm and pink. Remove the shrimp and set aside. Add cream to the pan and reduce. When this thickens, add some pieces of grapefruit and a little juice. Season with salt, cracked black pepper, and a little lemon juice. Add the shrimp; heat and serve.

It is optional to finish this sauce with a little Hollandaise. After adding the shrimp, remove from heat and add Hollandaise. Serve immediately. — RH

CRAWFISH LERUTH FRÈRES

1 medium onion, chopped
   fine, (1 cup) half green
   onion and onion can be
   used)
1½ sticks butter
¼ tsp. red pepper

1½ tsp. salt
1 lb. peeled, blanched
   crawfish tails
1¼ cups water
2 tbsp. flour
¼ cup chopped parsley

Sauté onion in butter until soft. Add salt, pepper, crawfish, and 1 cup water. Cover and boil for 5 minutes. Dissolve flour in ¼ cup water. While stirring, add flour dissolved in water to the boiling crawfish. Return to good boil, and add chopped parsley.

Serve over rice.

– LLL

SHRIMP VICTORIA

1 cup butter
¾ cup thinly sliced green
   onions
½ cup sliced mushrooms
1 bunch fresh basil, cut up
4 lbs. raw shrimp, peeled
   and deveined (about 7 to
   8 lbs. in the shell)
⅔ cup dry white wine

⅔ cup heavy cream
1¼ tsp. salt
½ tsp. white pepper
3 tbsp. Worcestershire sauce
⅓ cup white roux (1 tbsp.
   butter, 1 tbsp. flour, ¼ cup
   hot milk)
½ cup heavy sour cream

Melt the butter in a large heavy sauté pan or saucepan. Add the green onions, mushrooms, and basil, then sauté the shrimp until they begin to appear glazed and slightly translucent. Stir in the white wine and cook for about 2 minutes, then add the cream, salt, pepper, and Worcestershire sauce. Mix thoroughly, then add several tablespoons of the white roux and cook for a minute or so. If the sauce still appears thin, add the rest of the roux. Remove the pan from the heat and allow to stand for a few minutes, uncovered, then stir in the sour cream. Serve immediately on preheated dinner plates, taking care to divide the shrimp and the shreds of basil evenly and to arrange them attractively.

Serves 8.

– MR

RED SNAPPER CARIBBEAN

6 6-oz. red snapper fillets
6 lemons, cut in quarters
1 lb. 21- to 35-count
   shrimp
1 lb. butter
1 tsp. whole thyme
1 tsp. white pepper
3 eggs
1 oz. Lea & Perrins
   Worcestershire sauce

1 bunch green onions,
   chopped
1 lb. crawfish tails
2 doz. large mushroom caps
4 bay leaves
3 tsp. salt
8 oz. white wine
1 pt. milk
flour
½ lb. shortening

Make egg wash by mixing the eggs with the pint of milk; this is for the snapper.

In sauté pan melt ½ pound shortening. Place the snapper in the egg wash, dust the snapper in flour, then place the snapper in sauté pan and cook until brown on both sides. Take out of the pan and place on a plate.

In medium saucepan place 1 pound butter, shrimp, and mushrooms. Cook for 20 minutes on low heat. Then add green onions, crawfish tails, white wine, squeeze lemons (add the squeezed lemon quarters as well), thyme, bay leaves, salt, pepper, and Lea and Perrins. Cook for 15 more minutes on low heat, stirring constantly. Then pour over red snapper and serve. Suggest served with stuffed tomatoes or parslied boiled tomatoes.

Serves 6.

   – LE

FILLET OF FLOUNDER IN BUTTER

1¼ lbs. fillets of flounder
½ cup flour
½ cup butter

½ tsp. salt
½ tsp. pepper
3 tsp. lemon juice

Roll flounder in flour. Melt butter in skillet. Add floured fillets, sprinkle with salt and pepper and cook over low flame 10 minutes each side. Remove from pan. Sprinkle with lemon juice and serve.

Serves 4.

   – GF

CRYSTAL SHRIMP

1 lb. medium shrimp
3 pieces sliced ginger
¼ tsp. chopped garlic
3 green onions, cut into 2-
   inch pieces

peas and carrots, amounting
   to ¼ cup combined
3 tbsp. dry sherry or Chinese
   rice wine

GRAVY

Mix together:
½ tsp. salt
¼ tsp. accent
½ tsp. sugar
dash of white pepper

½ cup soup stock
1½ tsp. cornstarch
½ tsp. sesame seed oil
2 tsp. oil

MARINADE

1½ tsp. cornstarch
½ egg white

a pinch of salt and pepper

Peel and devein shrimp, and mix with 1 teaspoon salt. Run under cold water for 10 minutes. Dry out shrimp, then marinate with cornstarch and egg white for 20 minutes. Cut onions and carrots into small pieces.

Heat wok or heavy skillet until very hot. Add 2 cups of oil for about 45 seconds. Add shrimp. Cook until about 80 percent done. Remove shrimp and drain oil.

Reheat pan until very hot, adding 3 tablespoons oil. Add ginger, garlic, onion, carrots, and peas. Stir, then add shrimp and wine.

Stir for 30 seconds, then add gravy mixture. Stir until gravy is thick.

       – TW

ARTICHOKE AND CRAB BEIGNETS

1 bunch green onions
  (white part only)
¼ cup chopped pimentos
4 oz. chopped artichoke
  hearts
2 large toes fresh garlic,
  chopped fine

1 tbsp. chopped parsley
¼ tsp. red pepper
¼ tsp. salt
1 pt. flour
1 pt. water
2 tsp. baking powder
16 oz. jumbo lump crabmeat

Mix flour and baking powder. Add chopped artichokes, green onions, garlic, parsley, and pimentos. Add salt and red pepper. Add water and mix until batter is well blended. Fold in 16 ounces jumbo lump crabmeat. Fry in peanut oil at 350° until golden brown. Use tablespoon to drop batter into oil.   – LLL

REDFISH ETOUFFÉE

4 to 6 fillets redfish, 6 to 8
  oz. each
salt and pepper
Lea & Perrins
  Worcestershire sauce
lemon juice
2 oz. sherry wine
1 tbsp. tomato paste
thyme
stock

crawfish, shrimp, or
  crabmeat
1 cup butter
1 cup flour
½ bell pepper, minced
1 celery stalk, minced
1 garlic toe, minced
½ large onion, minced
2 green onions, minced
1 large tomato, minced

Take fillets of redfish and season lightly with pepper, salt, Lea & Perrins Worcestershire sauce and lemon juice. Sauté in skillet for 10 minutes at moderate heat.

Melt butter in saucepan, add flour while stirring constantly. Cook until dark brown. Add the vegetables and stir till limp, then add sherry, tomato paste, thyme, black pepper, and salt to taste. Add stock to desired thickness, and add your choice of seafood.

Top redfish with etouffée, garnish with lemon slices, and serve hot. Serves 4 to 6.   – WC

SMOKED FISH WITH PASTA

1 lb. fresh pasta　　　　　　　1 tbsp. olive oil
1 lb. fish fillet　　　　　　　　1 pt. whipping cream
3 diced red bell peppers

In a large bowl mix 1 quart of cold water and 1 cup salt together. Place the fish in it and marinate for 20 minutes. Remove the fish and smoke it in a smoker on the coolest temperature possible and with the most smoke possible. Remove the fillet or fillets before they are cooked.

Poach the fillets in a courtbouillon (one cup white wine, 2 cups water, pinch of salt and cracked peppercorns). Cool the fish in this liquid. (This can be done a day ahead.) The fish fillets must be drained and flaked apart before using them in the recipe.

Cook the pasta, rinse in hot water and drain. In a large skillet sauté the red peppers in the olive oil. Add heavy cream and bring it to a boil. Add the fish. Reduce to sauce consistency and add the hot pasta.

Season to taste with salt, pepper and cayenne and toss. Place on a plate and garnish with cracked pepper and chopped parsley.

Serves 4 to 6.　　　　　　　　　　　　　　　　　　　　　　　　　– RH

WHITE TROUT EN PAPILLOTE
PETIT LEO

6 oz. fresh fillet of trout　　　　salt and pepper
2 oz. butter　　　　　　　　　　1 heart-shaped piece of
½ tsp. minced fresh garlic　　　　　parchment paper (brushed
1 tsp. fresh chopped　　　　　　　with oil)
　parsley　　　　　　　　　　　1 tsp. chopped white onion
1 tsp. fresh chopped　　　　　　½ tsp. paprika
　oregano　　　　　　　　　　　1 fresh artichoke bottom cut
½ tsp. fresh diced green　　　　　　into small dice
　pepper

In a bowl, mix all ingredients except the trout. Place half of the filling on half of the paper. Put the fillet of fish on top of the filling. Place remaining filling on top of fish. Fold and seal paper all around fish. Place in baking pan and bake at 375° for 16 to 20 minutes.　　　　– LED

STUFFED SHRIMP

3 lbs. (about 36) fresh
  jumbo shrimp, with
  fantails
2 cups flour

egg wash
1 box commercial fish fry
oil for frying

CRABMEAT DRESSING

1 stick margarine (or 3 oz.
  butter)
4 sprigs parsley, finely
  chopped
1 celery rib, finely chopped

1 onion, finely chopped
1 lb. crabmeat
1 loaf French bread
2 eggs
salt and pepper to taste

Melt margarine or butter in skillet with seasonings (parsley, celery, and onion) and sauté 10 to 15 minutes. Add crabmeat and sauté an additional 10 to 15 minutes. While crabmeat sautées, moisten bread (it should be wet but not soggy) in a bowl and then chop it. Add eggs and mix. Add crabmeat mixture to bread and eggs. Season with salt and pepper. Place in a baking pan and bake for 1 hour. Stir after the first half hour of cooking. Remove from oven and place in refrigerator and cool to refrigerator temperature (approximately 45°.). Peel shrimp (make sure to leave on fantails) and devein. Sprinkle shrimp with salt and pepper. Take dressing from refrigerator. For each shrimp, place 1 tablespoon of dressing in palm of hand, spread evenly to 1/8 inch thick. Place shrimp in dressing, roll, and pat well. Roll shrimp in flour, then in egg wash, then in fish fry. Place in frying pan and brown evenly by moving shrimp around for 10 minutes on each side (20 minutes in all.)

Serves 6.

– AL

QUENELLES

8 oz. panada
9 oz. fresh fish*
4½ oz. butter
2 eggs

1 egg yolk
1 dash nutmeg
2 dashes cayenne pepper
1 tsp. salt

*Frozen fish will not make firm quenelles.

PANADA:

4 to 5 oz. (depending upon
gluten content) bread
flour

1 cup water
1 oz. butter

To make panada, boil water and butter with a pinch of salt. When it reaches a rolling boil, turn off heat and add all the flour at the same time. Stir with a wooden spoon until smooth, then turn on heat and continue stirring until mixture balls up and is free from the pan. Then place dough on plate and chill.

Blend fish in food processor; add cold panada and cold butter cut in cubes and blend until smooth. Add seasonings and eggs, blend again, and chill.

When thoroughly chilled, use pastry bag and greased waxed paper. Pipe into 2-inch lengths. Two spoons can also be used to form the quenelles.

Place quenelles into a boiling pot of salted water, and cook at a simmer until they are firm in the center. Test by pulling one out and cutting it in half with a knife. When done, chill the quenelles quickly in cold water.

To serve, heat quenelles in simmering, salted water. When they are hot, pull them out, pat them dry, and place in dish. Spoon Americaine sauce over them, being sure to cover them completely.   – RH

SQUID AND SHRIMP STEW, CREOLE STYLE

1 tbsp. olive oil
1 large onion, peeled and
  chopped
4 cups tomatoes, coarsely
  chopped, with their juice,
  or 4 cups canned
  tomatoes and their juice
  plus 1 tablespoon tomato
  paste

2 tbsp. Brennan's Shellfish
  Seasoning
1 tbsp. sugar
1 lb. squid, cleaned and
  sliced into ½-inch rounds
1 lb. shrimp, shells removed
  and cleaned

Heat the oil in a 7-quart casserole or saucepan. Add the onions and cook for 5 minutes; the onions should be milky in color and just about to start browning.

Mix in the tomatoes, Seasoning, and sugar. Bring the sauce to a simmer and cook for 30 minutes. Stir often. Add the squid, cover, and cook at a simmer for 20 minutes.

Mix in the shrimp, cover, and cook at a simmer for 3 minutes. Serve over cooked brown rice.

Serves 6.   – MR

SALMON WITH VEGETABLES AND CHABLIS

4 5-oz. boneless fillets of
  salmon
1 leek (white only)
1 celery branch, peeled
1 medium carrot

1 cup sliced mushrooms
1 cup cream
4 oz. butter
1 cup Chablis

Cut vegetables in slices and boil in salted water until tender. Drain and stew in butter for 4 minutes.

In a saucepan arrange vegetables and mushrooms. Season. Put salmon on top of vegetables. Add wine and cook for 10 minutes.

Put fish on platter. Reduce stock with cream. Before serving add butter, check seasoning, and pour over fish.   – GP

LERUTH'S CRAB SOUFFLÉ

2 oz. butter and 1 tsp. paprika
1 bunch chopped green onions
¼ tsp. salt
¼ tsp. red pepper
¼ tsp. thyme
¼ tsp. ground bay leaf
¼ tsp. white pepper
1 tbsp. tomato paste

1 tsp. Creole mustard
¼ cup flour
1 cup cream (marinate 1 toe garlic 1 hour and strain)
6 egg yolks
6 egg whites
8 oz. jumbo lump crabmeat
3 tbsp. grated Romano cheese

Sauté green onions with butter and all spices and salt. Add tomato paste. Cook for five minutes. Stir in flour. Add garlic-cream. Cook until thickens. Remove from heat. Whisk in egg yolks and add mustard. Gently stir in jumbo lump crabmeat. (Be very careful not to break up lumps of meat.) Whisk egg whites until they peak. Add crabmeat mix a little at a time to whites. Fold in very easy. Place in buttered and floured 10-inch soufflé dish. Dust top of soufflé with cheese. For about 25 minutes bake at 375°.

– LLL

MOUSSELINE DE POISSON

1 lb. fresh fish
1 egg white
1 qt. cream (approximately)

salt and pepper
nutmeg
red pepper

Puree the fish, making sure to scrape down the sides of the food processor to insure that all is well pureed.

Add the egg white. Puree for 30 seconds, then add half the cream and puree for another 30 seconds. Remove this mixture into a mixing bowl over ice and beat in cream with a wooden spoon until light.

Season with salt, pepper, a dash of nutmeg, and red pepper. Cook a sample – place a large tablespoon in a ramekin, place ramekin in small baking pan with hot water about ⅓ inch deep, and place in 350-degree oven until done, about 5 to 8 minutes. Adjust cream and seasonings.

– RH

FILET OF TROUT NIÇOISE

You can use any local fish in your area, such as catfish, trout, redfish, drum, or salmon.

1 8-oz. fillet per person	1 tbsp. fresh rosemary
1 eggplant	1 tbsp. chives or green of
1 tomato	green onion
1 zucchini	1 tbsp. parsley
1 red onion	4 tbsp. butter
1 lemon	salt and pepper to taste
4 bay leaves	½ cup water
½ cup olive oil	¼ cup white wine
1 tbsp. fresh tarragon,	½ stick butter
chopped	

In a very shallow pan, marinate fish with oil and herbs for a couple of hours. Just before cooking, slice eggplant with skin on, and cut slices in half. Squeeze lemon on eggplant (use rest on fish), slice tomato, and cut slices in half. Thinly slice zucchini and onion. In a shallow baking pan, arrange fish and interlace eggplant, tomato, zucchini and onion over each fillet (remove excess oil). Season with salt and pepper. Place bay leaf on each fish. Add tablespoon of butter on each fillet; add water, bake at 450° for approximately 10 minutes. Do not overcook, be sure to watch that vegetables do not burn. Remove fish and vegetables from pan. Just before serving, add wine and ½ stick of butter into pan. Reduce until cream consistency. Pour over fish and serve. (Can be served with angel hair, pasta, rice, etc.) – CK

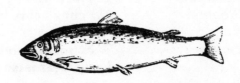

STUFFED LOBSTER

3 live Florida or Maine
  lobsters
1 box commercial seafood
  seasoning
salt and pepper to taste
1 tsp. cayenne pepper
1 lemon, sliced
1 recipe Crabmeat Dressing
  (see Stuffed Shrimp
  recipe)

¼ cup bread crumbs
2 oz. margarine, melted
½ clove garlic, finely
  chopped
4 sprigs parsley, chopped
dash of paprika
6 lemon slices

Put lobsters in large pot of boiling water along with seafood seasoning, salt and pepper, cayenne, and lemon slices. Make sure water covers the lobsters. Cover pot and bring water back to boiling. Turn flame off, remove lobsters and let them sit for 5 minutes before placing in refrigerator to cool. When cool, cut lobsters in half. Clean the heads and devein the tails. Stuff heads with crabmeat dressing and pack well. Cover dressing with bread crumbs. Sprinkle melted margarine on each lobster half. Place under broiler for 10 minutes. Before serving, place slice of lemon on each lobster half, top with garlic and parsley and a sprinkling of paprika.

Serves 6 (½ lobster each).
                                   – AL

GRATIN DE CRABE AU BEURRE D'ÉCREVISSES

2 tbsp. butter
1 tbsp. chopped shallots
6 medium mushrooms,
  thinly sliced
2 lbs. lump crabmeat
salt and pepper

cayenne pepper
1 splash brandy
1½ cups heavy whipping
  cream
¼ cup crawfish butter
1 cup Beárnaise sauce

Heat butter in 10-inch sauté pan. Bring to high heat and quickly stir in shallots, mushrooms, and crabmeat. Add dashes of salt, pepper, and cayenne to taste and flame with brandy (it is important that this be done quickly to avoid overcooking the crabmeat). Remove contents from pan and place aside.

In the same pan, reduce whipping cream by one half, then stir in crawfish butter until well blended.

Into this sauce fold the previously prepared crabmeat. Then fold in the Béarnaise sauce.

To serve, place individual serving in 5-inch metal au gratin dish and put close to heat under broiler until surface is lightly browned. Remove from heat, and serve.   – CK

LES CREVETTES EN ROBE VERTE
DU FAIRMONT
(Shrimp Vermicelli Wrapped in
Lettuce Leaves With
Creole Mustard Sauce)

1½ lbs. small shrimp – 90
   count
4 shallots, minced
4 cups cooked vermicelli
36 large Boston lettuce
   leaves, blanched for 45
   seconds and placed in ice
   water
2 oz. butter
3 oz. fresh grated Parmesan
   cheese

1 tbsp. chopped fresh basil
1 pinch nutmeg
3 tomatoes, cut in fine dice
4 fresh artichoke bottoms
   cut in small julienne
12 oz. whipping cream
salt and white pepper to
   taste
2 tbsp. Creole mustard

In heavy saucepan melt butter. Add shrimp and shallots and sauté approximately 4 minutes. Add basil, nutmeg, cream. Bring to a boil and add vermicelli, artichoke bottoms, salt, pepper, cheese, and mustard. Mix lightly until ingredients thicken. Place in bowl and let cool slightly. Place two lettuce leaves face side down and place approximately 1½ ounces of vermicelli mixture in leaves. Fold leaves around vermicelli to form little pouches. (These can be made a day ahead if you desire.) Store in refrigerator and re-heat in pans with a little chicken stock in 400° oven.   – LED

SHRIMP CURRY

3 tbsp. butter
3 tbsp. flour
2 lbs. medium-size peeled
and deveined shrimp
½ cup sliced green onions
1 tbsp. chopped shallots
1 tbsp. chopped parsley
2 tbsp. curry powder (or to
taste)

1½ tbsp. apple sauce
1 tsp. diced red pimento
1 tbsp. chutney
2 tbsp. sliced hearts of palm
2 cups heavy cream
salt to taste

Melt butter, add flour, and cook 5 to 10 minutes slowly. Add shrimp, green onions, shallots, parsley, and curry powder and cook 3 to 4 minutes. Now add apple sauce, pimento, chutney, and hearts of palm. Add cream slowly. Salt to taste and simmer 10 to 12 minutes and serve. Pass chutney on the side.
Serves 4.   – GP

CRAWFISH EVANS

1 lb. crawfish tails, cooked
and peeled
1 small bunch of green
onions
1 cup half-and-half
4 bay leaves
½ tbsp. sweet basil
½ tbsp. oregano
½ lb. butter

2 cups white wine
1 tsp. salt
6 oz. flour
½ qt. shrimp stock
1 tsp. chicken base
½ tbsp. Lea & Perrins
Worcestershire sauce
1 tbsp. jalapeño green
pepper sauce

In sauté pan, add butter; melt. Add chopped green onions and flour, and cook for 5 minutes. Add oregano, bay leaves, basil, green pepper sauce, chicken base, and Lea & Perrins and mix well.
Add shrimp stock, crawfish, white wine, and salt. Let come to a boil. Cook for about 5 to 8 minutes on slow heat.
Add half-and-half. Let come to a boil; cook slowly for about 3 minutes and serve.   – LE

POMPANO VERMOUTH

pinch of minced garlic
pinch of minced dry
  shallots
pinch of salt and white
  pepper
1 tbsp. sliced green onions
1/3 cup peeled and deveined
  shrimp (raw)

1/4 cup dry Vermouth
1 6 to 8-oz. skinless
  pompano fillet (folded
  once, head to tail)
3/4 cup heavy cream
1/4 cup lump crabmeat

Place garlic, shallots, salt, and pepper in oven-proof skillet. Add onions, shrimp, Vermouth, and pompano. Cover with foil and cook in a hot oven approximately 20 minutes. Remove pompano to heated plate and keep warm.

To the pan juices add the cream. Reduce on top of stove until sauce begins to thicken, then add crabmeat and heat thoroughly. Pour over pompano and serve.

Serves 1.

– GP

STUFFED CRAB A LA PONTCHARTRAIN

1 lb. lump crabmeat
2 hard French loaves
8 eggs
1/2 bunch green onions,
  chopped
1/2 bell pepper, chopped
2 bay leaves

1/2 clove garlic, chopped
1/2 tsp. cayenne pepper
1 lb. butter
1 rib celery, chopped
1/2 bunch parsley, chopped
1 lb. bread crumbs

Soak hard French bread in cold water. Place 1/2 pound of butter in sauté pan with celery, bell pepper, and green onion. Cook until vegetables are tender; add the soaked French bread, crabmeat, eggs, and remaining ingredients (except bread crumbs). Mix well. Place in a baking pan in the oven at 450° for 30 minutes, then stuff in crab shells and sprinkle with bread crumbs and butter. Return to oven until brown.

Serves 4.

– LE

POMPANO GRAND DUC

3 tbsp. butter
¼ cup finely chopped green
  onions
¼ cup flour
¾ cup fish stock
3 tbsp. white wine
¼ tsp. salt
dash cayenne
1 egg yolk, beaten
2 cups seasoned mashed
  potatoes

6 warm green asparagus
  spears
1½ lbs. poached fillet of
  pompano (save head, skin
  and bones for stock)
6 each boiled shrimp and
  scalded oysters
½ cup Hollandaise sauce
½ cup unsweetened whipped
  cream

Over medium heat in 7-inch skillet, melt butter and sauté onions until tender. Blend in flour thoroughly. Cook slowly about 5 minutes, stirring constantly; do not brown. Remove from heat. Blend in fish stock, wine, salt, and pepper until smooth. Blend in egg yolk thoroughly. Return pan to heat and gently cook over low heat, stirring constantly, about 15 minutes. Remove from heat and keep warm.

With mashed potatoes in pastry bag, flute a wall around extreme edge of large, warm platter. In center of platter place bundle of asparagus. Cover with fish sauce, made above, and arrange pompano on this bed of fish sauce. Garnish pompano with shrimp and oysters. Combine Hollandaise sauce and whipped cream and pour over fish. Bake at 375° (quick moderate oven) until potatoes brown lightly on edges.

Serves 3 to 4.

– MR

ESCALOPE DE SAUMON AU
BEURRE DE PISTACHE

fresh salmon   1 tsp. dry vermouth

Fillet salmon (remove bones). Slice very thin, with grain, approximately ¼-inch thick. Use clarified butter to barely sauté salmon, approximately 5 seconds on each side. Remove from pan. Make glace with dry vermouth. Finish with pistachio butter. Cover salmon and serve at once.

PISTACHIO BUTTER:

1 lb. butter, at room
   temperature
¼ lb. fresh pistachios (from
   health food store)

1 fresh lime

Remove shells and skins from nuts and pulverize. Add to butter with juice of lime, making a paste. Remainder can be refrigerated for later use.

I recommend serving this with julienne of leeks, sautéed in butter with salt and pepper.
          – CK

TROUT KOTTWITZ

5 tbsp. butter
8 fillets of speckled trout
1 cup artichoke bottoms,
   cut into large pieces

1¼ cups sliced mushrooms
1 tsp. salt
¼ tsp. pepper

LEMON BUTTER SAUCE:

½ cup brown sauce (rich
   beef stock and flour
   cooked together to a
   medium-thick
   consistency)

2 tbsp. lemon juice
1½ lbs. melted butter

Melt the butter in a large heavy skillet and sauté the trout, artichoke bottoms, and mushrooms over medium heat for about 7 to 8 minutes, until the fish is cooked through. Sprinkle in the salt and pepper while sautéeing. Remove the trout and vegetables to heated plates while you prepare the sauce. If possible, set the plates in a warm (175-degree) oven. To make the lemon butter sauce, combine the ingredients listed and heat over a low flame, mixing with a whisk to get a smooth, even texture. To serve, ladle about ⅓ cup sauce over each portion.

Serves 8.
          – MR

ALLIGATOR SAUCE PIQUANTE

3 lbs. alligator meat (cut in
  small pieces and
  preferably meat other
  than from the tail)
4 tbsp. butter
½ cup chopped onions
½ cup chopped celery
½ cup chopped green
  peppers
6 cloves garlic, chopped
2 tbsp. tomato paste
2 cups fresh peeled,
  seeded, chopped
  tomatoes

1 tsp. sugar
Louisiana hot cayenne
  pepper
salt and pepper to taste
2 cups white wine
1 qt. chicken stock
½ tsp. thyme
3 bay leaves
1 cup mushrooms (stems
  and pieces), sautéed in
  butter
½ cup chopped black olives
chopped parsley
chopped green onions

Sauté onions in butter until lightly browned. Add green peppers, celery, and garlic and stir well. Add tomato paste, sugar, and chopped tomatoes. Simmer a few minutes. Add the seasonings, wine, chicken stock, bay leaves, and thyme. Pour in alligator meat; bring to boil and let it cook for 25 to 30 minutes on low heat until meat is tender. Add mushrooms and olives. Correct seasonings. Serve over steamed rice; sprinkle with chopped parsley and chopped green onions.   – JLA

ESCALOPE DE POISSON ROUGE AU
BASILIC

2 shallots
20 basil leaves
½ cup dry vermouth
2 cups fish stock
salt and pepper
½ lb. redfish fillet, cut into
  4 sections

2 tbsp. clarified butter
  (enough to sauté fish)
½ lemon
½ cup cream

Peel and chop shallots. Chop basil leaves thoroughly as well and place on side.

In a 10-inch saucepan, pour vermouth and reduce 50 percent over about half maximum heat. Add shallots and fish stock and continue reduction until about 1 cup remains. Strain and place aside.

Salt and pepper one side of each redfish section to taste and sauté over high heat for 2 minutes on each side. Place the cooked fish aside in a warm place (i.e., a low oven) until sauce is completed.

Pour strained reduction into a 10-inch saucepan and stir in, over low heat, chopped basil and cream. Allow to reduce slowly until smooth and creamy. Stir in a squeeze of fresh lemon to finish.

Cover the surface of a plate with the sauce and place sections of the warm redfish on top.   – CK

TROUT BLANGE

½ cup butter
1 tbsp. minced garlic
¾ cup raw shrimp, peeled
¾ cup raw oysters
½ cup sliced cooked
  mushrooms
½ tsp. Spanish saffron
2 cups whole canned
  tomatoes
1 cup fish stock
¼ tsp. cayenne
1 tsp. salt

2 tbsp. cornstarch
¼ cup water
¼ cup chopped parsley
2 2-lb. trout, cleaned and
  boned (save heads, skin,
  and bones for making
  stock)
2 cups seasoned mashed
  potatoes
1 doz. whole mushrooms
1 doz. peeled, boiled shrimp

In a 10-inch skillet melt butter and sauté garlic, shrimp, oysters, mushrooms, and saffron. Add tomatoes, fish stock, cayenne, and salt. Simmer 15 to 20 minutes. Combine cornstarch and water; add to sauce to thicken. When desired consistency is obtained, remove pan from heat and add parsley. Keep warm. Grill or broil trout to a golden brown and remove to warm serving platter. Place mashed potatoes in a pastry bag and flute a wall around extreme edge of platter. Cover fish with warm sauce. Garnish with whole mushrooms and peeled, boiled shrimp. Sprinkle potatoes with paprika. Place under flame until potatoes are lightly browned.

Serves 4.   – MR

FILLET OF TROUT BAYOU STYLE

8 trout fillets
3 cups heavy cream
2 tbsp. Creole mustard
½ lemon
2 lbs. crawfish, live
1 carrot, whole
4 pieces shallots

2 celery ribs
1 tsp. tarragon
1 tbsp. tomato paste
8 oz. butter
2 oz. brandy
salt and pepper

Pound trout fillets until they are ¼-inch thick. Put 1 cup heavy cream in a bowl and whip until you have a firm consistency. To this, add Creole mustard, juice of half lemon, and salt and pepper.

Place inside refrigerator.

Cook crawfish in a courtbouillon, (water, celery, carrot, onion, bay leaves, thyme, whole peppercorns, and ½ cup white wine) for 5 minutes after it begins to boil. Peel crawfish. Keep crawfish tails in a bowl on the side.

Dice shallots, carrots, and celery into ¼-inch cubes. Place 4 ounces butter in a sauté pan and sauté, very slowly, the diced vegetables. Add the crawfish shells and flambé brandy over. Add 2 cups cream, tarragon, and tomato paste. Cook 20 minutes, strain, and finish with butter.

Season to your taste.

Butter a broiler tray, place fish fillets inside tray, and pour cream sauce over fish. Place under broiler for 3 minutes (or more, if needed). Fish will cook and cream will turn golden brown.

Place fillets in serving platter, pour sauce around fillets, place sautéed crawfish tails over fillets, and serve.   – LED

FISH VELOUTÉ

2 sticks butter
1 cup flour

1 qt. fish stock
1 cup California Chablis

Melt butter in a saucepan. Stir in flour, fish stock, and Chablis until well blended. Bake at 450° for 20 minutes. Stir again and use.   – CK

CRABE MOU AU STYLE DE LA LOUISIANE

6 medium soft-shell crabs
1 cup flour
clarified butter (enough to
  sauté crabs)
6 oz. fish velouté*
6 oz. heavy whipping cream
2 lemons
salt and pepper

¼ lb. butter
1 tbsp. butter
1 tbsp. chopped shallots
2 fresh artichoke hearts,
  cleaned and sliced
6 medium fresh mushrooms,
  sliced
¼ cup California Chablis

*See Fish Velouté recipe.

Remove gills and eyes from crabs and wash. Pat dry and turn over in flour in small saucepan. Sauté floured crabs in clarified butter until brown on both sides. Pour off butter and place crabs aside.

Whip together (in sauté pan) over high heat fish velouté, whipping cream, juice of 2 lemons, and salt and pepper to taste. Reduce for 2 minutes (continue whipping during reduction). Remove from heat and whip in the ¼ pound of butter (in fragments) to achieve a creamy consistency. Place aside.

Sauté shallots, artichoke hearts, and mushrooms in 1 tablespoon butter for 2 minutes over high heat. Deglaze with Chablis.

To serve, place 1 tablespoon of cream sauce on plate. Situate crab atop sauce and pour artichoke and mushroom sauté over crab (should be surrounded with garniture of sauté of various fresh steamed vegetables).   – CK

SHRIMP CREOLE BRENNAN

½ lb. butter
1 cup chopped green
  pepper
3 cups chopped white
  onions
½ cup chopped celery
2 tbsp. very finely chopped
  garlic
⅓ cup flour
3 cups whole canned
  tomatoes

2 tsp. salt
½ tsp. black pepper
¼ tsp. cayenne
3 bay leaves, broken up
1½ tsp. leaf thyme
4 to 5 cups water
4 lbs. raw shrimp, peeled
  and deveined (about 7 to 8
  lbs. in the shell)

In a large heavy saucepan melt the butter over medium heat, then add the green pepper, onions, celery, and garlic. Cook, stirring frequently, until the vegetables begin to turn brown. Quickly stir in the flour and continue cooking, stirring constantly, until the base is a rich light brown color. Add the tomatoes and mash them in with the back of a large spoon. Cook for about 3 minutes, stirring to mix thoroughly, then add the salt, pepper, cayenne, bay leaves, and thyme. Stir to mix, then gradually add the water, keeping the heat on high. When you have added 4 cups of water, allow the sauce to come to a boil, then lower the heat and simmer for about 10 minutes to develop the flavor. Stir frequently. Toward the end of the 10 minutes, check to see if the sauce has thickened too much; if so, add the remaining cup of water. Add the shrimp. Bring the sauce to a boil again, then lower the heat slightly and cook until the shrimp are done, about 5 to 7 minutes, depending on size. Taste one to check. Be careful not to overcook the shrimp. Serve with boiled rice. — MR

PAUPIETTES DE TRUITE MAÎTRE MARCUS
(Poached trout with tomatoes and artichokes)

2 6-oz trout fillets
1 tbsp. sliced green onions
pinch chopped garlic
pinch chopped dry shallots
¾ cup red wine
butter

1 medium tomato
3 artichoke hearts (or 2
  bottoms)
⅔ cup brown sauce
  (optional)

Preheat oven to 375°. Split trout lengthwise and roll into 4 paupiettes. Lightly butter a 6-inch skillet, then add green onions, garlic, shallots, and wine.

Place paupiettes in mixture; cover with buttered wax paper. Bake until done (15 to 20 minutes).

Meanwhile, peel and seed tomato and cut into 6 wedges. Cut artichoke hearts into quarters.

Remove fish from skillet and keep warm. To remaining juices in pan add brown sauce, tomato wedges, and artichokes and heat thoroughly.

To finish, add 2 tablespoons fresh butter. Stir constantly to emulsify the butter and wine. Pour sauce and garniture over each serving.

Serves 2.

– GP

Meats

RABBIT (OR CHICKEN) JAMBALAYA

1¼ cups margarine
1½ cups chopped onions
(in ¼-inch pieces)
1½ cups chopped green
bell pepper (in ¼-inch
pieces)
1½ cups chopped celery (in
¼-inch pieces)
2 large bay leaves
1 tsp. salt
½ tsp. ground red pepper,
preferably cayenne (if you
want a Cajun pepper
taste, use an additional
½ teaspoon red pepper)
1 tsp. white pepper

½ tsp. black pepper
1 tsp. granulated garlic
¼ tsp. red sandalwood,
optional
½ tsp. Tabasco sauce
1⅔ cups tasso, diced ⅛ inch
thick (ham may be
substituted)
¾ cup crushed tomatoes in
tomato puree
2 cups rabbit (or chicken),
diced ¼ inch thick
2 cups raw rice
3 cups rabbit or chicken
stock

Melt the margarine in a 2-quart saucepan. Add ¾ cup each of the onions, bell pepper, and celery, and the bay leaves, salt, red pepper, white pepper, black pepper, garlic, sandalwood, Tabasco sauce, and tasso. Cook over high heat for 20 minutes, continually stirring. (By the end of 20 minutes the onions will be dark brown, but don't allow them to burn.) Then add the remaining ¾ cup each of onions, bell pepper and celery. Cook 5 more minutes, uncovered, stirring as needed. Add tomatoes and simmer 5 minutes, stirring constantly. Add the rabbit and cook over high heat, uncovered, for 15 minutes, stirring occasionally. Fold in the rice while the heat is on high until ingredients are well mixed. Lower the heat to medium. Simmer uncovered 12 minutes. Add the stock. Bring the mixture to a boil uncovered. Lower heat enough to achieve a gentle simmer, and simmer covered over a very low fire for 15 minutes or until the rice is tender. Turn off heat, leaving pot covered an additional 15 minutes. Rice will be somewhat crunchy.

To serve, mold in a rice ring, cup, or decorative mold. You may wish to serve this with Creole Sauce or Sauce Piquant.

Serves 5 as a main course, 9 as an appetizer.   – PP

BLACK PEPPER STEAK
(Steak au poivre)

2 lbs. good cut of beef, trimmed, cut at least 1 to 1½ inches thick	butter
	oil
	½ cup dry white wine
peppercorns	1 tbsp. brandy (optional)

Cover both sides of the steak very generously with peppercorns, first coarsely crushed with a mortar or on a board with a potato masher. Pound the pepper firmly into the meat with the potato masher. In an iron skillet, over a high flame, brown both sides of the steak in 1 tablespoon butter and a few drops of oil. (A French cook would, of course, leave the steak rare.) When it is done, remove it to a hot platter. Stir white wine (and 1 tablespoon of brandy, if you wish) into the pan juices, simmer the sauce for 2 minutes, add a lump of butter, and pour sauce, loose pepper and all, over the steak. Serve with French fried potatoes.

Serves 4.   – LE

VEAL FINANCIÈRE

6 veal steaks	green onion, chopped
6 1-oz. pieces of sweetbread	parsley
	green olives, sliced
egg wash	2 cups brown sauce
flour	red wine
diced shallots	

Take veal steaks and pieces of sweetbread and season, flour, and run through an egg wash.

Sauté in clarified butter until golden in color.

Make a sauce of diced shallots, chopped green onion, a little parsley, sliced green olive, brown sauce, and a dash of red wine. Simmer 15 minutes.

Place veal steak on each plate with a piece of sweetbread on each one. Serve sauce over each.   – GP

VEAL JASON

8 4- to 5-oz. medallions of
  baby veal, pounded very
  thin
salt and pepper to taste

2 cups Progresso Italian
  bread crumbs
2 eggs
1 cup milk

JASON SAUCE:

3 cups ketchup
1½ cups sour cream
juice from 1 lemon
2½ tbsp. Worcestershire
  sauce

¼ tsp. white pepper
½ tsp. salt

Beat egg thoroughly in a mixing bowl then add milk and mix. Sprinkle veal lightly with salt and pepper then dip in egg wash and place in bread crumbs; cover well with the crumbs. Sauté veal in butter until golden brown. Place the finished pieces on a platter, then set the platter in a 175-degree oven to keep warm while you prepare the sauce. To prepare the sauce place ketchup in a saucepan over low heat, gradually blend in sour cream with a wire whisk, add remaining ingredients, and heat, stirring frequently. To serve, place a portion of veal on preheated plate and top with ¼ cup of sauce. Pour remaining sauce into sauce boat and pass around for "seconds."
Serves 8.

– MR

PEPPER STEAK ROBERT AYMES

4 steaks
1 tbsp. green peppercorn
2 tbsp. shallots
1 pt. heavy cream

2 tbsp. lemon juice
salt and pepper
brandy

This dish features prime fillet of beef, cut into 8-ounce steaks. Cook steaks as desired in pan, and add to sauce when almost done. To make sauce, sauté butter, green peppercorn, and shallots. Flame with brandy. Add heavy cream, lemon juice, salt, and pepper. Remove steaks, reduce liquid until thickened. Pour sauce over steaks.

– CK

HOMEMADE ITALIAN SAUSAGE

2 lbs. ground pork (Boston
   Butt)
½ oz. salt
1 pinch sodium nitrate
¾ oz. black pepper

1 tsp. anise seed
1 pinch crushed red pepper
2 cloves minced garlic
2 tablespoons grated
   Pecorino cheese (optional)

Mix above ingredients together and stuff sausage casing (obtainable from butcher). Use pastry bag or make one with heavy foil rolled in a cone shape. Tie off in sausage length with string or #8 thread.

Makes about 2 dozen medium sausages.   – GF

AUSTIN'S SAUSAGE, HAM, AND
SHRIMP JAMBALAYA

2 lbs. ham
2 lbs. smoked sausage, cut
   into ½-inch pieces
2 lbs. deveined shrimp
1 large onion, chopped
½ cup chopped shallots
½ cup chopped parsley
1 cup chopped celery

4 pods garlic, chopped
16-oz. can whole tomatoes
1 tsp. thyme
2 bay leaves
salt and pepper to taste
2 cups rice
2 cups water

Brown sausage and ham in thick skillet; pour off excess drippings. Add onions; let cook until golden in color and limp. Add parsley, shallots, celery, garlic, water, tomatoes, thyme, bay leaf, salt, and pepper. Bring to a boil; mash tomatoes with spoon as they're cooking. Add rice and shrimp. Stir once and put heat on low and cover. Do not stir again. Lift with fork if mixture is sticking. If it's not quite cooked, add about ½ cup more of water. The rice will take approximately 30 minutes to cook. Cook rice until tender and it separates easily.

Serves 10.   – AL

BEEF WITH BROCCOLI

½ lb. flank steak, cut into
  2- to 3-inch strips
1 bunch (3 to 4 stalks)
  broccoli

½ tsp. garlic, minced
1 tbsp. sherry wine

MARINADE:

1 tbsp. water
1 tbsp. soy sauce
1 tsp. cornstarch

1 tbsp. oil
½ egg white

GRAVY:

Mix together:
2 tsp. oyster sauce
½ cup chicken broth
1½ tsp. cornstarch
1 tbsp. soy sauce

½ tsp. sesame seed oil
1 tbsp. oil
salt and pepper to taste

Place beef in bowl and cover with marinade. Place in refrigerator for 2 hours, stirring occasionally to keep meat coated. Take meat out 1 hour before cooking.

Cut broccoli into individual flowerettes; trim excessive stems. Cut in half if flowerettes are large. Bring 4 cups of water to a rolling boil, add flowerettes and boil for 2 minutes or until crisp. Drain, spray with cold water, and set aside.

Heat wok over high heat until hot, add 2 tablespoons oil, toss in garlic and beef. Stir in fast, using turning and flipping motions until 75 percent done. Add broccoli and sherry and stir a few minutes. Stir gravy and pour into the wok. Stir vigorously until sauce thickens. Serve.　　– TW

VEAL CUTLETS FROM THE CARIBBEAN

8 veal cutlets
4 oranges
4 Creole tomatoes
2 heads garlic
1 onion, chopped

1 bunch mint
1 cup beef stock (beef bouillon)
1 whole lemon
butter

Peel oranges and slice. Slice the tomatoes, seed if necessary. Peel garlic, cut in half, remove green center, and boil for 2 minutes.

Sauté veal cutlets.

In a sauté pan with a little melted butter, sauté the chopped onion and boiled garlic together. Then drain off butter and deglaze pan with lemon juice. In same sauté pan with drained onions and garlic, add 6 mint leaves, sliced oranges, sliced tomatoes, and beef stock.

Reduce a little. Season and finish with butter.

Place veal in serving platter topped with sauce.

– LED

STUFFED PORK CHOPS

6 loin pork chops, center cut (have butcher cut a pocket in each)
Stuffing (follow recipe for stuffed peppers)

4 oz. margarine
1 cup water
1 cup brown gravy

Preheat oven to 350°. Stuff pork chops with filling and close pockets with heavy toothpicks. Place in baking pan and pour melted margarine over the top of each chop. Add approximately 1 inch of water to the pan and place it in preheated oven. Cook for 1½ hours, turning after 45 minutes so that chops brown evenly on both sides. Cover with brown gravy before serving.

Serves 6.

– AL

JEAN PAUL'S SWEETBREADS MADEIRA

1½ lbs. cleaned veal
  sweetbreads
1 cup brown sauce
½ cup madeira wine

1 stick butter
2 eggs
flour
salt and pepper

Blanch sweetbreads in simmering water for 10 to 12 minutes. Allow blanched sweetbreads to cool, then slice in half, dip in seasoned flour and then in beaten eggs. Immediately drop into bubbling butter and sauté. Brown on both sides, drain half the butter from pan and place all into a hot oven (475°) for 5 minutes. Then drain excess butter, add madeira and brown sauce and bring to boil. Flame madeira and serve.

– WL

BAR-B-QUE AUSTIN LESLIE STYLE

8 lbs. spareribs (2 slabs)
½ cup commercial smoke
  flavoring
salt
pepper
½ lb. margarine
1 rib celery, chopped

1 onion
4 sprigs parsley, chopped
⅓ cup flour
1 can tomato paste
2 tsp. brown sugar
6 cups water

Preheat oven to 350°. Salt and pepper ribs and sprinkle with some smoke flavoring. Put ribs in baking dish with 2 cups water. Bake for 1½ hours, turning occasionally so as to brown on all sides. Remove and set aside.

Melt margarine in large pot and add the chopped seasoning (celery, onion, parsley). Sauté lightly and simmer until tender. Add flour, tomato paste, smoke flavoring, and brown sugar and sauté for 20 minutes. Add water (approximately 4 cups) to half fill the pot and cook for 1 hour. If sauce is too thick, thin with a little water or drippings from ribs in baking pan. Drain dripping from meat in pan and pour sauce over ribs. Return to oven for 30 minutes to glaze.

Serves 6.

– AL

GRILLADES AND GRITS

3 lbs. beef or veal round
¼ lb. butter
¾ cup olive oil
3 cups coarsely chopped
  white onions
1 bunch green onions,
  chopped
5 cloves garlic, finely
  chopped
3 cups chopped green
  pepper

¾ cup chopped celery
3 bay leaves, broken up
2 tbsp. Worcestershire sauce
8 ripe tomatoes, diced
2 qts. rich beef stock
4 tbsp. cornstarch
about 2 to 3 tsp. salt
about ½ tsp. black pepper
freshly cooked butter grits

Pound out the beef or veal rounds with the scored side of a mallet and, if necessary, cut into large pieces (about 5 inches by 5 inches). Melt the butter in a heavy skillet and sauté the meat for about 6 to 8 minutes on each side in the hot butter, until nicely browned. (Cook in several batches if necessary.) Place the cooked meat on a platter and set the platter in a 175-degree oven to keep warm while you prepare the sauce. To prepare the sauce, heat the olive oil in a large heavy saucepan, then cook the onions, green onions, garlic, green pepper, and celery in the hot oil until browned. Add the bay leaves, Worcestershire sauce, and tomatoes and stir to mix thoroughly. Gradually add the beef stock and cook, stirring frequently, for about 5 minutes. Stir in the cornstarch, salt, and pepper. To serve, spoon some of the sauce on each plate, then place the meat over it. Place a serving of freshly cooked grits to one side of the meat, then ladle another, slightly larger quantity of the sauce over the meat and the grits.
Serves 8.

– MR

MÉDAILLON DE VEAU
A LA PETIT FILS
(Medallions of veal stuffed with crabmeat duxelle)

8 veal slices, thick as 2
 nickels (about ¾ lb.)
salt and fresh ground white
 pepper
¾ to 1 cup crabmeat
 duxelle (recipe follows;
 prepare first and keep
 warm)

2 tbsp. oil
2 tbsp. clarified butter
½ cup champagne, still
¾ cup heavy cream (reduce
 by 40 percent)
½ cup veal stock (reduce by
 50 percent)
crushed red pepper flakes

Pound the sliced veal with mallet and season with salt and white pepper. Heat oil and butter and sauté veal quickly on both sides. Keep warm.

Spread duxelle over 4 cooked veal slices and "sandwich" together with the other 4 veal slices. Keep warm.

Drain fat from pan and deglaze with still champagne. Add reduced cream and veal stock. Adjust salt and add crushed red pepper flakes.

Top the veal with sauce and enjoy.

Serves 2.

– LLL

CRABMEAT DUXELLE

6 slices bacon
4 tbsp. butter
1¼ cup finely chopped
 mushrooms
2 tbsp. chopped green
 onion

¾ cup lump crabmeat
2 tbsp. chopped parsley
salt and pepper to taste

Sauté bacon till crisp. Cool and chop. Sauté green onions in butter. Add mushrooms and continue cooking. Gently stir in crabmeat and parsley. If necessary sprinkle 1 or 2 tablespoons of fine cracker meal over mixture.

– LLL

BEEF TIPS BOURGUIGNONNE

8 lbs. beef tips
2 white onions, chopped
  fine
1 lb. butter
11 oz. all-purpose flour
3 bay leaves
2 tbsp. salt
1 tsp. white pepper

1 tbsp. whole thyme
3 cups tomato puree
5 cups Cabernet Sauvignon
1½ gals. beef stock
1 tsp. beef base
3 #303 cans pearl onions
egg noodles

In roasting pan add butter, beef tips, and onions, and cook in oven at 400° for 45 minutes. Then add flour and cook for 30 minutes more. Add bay leaves, salt, white pepper, whole thyme, tomato puree, Cabernet Sauvignon, beef stock, and beef base and mix well.

Lower oven temperature to 350° and cook for 1 hour more. Add pearl onions and serve with egg noodles.   – LE

VEAL PICCATA

12 veal escallops
3 oz. butter
2 tbsp. parsley, finely
  chopped

2 tbsp. hot stock
juice of 1 lemon
flour
salt and pepper

Beat the escallops until thin and flat, but not broken. Sprinkle them with salt, pepper, and flour. Melt ⅔ of the butter in a wide pan, add the veal, turn up the heat, and fry the veal quickly. Salt lightly. When meat is done put it in a heated serving dish and keep it hot. Add the parsley, lemon juice, remaining butter, and stock to the pan. Stir well and as soon as the sauce is bubbling, pour it over the veal. Serve immediately!

Serves 6.   – GF

FRICASSÉ OF VEAL WITH CAPERS AND DILL

4 lbs. veal (not too lean or too fat), cut into 1-inch strips
2 cups white wine
1 onion, peeled and cut in half
3 bay leaves
5 cloves
3 tsp. capers
1 tsp. chopped dill
salt and white pepper
nutmeg
1 cup heavy cream
2 egg yolks

Evenly cover veal with water and bring to slow boil. Rinse clean.

Cover veal with water, season with salt, white wine, onion, bay leaves, and cloves. Simmer until cooked.

Make a white roux and use strained stock for sauce. Cook until flour taste is gone. Add capers, chopped dill, white pepper and a pinch of nutmeg. Adjust taste, add cooked veal to sauce and simmer 10 more minutes.

Before serving, mix cream and egg yolks and pour very slowly in fricassé.

Serve with rice or noodles.

Serve 6.   – GP

LAPIN BRAISÉ AUX OIGNONS DOUX
(Braised rabbit with onions)

1 3- or 4-lb. rabbit, cut in pieces
4 onions, sliced
1 tsp. thyme
2 bay leaves
½ bottle sweet Sauvignon Blanc
1 stick butter

In a large pan, add ½ stick butter. Sauté rabbit until all brown. Remove rabbit from pan. Add ½ stick butter and sauté onions very slowly. Add wine. With spatula, clean bottom and side of pan. Boil for about 10 seconds. Replace rabbit in pan to cook. Season to taste. Add bouquet garni (thyme and bay leaves). Cook for 45 minutes until done.   – CK

MIGNON OF FILET GRILLÉ, SAUCE BÉARNAISE

6 11-oz filets mignons
salt, black pepper
clarified butter

12 breaded onion rings
6 tbsp. garlic butter

Salt and pepper filets, dip in clarified butter, and grill or broil to desired doneness. Deep-fry onion rings until golden.

To serve, spoon garlic butter over each filet, place two onion rings on each, and sprinkle with chopped parsley. Serve Béarnaise in a sauce boat separately.
— GP

NOISETTES DE PORC A L'ANCHOIADE
(Medallions of Pork with Anchovy-Cream Sauce)

1¼ lbs. pork tenderloin
5 anchovy fillets
2 tbsp. chopped shallots
4 tbsp. butter

½ cup ruby port wine
½ cup cream
fresh ground pepper to taste

With a mortar and pestle, lightly pound the anchovies to a paste and set aside. Cut the tenderloin into 8 equal slices. Gently pound into medallions.

Melt 2 tablespoons of the butter in a sauté pan. Add the pork, sprinkle with the shallots and cook the pork lightly till done, turning once. Remove the medallions from the pan, set aside, and keep warm.

Add the anchovies to the pan and cook briefly. Deglaze them with the ruby port, bring to a boil, and whisk in the cream. Reduce for a few minutes until lightly thickened. Whisk in the remaining butter and adjust the seasoning. Strain the sauce and pour over medallions. Serve at once.

Note: Recipe will serve 4 people with 5 ounces of pork per serving.
— CK

GRENADIN DE VEAU AUX HERBES

6 oz. grenadin of veal
2 tbsp. cooking oil
1 large Creole tomato,
  peeled and diced
½ tsp. fresh chopped basil
½ tsp. fresh chopped
  parsley

touch of fresh thyme
touch of fresh chopped
  garlic
½ cup pureed tomatoes
1 cup fresh sliced
  mushrooms
salt and pepper

Preheat oil in skillet. Season and flour the veal. Sauté quickly. Remove onto platter when done and keep warm. In skillet, add mushrooms, diced tomato, herbs, seasonings, and pureed tomatoes. Cook for 5 minutes. Season to taste. Pour over top of veal.   – LED

MEDALLIONS OF PORK WITH
OYSTERS

6 3-oz. medallions of pork
30 oysters
12 mushrooms, sliced
2 heads shallots, chopped
1 cup red wine
2 oz. brandy

4 oz. brown sauce
1 oz. butter
3 oz. margarine
1 oz. flour
salt, pepper, and sage to
  taste

Season medallions with salt, pepper, and sage. Dust with flour.

Place margarine in sauté pan and heat to cooking temperature. Place medallions in pan and cook 3 to 5 minutes each side. Add shallots and mushrooms. Cook until shallots start to turn clear. Degrease pan and flambé brandy.

Set medallions aside. Return pan to fire and add red wine. Reduce by 90 percent. Add brown sauce and bring to boil. Place oysters in sauce and poach slowly for 1 minute.

Remove oysters and reduce sauce until it will glaze spoon. Finish with 1 ounce butter. Check seasoning.

Cover medallions lightly with sauce and arrange oysters around medallions.   – LED

PORK TENDERLOINS WITH
CALVADOS

2 pork tenderloins   1 cup demi-glace
3 apples   sugar
½ cup Calvados   butter

Clean the tenderloins and slice them into medallions. Pound them some to tenderize them. Pour the Calvados in a saucepan and reduce it by half. Add the demi-glace, boil it, and keep this sauce warm.

Peel and core the apples. Cut them in halves and poach them in sugar and water until they are tender but still firm. Keep them warm. Slice 2 of the apple halves for a garnish on the pork.

Heat up the demi-glace and finish it with butter. Meanwhile sauté the pork medallions in butter. Place them on a plate, fan some apple slices over the pork, and spoon on the sauce. Place the apple halves next to the pork and place a mint leaf or a dollop of jelly on the apple where the core was.

Serves 4.   – RH

SCALOPPINE ALLA TOSCANA
(Veal cutlets Tuscany-style)

1 lb. thin veal cutlets   1 stick butter
1 egg, beaten   ½ cup grated Parmesan
½ tsp. pepper   cheese
½ tsp. salt   1 tsp. oregano
½ cup flour   4 slices lemon

Pound cutlets, then cut into 4-inch pieces. Dip veal into beaten egg then into flour mixed with salt and pepper.

Heat skillet, melt butter in it, and brown cutlets quickly on both sides. Sprinkle with cheese and oregano, cover pan, and cook over low heat 5 minutes until cheese is "set" and about to melt on meat. Serve at once garnished with lemon.

Serves 4.   – GF

COTOLETTE ALLA PALERMITANA
(Breaded Veal Cutlets Palermo Style)

1½ lbs. top round of veal,
cut into slices ½ inch
thick, or 4 veal rib chops,
pounded until they are no
more than ½ inch thick.
2 tbsp. olive oil

1½ cups unflavored bread
crumbs, spread on a plate
salt and freshly ground black
pepper
2 tsp. rosemary
1 lemon, cut into 4 wedges

Preheat the broiler 15 minutes in advance of cooking, placing the broiler pan and grid as close as possible to the source of heat. Rub both sides of all cutlets with olive oil. Turn the cutlets in the bread crumbs, pressing the crumbs against the meat with the palm of your hand. Lay the cutlets on a platter without overlapping them. Sprinkle with salt, pepper, and the rosemary leaves.

Place the meat on the broiler grid with the salted side facing upward. Cook for about 1½ minutes until the bread crumbs begin to brown. Turn the cutlets and cook for another 1½ minutes.

Serve piping hot, with wedge of lemon on the side.

If you like, you can trickle a little olive oil over the cutlets when serving them.

Serves 4.   – GF

LAMB NOISETTES WITH HERBS

2 racks of lamb
1 cup demi-glace
4 large red potatoes
1 lb. mushrooms

fresh thyme
fresh rosemary
butter
salt and pepper

Remove the eye from the racks of lamb and take off any nerves. Slice each eye into 6 noisettes (medallions).

Heat up the demi-glace and add a little fresh rosemary and fresh thyme. After it boils, remove it from the heat so the herbs can steep and the full flavor develops. Let this sauce set while you make the garnish.

Peel and cut the potatoes into uniform shapes about the size of your thumb. Blanch them slightly and let them drain. Then cut the mushrooms into random pieces that are over ½ inch square. Sauté these mushrooms in oil in a very hot skillet. Strain them and reserve the oil. Heat up the oil until the water from the mushrooms has evaporated. Then sauté the potatoes over a very high heat in this oil. When the potatoes are golden, drain them and discard the oil.

Sauté the mushrooms and potatoes in the skillet with butter; season them with salt and pepper. Meanwhile heat up the demi-glace sauce and finish it with butter.

Sauté the noisettes of lamb in butter; spoon the sauce on the plate before placing the noisettes on it. Spoon the garnish next to them on the plate. Sprinkle cracked black pepper over the lamb before serving.

Serves 4. — RH

POINTES DE BOEUF AVEC LAURIER FRAIS MARINÉ
(Beef tenderloin points marinated with fresh bay leaves)

2 lbs. beef tenderloin points (tails) cut into 1¼-inch cubes	1 tsp. freshly ground black pepper
½ cup olive oil	¾ tsp. Greek oregano
¼ cup salad oil	4 toes garlic, finely chopped
4 tbsp. red wine vinegar	20 quartered onion cups
1¼ tsp. kosher or sea salt	15 fresh bay leaves
	½ cup white wine

To make onion cups: cut off stem end and opposite end of onion and peel onion. Quarter onion and break quarters into natural layers. These are the "cups."

Marinate beef in the next 7 ingredients listed. Add 5 of the fresh bay leaves. Cover and refrigerate for 24 hours. When ready to assemble the brochettes, simmer the onion cups and bay leaves in white wine, covered, for 2 to 3 minutes. On 4 skewers (10 inches long) string pieces of onion, beef, and remaining laurel leaves. Broil 3 to 4 inches from heat to desired doneness. Brush with leftover marinade while cooking. To serve, top with Béarnaise sauce or hot butter. Sprinkle with chopped parsley.

Serves 4. — LLL

SPICY LAMB SHANKS

4 lamb shanks   ½ cup sugar
salt, pepper, and flour   ½ tsp. cinnamon
1 cup water   ½ tsp. allspice
1 cup cooked prunes,   ¼ tsp. cloves
   pitted   3 tbsp. vinegar
1 cup cooked dried apricots   ¼ tsp. salt

Season meat with salt and pepper, dredge with flour, and place in greased baking dish. Cover and bake in moderate oven (350°) until meat is tender, 1¾ to 2 hours.

Combine remainder of ingredients, heat to boiling, and simmer about 5 minutes. Drain most of fat from cooked shanks, add fruit mixture to meat, cover dish, and bake in hot oven (400°) about 30 minutes. Serves 4.   – LE

VITELLO CON ACCIUGHE
(Veal rolls with anchovies)

1 lb. veal cutlets (slice thin)   salt and pepper to taste
½ lb. mozzarella cheese   ½ cup stock or water
1 can anchovy fillets   6 sprigs parsley, chopped
¼ cup butter

Cut the veal into pieces no larger than 4 by 6 inches. On each slice place a small piece of mozzarella cheese, one fillet of anchovy, and a little pepper. Roll the little slices and tie with heavy thread. Melt half of the butter in frying pan, add rolls and brown well on both sides. Add salt and pepper, a little water, if necessary, and cook about 15 minutes. Remove rolls and place on serving plate, removing threads. Pour stock or water in frying pan over low fire and scrape bottom and sides of pan. Cook for few minutes, remove pan from fire, and add the rest of the butter. Mix well, add chopped parsley, and pour over rolls. Serves 4.   – GF

ESTOUFFADE DE BOEUF A LA BOURGUIGNONNE
(Beef Burgundy)

4 lbs. chuck of beef, diced into 1-inch by 1½-inch cubes
3 carrots, peeled and sliced
2 large onions, diced
2 celery ribs, diced
8 cloves garlic, crushed
4 bay leaves
½ tsp. thyme leaves
pinch of marjoram and rosemary
4 cloves
2 tbsp. crushed black pepper

1 bottle Burgundy table wine
3 tbsp. olive oil
butter
3 tbsp. brandy
½ cup flour
3 cups beef consommé or stock
½ cup whipping cream
mushrooms
pearl onions
parsley

Combine first 12 ingredients in a bowl. Cover with waxed paper or plastic wrap. Keep in the refrigerator and marinate for at least 48 hours.

Drain off the meats and vegetables, separate. Sauté the meat in butter to a real golden brown. Do the same to the vegetables.

In a braising pan, heat ½ cup butter, add meat and vegetables, then flame with brandy. Dust with flour, stir well, then place in oven to cook off flour, for 15 minutes.

Bring marinade to a boil. Strain in a fine strainer and pour over meat. Add beef consommé or stock. Season with salt and bring to a boil, slowly, while stirring. Cook covered in oven at 325° for 1½ to 2 hours until meat is done.

Separate meat from vegetables. Put meat aside. Reduce sauce to thicken very slowly, stirring on top of range. Season to taste. Finish sauce with whipping cream.

Garnish the stew with sautéed fresh mushrooms and glazed pearl onions. Decorate with toasted heart-shaped bread and fresh chopped parsley.

Serve with boiled potatoes, buttered noodles, or even steamed rice.

– JLA

SWEET AND SOUR PORK

1 lb. pork (Boston Butt or any lean cut)
1 tsp. soy sauce
1 tsp. sherry wine
1 egg, beaten

pinch of white pepper and salt
enough cornstarch that when mixed with water it will coat the pork

SWEET AND SOUR SAUCE:

1 small can pineapple chunks
4 tbsp. catsup
3 tbsp. white vinegar
1 tbsp. oil
pinch of salt

4 tbsp. sugar
1¼ tbsp. cornstarch mixed with water
½ cup sweet pickle chunks
½ cup pineapple juice

First make sauce by adding juice from pineapple chunks to about 2 tablespoons water and oil. Add vinegar, catsup, salt, and sugar, and bring to boil. Stir in cornstarch and water mixture.

Cut pork into 1-inch cubes and mix with salt and white pepper to taste. Add soy sauce and wine and the beaten egg. Add cornstarch which has been previously mixed with water to consistency that is thick but not sticky to the fingers. This will give the pork chunks a nice coating. Next sprinkle the pork with flour.

Have the wok or skillet very hot and add enough oil to deep fry the pork. (A deep fryer is best for this step.) Cook until about 80 percent done and remove from heat. Let the pork chunks sit until the coating becomes soft (usually about 10 to 15 minutes), then return to the hot oil and refry until complete done. This second frying will make the coating extra crispy.

After draining, place pork on small platter and top with pineapple chunks and sweet pickle chunks. Next pour the sweet and sour sauce over the entire mixture and serve. — TW

BEEF ROULADES

enough thinly sliced top beef round for 4 to 6 persons (sliced ½ inch thick)
dill pickles

Dijon mustard
1 medium onion, thinly sliced
4 to 6 slices bacon

Sprinkle salt and pepper over thinly sliced beef round. Spread lightly with Dijon mustard. On one end of the meat, place ½ slice of dill pickle, a few onion slices, and 1 uncooked slice of bacon. Roll up and secure with a toothpick. Brown lightly in a fry pan containing a little oil. Remove and keep warm while sauce is being prepared. — WC

SAUCE

3 stalks celery, diced
1 large onion, diced
½ large carrot, diced
1 toe garlic, minced
1 tsp. tomato paste

¾ cup flour
1 cup red wine
2 bay leaves
3 whole cloves
1 qt. beef stock

Sauté celery, onion, carrot, and garlic in a frying pan with meat juices left over from frying beef roulades. Dust with ¾ cup of flour and stir, mixing until smooth. Add red wine, bay leaves, and cloves. Add beef stock, stir, and bring to a boil. Remove from heat when thickened. Place roulades in sauce and simmer over low heat for 25 minutes or until tender. Serve over rice, noodles, or French bread. — WC

HUNGARIAN PORK GOULASH
WITH SAUERKRAUT

4 oz. bacon
½ lb. onions, diced
4 lbs. pork shoulder, cubed
¼ cup paprika
4 cloves garlic, crushed
½ tbsp. marjoram
1 tbsp. caraway seeds
1 bay leaf

4 oz. tomato puree
½ pt. water
8 oz. bell peppers, sliced
2½ lbs. sauerkraut, drained
salt
sour cream
chopped parsley

In a heavy duty brazier, render bacon. Sauté onions until light brown. Cook pork for several minutes. Add all spices, tomato puree, and water. Cover and braise slowly for 15 minutes.

Add green peppers and sauerkraut with some water to substitute for the drained liquid. Adjust seasoning, cover, and slowly cook for 1 hour.

Serve individual portions of goulash topped with 1 tablespoon sour cream and chopped parsley.

Serves 8 to 10.   — WC

VEAL ALL'AGRO DI LIMONE

1 lb. veal
1 cup flour
1 tbsp. Wesson oil
1 cube butter

2 oz. white wine
lemon juice
chopped parsley

Cut tender slices of veal; pound them thin to 3 inches by 4 inches. Dip in flour. Heat Wesson oil and butter; put in veal slices and brown on both sides. Remove veal and set aside. Pour in lemon juice and chopped parsley; shake pan then add white wine while still shaking pan. Gradually add cube of butter until it is completely blended with all ingredients to serve as a sauce.

Arrange the veal slices on a hot platter. Pour the lemon sauce over the veal; garnish with slices of lemon.

Serves 4.   — LE

SALTIMBOCCA ALLA ROMANA
("Jump in the Mouth")

12 small veal escallops
12 thin slices Parma Ham
  or Country Ham
4 tbsp. butter
½ cup finely minced
  parsley

salt and pepper
sage to taste
½ cup dry white wine

Carefully beat the escallops until very thin. On each slice of veal put a slice of ham and sprinkle with sage. Secure with a toothpick. (Don't roll up.) Melt the butter in a pan, add the veal slices, and brown on both sides over brisk heat. Sprinkle with pepper and parsley. Put the veal on a warm platter. Add the wine to the pan and increase the heat. Deglaze the pan. Spoon over the veal and serve immediately.
Serves 6.
    – GF

VEAL WITH SWEET POTATOES IN
PORT WINE SAUCE

8 thin veal slices (about ¾
  lb.)
pinch salt and black pepper
2 tbsp. butter
2 tbsp. oil
1½ pts. port (vintage
  preferred)
1 pt. veal demi-glace sauce
6 toes garlic

2 oz. soft butter
2 sweet potatoes (cut in
  small squares and blanch
  in peanut oil at 350° for 5
  minutes; set aside and
  keep hot)
1½ doz. fresh snow peas
4 sprigs fresh parsley,
  chopped fine

To make the port sauce, reduce port wine by 50 percent. Add demi-glace and garlic. Return sauce to boil and simmer for a few minutes. Add soft butter and reduce until velvety.

Heat oil and butter, sauté and brown veal quickly on both sides with high flame. Set aside and keep hot. Add snow peas and sweet potatoes. Add sauce; return to boil and garnish and sauce veal slices. Finish the dish with fresh chopped parsley.
    – LLL

EGGS ST. CHARLES

4 trout fillets, each cut in
  half
1¼ cups milk
1½ cups flour
1 tsp. salt

¼ tsp. black pepper
vegetable oil for frying
16 eggs
Hollandaise sauce

To fry the trout, soak the halved fillets in milk for about 5 minutes, then roll in the flour, salt, and pepper to coat evenly. Deep or shallow fry in hot oil (375°) until crisp and nicely browned, about 5 minutes. Remove from the oil with tongs or a skimmer, allowing the excess oil to drain off. Place the fillets on paper towels to drain. Poach the eggs. Place a piece of trout on each of 8 heated plates, top with 2 poached eggs, then cover evenly with Hollandaise sauce.
Serves 8.

– MR

OSSO BUCO CON FUNGHI
(Veal Shanks with Mushrooms)

1 onion, finely chopped
1 carrot, finely chopped
1 stalk celery, finely
  chopped
½ cup olive oil
8 oz. mushrooms (fresh or
  canned)
16 oz. tomato puree
6 veal shanks, about ½ lb.
  each

3 tbsp. flour
salt and pepper
¾ cup white wine
2 tbsp. chopped parsley
2 cloves garlic, chopped
  finely
1 tsp. rosemary, chopped

Brown the onion, carrot, celery, garlic, and parsley in the oil in a casserole. Dredge the shanks in flour and add them to the vegetables. Brown evenly and then set upright to retain the marrow. Season with salt and pepper and pour the wine over them. When the wine has partially evaporated, dilute the tomato puree with a little clear stock and pour it over the meat. When the liquid begins to boil, cover the casserole, reduce the heat. Add the rosemary and simmer slowly for 1½ to 2 hours. Before removing from the heat add the mushrooms, simmer for a few minutes. Place the meat in a warm oven-proof dish and cover with the sauce.

Serves 6.

– GF

PAN-FRIED LEMON PORK

1 lb. pork tenderloin, cut
   diagonally into pieces
   1/5-inch thick
1 tbsp. cornstarch

1 tbsp. sherry
sesame seeds
lemon slices

MARINADE:

2 cloves garlic, minced
1 egg, beaten
2 tbsp. cornstarch
2 tbsp. water

1 tsp. salt
½ tsp. sugar
½ tsp. sesame seed oil
dash white pepper

SAUCE:

1 tsp. lemon peel
1 tbsp. lemon juice
1 tbsp. vinegar
1 tbsp. ketchup
1 tsp. Tabasco (or hot
   pepper sauce)

½ cup water
2 tbsp. sugar
dash salt

Combine the ingredients for the marinade and marinate pork for ½ hour. Combine the ingredients for the sauce. Heat wok. Add 3 tablespoons oil. Fry pork until both sides are brown. Remove pork and drain oil. Add 1 tablespoon oil. When hot, add sherry, then add sauce. When sauce comes to a boil, add the tablespoon cornstarch, stirring until thickened. Add pork and stir to coat with sauce. Remove and place on a serving platter. Garnish with lemon slices and sprinkle with sesame seeds.

– TW

SCALOPPINE DI VITELLO AL POMODORO
(Veal Cutlets in Tomato Sauce)

1 onion, chopped
¼ cup olive oil
2¼ lbs. tomatoes, peeled
salt and pepper
6 sage leaves, finely
   chopped

6 veal cutlets
½ cup flour
5 tbsp. butter
¼ cup dry white wine

Sauté the onion lightly in a saucepan with the oil. Add the tomatoes and let them absorb the tomato juice and onion flavor. Cook slowly, adding salt, pepper, and sage leaves. Flatten the veal cutlets with a meat pounder. Season them with salt and pepper and coat them lightly with flour. Melt the butter in a large skillet and brown the cutlets on both sides over a high heat, keeping them well apart. Sprinkle the white wine over them and when it has evaporated add the tomato sauce. Taste for seasoning. Cook the sauce and cutlets together for a few minutes, keeping the lid on the pan to bring out the full flavor. Arrange the cutlets in sauce on a hot oven-proof dish and serve at once.

Serves 6.

          – GF

PRIME RIB DIABLO

1 cup all-purpose flour
prime rib, cooked, cut in
   four ½-inch slices
5 oz. A-1 sauce
½ cup water

¼ cup chopped parsley
2 oz. yellow mustard
4 cups bread crumbs
8 oz. brown sugar

Mix brown sugar, yellow mustard, A-1 sauce, and water together in a bowl. Place the sliced prime rib in the mixture.

In another pan mix the bread crumbs, parsley, and flour. Place prime rib into the bread crumb mixture. Grill on slow fire for 10 minutes and serve.

          – LE

GREEN PEPPER STEAK

½ lb. flank steak
½ medium onion, cut in 1-inch squares
1 bell pepper, cut in 1-inch squares

2 tbsp. dry sherry
2 dry chili peppers (optional)
1 tbsp. black beans
1 slice ginger root
1 clove garlic

MARINADE:

1 tbsp. water
1 tsp. soy sauce
1 tsp. corn starch
½ egg white

1 tbsp. oil
dash salt
dash white pepper

SAUCE:

1½ tbsp. soy sauce
½ cup chicken (or beef) stock
½ tsp. sesame seed oil

1 tsp. cornstarch
1 tsp. sugar
salt and white pepper to taste

Rinse black beans. Mix with ginger and garlic and chili peppers, if used. Chop finely. Combine marinade ingredients and marinate beef for ½ hour in refrigerator.

Heat 2 cups oil in wok to 350°. Add beef; stir to separate for 20 to 30 seconds. Remove from heat to drain oil, leaving 2 tablespoons oil in wok. Set wok over high heat; add black bean, ginger, and garlic mix. Stir for 10 to 15 seconds. Add onion, bell peppers, and beef. Stir fry; add sherry; cover for 30 seconds. Add sauce mix and stir until thickens.   – TW

BARBECUED SPARERIBS

2 sides spareribs, cut in
  sections
salad oil
salt and freshly ground
  pepper

barbecue sauce (recipe
  follows)

Place spareribs in large pot. Cover with boiling water. When water returns to boil, reduce heat and simmer for 30 minutes. Remove ribs from pot and place on baking pans. Oil ribs lightly, sprinkle with salt and pepper to taste, and brown both sides under broiler.

Place ribs flat in roasting pans and cover with barbecue sauce.

Bake at 350° 1 to 1½ hours or until tender. Baste and turn ribs every 15 minutes.

BARBECUE SAUCE

1 stick butter
1 cup chopped onion
3 garlic cloves, finely
  chopped
½ cup catsup
¼ cup brown sugar

1 tsp. salt
½ tsp. pepper
½ tsp. Tabasco
¼ cup white vinegar
1 tbsp. chili powder
dash Worcestershire sauce

Sauté onions and garlic in butter till tender. Add the remaining ingredients and simmer for 10 minutes. — AL

HAMBURGER BRENNAN

2 lbs. ground beef
¼ cup minced shallots
¼ cup minced white onion
½ cup toasted Holland rusk
  crumbs
dash nutmeg

1½ tsp. salt
½ tsp. pepper
2 tbsp. Worcestershire sauce
1 tbsp. chopped parsley
2 eggs

Combine all ingredients together thoroughly and shape into 6 patties (oval in shape) and grill.
– MR

MEATBALLS

1 lb. ground beef
½ lb. ground pork
½ cup minced shallots
3 cloves minced garlic
½ cup minced bell pepper

½ cup Italian bread crumbs
3 eggs
1 tsp. salt
1 tsp. pepper

Combine meat with seasonings (shallots, garlic, and pepper), eggs, bread crumbs, salt, and pepper. Form meat mixture into balls about the size of a golf ball. Roll in flour. Brown meatballs in large skillet.

SAUCE

½ cup finely chopped
  shallots
1 8-oz. can tomato paste
1 No. 2½ size can whole
  tomatoes

1 tsp. minced parsley
½ tsp. Italian seasoning

Sauté shallots over low heat until shallots begin to color. Stir in tomatoes and tomato sauce. Let simmer for 30 minutes. Add 1 pint water, parsley, Italian seasoning and add meatballs. Let simmer for 1 hour. Serve with spaghetti and grated Parmesan cheese.

Serves 6.
– AL

BARBECUED RIBS

**2 racks of spareribs, each
about 2 lbs.**

MARINADE:

3 tbsp. light soy sauce
1 tbsp. dry sherry
4 tbsp. catsup
1 tbsp. concentrated
   orange juice
4 tbsp. sugar

1 tsp. accent
2 tbsp. honey
1 tbsp. hoisin sauce
½ tsp. five spice powder
2 drops red food coloring

Trim off the fat and remove the overlapping piece of the meat on the bony side, if any.

Lay the ribs flat on the tray and mix the ingredients for the marinade. Rub ingredients on both sides of ribs and place in refrigerator for 4 hours (preferably overnight).

Place marinated meat on rack in oven.

Place a pan filled with 1 inch of water to prevent any sticking and burning on pan and oven.

Preheat oven to 375°. Cook ribs for 35 minutes. Increase oven to 450° for 10 more minutes.

To reheat, place in broiler for 5 minutes.   – TW

FILETS DE CHEVREUIL

8 filets de chevreuil
   (venison), each 1½
   inches thick
2 medium onions
3 carrots
5 stalks celery
1 bunch parsley

6 toes garlic
5 bay leaves
1 tbsp. thyme
1 tsp. black pepper
2 cups white wine
2 cups demi-glace

Chop the vegetables coarsely and place on top of the meat. Cover with the white wine, bay leaf, and pepper. Cover with plastic wrap and marinate for 48 hours.

Remove the filets from the marinade. Place the marinade in a saucepan and reduce until the liquid is almost dry. Add demi-glace and bring to a boil.

Strain the sauce from the vegetables and put aside.

Sauté the filets in a small skillet with butter.

In a small saucepan bring the demi-glace to a boil and finish with butter before serving over the filets.   – RH

ZIGEUNER SCHNITZEL
(Gypsy Cutlet)

2 lbs. pork tenderloins
2 medium bell peppers, cut
    into thin slices
1 medium onion, cut into
    thin slices
1 tomato, cut into thin
    slices
2 oz. ham, cut into thin
    slices
½ cup mushrooms, cut into
    thin slices
(bell peppers, onion,
    tomato, ham, and
    mushrooms should be
    cut julienne style)

1 tbsp. tomato paste
½ minced garlic toe
½ tsp. chopped tarragon
    leaves
black pepper, salt, and
    cayenne pepper to taste
1½ cups beef stock
2 tbsp. vegetable oil
1 tbsp. butter

Trim off fat and silverskin from pork tenderloins, cut into 2-ounce cutlets, and season lightly with pepper and salt. Sauté in hot skillet in 1 tablespoon vegetable oil until well done. Set aside.

Using the same skillet, add the butter, sliced bell peppers, tomatoes, onions, mushrooms, and ham, and sauté in 1 tablespoon of hot oil.

Turn down heat and add tomato paste, seasonings, and stock.

Simmer for 2 minutes and top pork tenderloins with same. Serve immediately.

Veal or chicken can be substituted for pork tenderloins.

Serves 5 to 6.   – WC

STEAK DIANE

4 small (approximately 3-
oz.) tournedos or fillets,
about 2 inches thick,
each sliced across to
make 8 slices
4 tbsp. salted butter
3 cloves garlic, finely
chopped
1 cup finely chopped green
onions
1½ cups finely chopped
mushrooms

3 sprigs fresh parsley, finely
chopped
¾ tsp. salt
¾ tsp. black pepper
1½ cups brown sauce
½ cup Lea and Perrins
Worcestershire sauce
½ cup A-1 sauce
3 drops Tabasco

Melt the butter in a large skillet over low heat. When the butter is melted place the slices of meat in the skillet and simmer until medium done. Turn the slices over and cook on the other side. When the meat is cooked, remove it to a large serving platter and set aside. Add the chopped vegetables, salt, and pepper to the remaining butter in the pan. Simmer for a few minutes, then add the Lea & Perrins, A-1 sauce, brown sauce, and Tabasco. Cook for a few minutes longer until the sauce is slightly thickened. Put the slices of meat back into the skillet and cook both sides for about 30 seconds. Place the slices on the serving platter again, then pour the sauce from the pan evenly over them. Serve from the platter with the sauce spooned over each portion and provide French bread to soak up the gravy.

Serves 8.

– MR

JULIENNE OF BEEF NOUVELLE ORLÉANS

1 lb. julienne of lean beef
1 cup sliced fresh
  mushrooms
1 cup julienne of green
  peppers
1 cup julienne of celery
½ soup spoon chopped
  garlic
1 cup minced onions
1 cup chopped fresh
  tomato

1 cup tomato puree
1 soup spoon chili powder
1 soup spoon oregano
1 cup dry white wine
2 cups stock or demi-glace
salt and pepper to taste
1 soup spoon fresh chopped
  parsley

Preheat the skillet and add cooking oil. Sauté the julienne of beef. Add all the vegetables (including all seasonings) then deglaze pan with white wine. Add puree of tomato and stock or demi-glace. Let cook until the meat is ready. Correct seasonings.

Serve on bed of rice and sprinkle with fresh chopped parsley. – LED

VEAL SCALLOPS A LA PROVENÇALE

1½ to 2 lbs. veal, sliced
  thin
¼ cup olive oil
½ lb. fresh mushrooms,
  sliced
1 clove garlic, minced

½ cup dry white wine
4 medium tomatoes, peeled
  and chopped
salt and freshly ground
  pepper to taste
chopped parsley

Pound the veal lightly until very thin. Dredge with flour. Heat the oil in a skillet. Season and dip veal in flour; brown lightly in hot skillet. Push veal to side of pan. Add mushrooms and cook for 2 minutes.

Arrange the mushrooms on the veal and spoon around them the garlic, wine, and tomatoes. Season to taste. Simmer for 10 minutes. Serve sprinkled with parsley.

Serves 6 to 8. – WC

COTOLETTE DI MAIALE CON CAPPERI
(Pork Cutlets With Capers)

8 small pork cutlets
3 tbsp. flour
¼ tsp. salt
⅛ tsp. pepper
1 egg, lightly beaten
½ cup bread crumbs
3 tbsp. oil
1 small onion (chopped)
1 tbsp. butter

2 anchovy fillets, cut into
  small pieces
2 tbsp. chopped capers
1 tbsp. chopped parsley
¼ tsp. flour
2 tbsp. vinegar
½ cup stock or water
½ tbsp. butter

Dredge cutlets in flour, sprinkle with salt and pepper, dip into egg, roll in crumbs, and fry in oil 10 minutes on each side, or until well browned. Place onion in saucepan with butter and brown. Add anchovies, capers, parsley, and flour. Cook 2 minutes, stirring well. Add vinegar and stock and cook 10 minutes longer. Add butter. Pour sauce over cutlets and serve.

Serves 4.   – GF

BEEF WITH OYSTER SAUCE

1 lb. flank steak
1 medium onion, cut in
  strips
3 scallions, cut in 2- to 3-
  inch lengths

3 ⅛-inch-thick slices fresh
  ginger root
3 cloves garlic, sliced

MARINADE:

1 tbsp. light soy sauce
1 tbsp. rice wine or sherry
1 tbsp. cornstarch

¼ tsp. salt
1 egg white
dash of white pepper

Cut beef into bite-size pieces and add ingredients for marinade. Mix thoroughly and marinate for 20 minutes.

GRAVY

Mix together:

¾ tsp. salt
¾ tsp. sugar
2 tbsp. oyster sauce

¼ tsp. white pepper
1 cup chicken or beef stock
1 tbsp. cornstarch

Heat 3 tablespoons oil in wok and sauté beef over high heat until color changes. Add onion, scallions, ginger root, and garlic and stir-fry for 15 seconds. Pour in gravy mix and stir until sauce thickens; serve hot.   — TW

SWEET AND SOUR PORK

1 lb. pork loin
1 medium green pepper,
  cut in 1-inch squares
½ cup sweet pickle
½ cup pineapple
½ cup onion, cut in 1-inch
  squares
1 egg, beaten

1½ cups flour and
  cornstarch mix (¾ cup
  each)
2 tbsp. cornstarch
1 tbsp. light soy sauce
2 tbsp. sherry
½ tsp. salt
1 tbsp. water

SAUCE

Mix thoroughly in bowl:

4 tbsp. catsup
½ cup pineapple juice
½ cup orange juice

4 tbsp. vinegar
4 tbsp. sugar

Cut pork into bite-size pieces. Sprinkle ½ teaspoon salt into 1 tablespoon sherry, egg, 2 tablespoons cornstarch, water, light soy sauce and marinate pork for 15 minutes. Mix thoroughly until pork separates. Heat 4 cups oil to 350° and fry pork until 90 percent done. Drain oil and set aside.

Heat skillet over high heat with 2 tablespoons oil. Toss in onion and green pepper and sauté for 20 seconds. Sprinkle remaining sherry before adding sauce. Stir and bring to a boil; add cornstarch mix until thickened. Mix pork, sweet pickle, pineapple, and sauce well, and serve.

                                                                — TW

MING STEAK

1 lb. beef tenderloin   ⅓ medium onion

MARINADE:

2 tsp. cornstarch   1 tbsp. soy sauce
½ egg white   dash white pepper
4 tbsp. water   1 tbsp. oil

GRAVY:

2 tbsp. catsup   ½ tsp. oyster sauce
1 tsp. Worcestershire   ½ tsp. cornstarch
2 tsp. sugar   dash white pepper
2 tbsp. rice wine or dry
  sherry

Take the tenderloin beef and slice it into pieces ½ inch thick and 3 inches long.

Mix together ingredients for the marinade, then add beef slices and marinate for 15 minutes.

Heat skillet or wok until hot, then put 4 tablespoons oil in wok. Fry beef slices until brown on both sides; remove from wok. Put steak back; add two teaspoons oil; put onion in and stir.

Mix together ingredients for the gravy. Add gravy and stir-fry beef tenderloin into the gravy. Sauté quickly and remove.

Garnish with tomato slices and parsley.   – TW

VEAL AND SHRIMP BARATARIA

1½ lbs. veal (leg), thinly   6 oz. brown sauce
  sliced   8 oz. heavy cream
1 lb. (21 to 25) shrimp   4 oz. clarified butter
2 oz. dry shallots, chopped   salt and white pepper to
1 pt. fresh mushrooms,   taste
  sliced   1 tbsp. chopped parsley
8 oz. dry white wine

Slice veal and sauté in 2 ounces clarified butter over high heat, coloring well. Remove veal and reserve in a warm place. Repeat this procedure with shrimp (but discard liquid).

Cook shallots in same pan as veal and shrimp. Add mushrooms and sauté lightly, adding wine and brown sauce; reduce by about half. Add cream and seasoning and cook over medium heat, reducing liquid to consistency of cream.

Immediately prior to serving, place veal and shrimp in the sauce; heat thoroughly but do not boil. If desired, thicken slightly with arrowroot or cornstarch.

May be served with rice, potatoes or spaetzle.

Serves 5 to 6.

– WC

SZECHUAN SPICED BEEF

½ lb. flank steak
½ cup celery
½ cup shredded carrot
½ cup shredded onion
2 green onions, cut into
   2-inch slices
3 dried cherry peppers
½ tsp. chopped garlic

½ tsp. salt
1 tsp. sesame seed oil
½ tsp. crushed Szechuan
   peppercorn
2 tbsp. soy sauce
1 tbsp. sugar
1 tbsp. vinegar
1 tbsp. sherry

MARINADE:

1 tbsp. water
1 tbsp. soy sauce

1 tsp. cornstarch
1 tbsp. oil

Slice beef and season with marinade ingredients for 20 minutes. Cut all the vegetables.

Heat the wok or heavy skillet until very hot, adding 5 tablespoons of oil for 30 seconds. Add beef; stir-fry until meat turns brown. Remove beef from pan and drain oil.

Reheat pan with 3 tablespoons of oil. Break cherry peppers in half into the oil until they turn brown. Add garlic. Then add vegetables. Stir-fry for 2 more minutes. Put beef back in pan. Then add sherry, vinegar, soy sauce, salt, peppercorn, sugar, and sesame seed oil, and stir for 30 seconds. Add cornstarch if needed.

– TW

Fowl

CHICKEN HASH PONTCHARTRAIN

4 1-lb. chicken breasts
1 gal. water
4 ribs celery
1 bell pepper
12 oz. butter
12 oz. all-purpose flour

3 bay leaves
1 white onion
2 tbsp. chicken base
1 tbsp. salt
½ tsp. white pepper
2 pieces pimento

Boil chicken breasts in 1 gallon water, along with 2 ribs of celery, chopped, ½ white onion, chopped, bay leaves, chicken base, salt, and pepper. Cook until tender.

In another pot add butter and melt. Add flour. Cook for 5 minutes. Add ½ chopped onion, chopped bell pepper, and remaining 2 ribs of celery, chopped. Cook for another 10 minutes on slow fire.

Strain broth from chicken breasts. Stir well. Add to butter and flour mixture. Break chicken breasts into small pieces and add to mixture.

Cook for 15 minutes and add chopped pimento and serve. Serve with Grits Soufflé.   – LE

CHICKEN CACCIATORA

3-lb. chicken, cut up
½ cup olive oil
½ cup butter
2 cups finely chopped
  onion
1 green pepper, chopped
4 garlic cloves, mashed
½ tsp. basil

1 cup Italian plum tomatoes
  (canned)
¼ cup dry red wine
1 tsp. salt
½ tsp. oregano
1 cup canned mushrooms,
  drained
ground black pepper

Sauté chicken in combined oil and butter for 10 minutes, or until golden brown. Add onions, green pepper, garlic, salt, basil, and black pepper. Simmer for 5 minutes. Add tomatoes and oregano; bring to a boil. Then reduce heat, cover and simmer for 20 minutes. Stir occasionally. Add wine and mushrooms and simmer for 10 minutes.

Serves 4.   – GF

UMBRELLA CHICKEN

40 chicken wings

MARINADE:

1½ tsp. salt
1 tsp. white pepper
1½ tbsp. light soy sauce
½ tsp. minced ginger
½ tsp. minced garlic

2 tbsp. minced green onion
3 tbsp. cornstarch
3 eggs, beaten
2 tbsp. sherry

SAUCE:

1 oz. brandy
3 oz. light soy sauce
½ oz. sesame seed oil
1 tsp. sugar

½ tsp. minced garlic
1 tsp. minced green onion
½ tsp. minced ginger

Remove wing tip at joint. Push meat to one end of bone. Mix all ingredients for marinade and marinate chicken for 1 hour. Roll wings in flour and deep fry until golden brown.

Mix all ingredients for sauce in separate bowl and use as dip or sprinkle over chicken.   – TW

CHICKEN BLACKBERRY VINEGAR

2 chickens, halved,
  partially boned
4 to 6 oz. blackberry
  vinegar

12 oz. demi-glace
4 to 6 oz. butter

To prepare blackberry vinegar, use 1 part blackberries to 2 parts white vinegar. Soak the berries in the vinegar and pass the mixture through a food mill. Discard the seeds.

Sauté chicken and remove from pan. Drain fat and deglaze pan with blackberry vinegar. Add the chicken and the demi-glace. Bring to a boil. Finish with the butter and serve the sauce over the chicken on a plate.

                                                                    – RH

CORN-GOOSE BREAST STUFFING
(For Small Chickens)

1 onion
3 ribs celery
3 large toes garlic
¼ tsp. red pepper
¼ tsp. black pepper
¼ tsp. thyme

1½ sticks butter
8 small corn muffins (about
8 oz.)
4 oz. smoked goose breast,
diced (chopped fine)
1 tbsp. chopped parsley

Sauté onions, celery and garlic in butter with black and red pepper and thyme. Crumble muffins and stir into cooked vegetables till thick. Add smoked goose breast and whisk in one egg (remove from heat when adding egg.) Add chopped parsley.

Stuffs 4 small chickens.

– LLL

POLLO ALLA CASALINGA
(Chicken Home Style)

1 3-lb. (approximately)
tender chicken
1½ tbsp. olive oil
4 tbsp. butter
1 onion, sliced
1 carrot, finely chopped
1 stalk celery, finely
chopped

½ cup dry white wine
10 oz. Italian peeled
tomatoes
salt and pepper
2 cloves
pinch ground cinnamon
4 oz. chopped mushrooms

Wash the chicken and cut into serving portions. Heat oil and butter in fairly large saucepan and gently sauté the onion, carrot, and celery. Add the pieces of chicken and brown them lightly. Then add the wine and the tomatoes. Season to taste with salt and pepper, and flavor with cloves and cinnamon. Continue cooking over a moderate heat until the chicken is tender. Add the mushrooms 5 minutes before serving.

Serves 4 to 6.

– GF

DUCKLING BERNARD

1 4½- to 5-lb. duck, whole
½ cup oil
2 sticks butter
1 tbsp. juniper berries
1 tbsp. whole black
  peppercorns
1 large onion, diced small
2 carrots, diced small
2 bay leaves
1 tsp. arrowroot

½ cup raspberry vinegar
3 stalks celery, chopped
3 lbs. fresh clean spinach
2 cups consommé
½ cup dry white wine
6 slices bacon, broiled and
  chopped
1 tbsp. chopped shallots
1 tsp. thyme
salt and pepper to taste

Preheat oven to 375°. Pour oil over bottom of a large roasting pan. Salt the duckling body cavity and stuff with celery, onion, carrots, juniper berries, black peppercorns, bay leaves, and thyme. Rub the duckling with softened butter and place on its side in roasting pan along with neck and giblets.

Roast the duckling for 20 minutes and turn on its other side. Roast an additional 20 minutes. Finish roasting duckling breast side up for another 15 minutes. When duckling is cooked, remove meat from the carcass and cut into serving portions. Place meat on a serving platter and keep warm.

Return roasting pan to stove top and add chopped duckling carcass, vegetables, and giblets. Remove the fat from the pan, deglaze with half of the raspberry vinegar. Add white wine and reduce by one third. Add the consommé and cook over medium heat for 8 to 10 minutes.

Preheat a large skillet and add ¼ pound butter, shallots, and bacon. Sauté briefly and add the spinach leaves and the rest of the raspberry vinegar. Sauté until the leaves just wilt and the spinach is bright green. Place the spinach in the center of a serving platter and arrange the pieces of duckling around it. Strain the sauce, thicken it slightly with arrowroot, and cook for 3 minutes. Reduce the sauce and finish with a few bits of butter. Pour sauce over duckling and serve very hot.

Serves 4.   – LED

CHICKEN SMOTHERED WITH BLACK-EYED PEAS

1 3½- to 4-lb. stewing or
  roasting hen, cut into 8
  to 10 pieces
1 cup all-purpose flour
cooking oil for frying
¼ cup chicken fat
  (preferred), pork lard, or
  shortening
9 slices bacon, cut into ½-
  inch pieces
2½ cups finely chopped
  onions
1½ cups finely chopped
  celery
3 bay leaves

1 tbsp. plus 1 tsp. Tabasco
  sauce
1 lb. dried black-eyed peas
1 tbsp. granulated garlic
  (preferred) or garlic
  powder
1½ tsp. rubbed sage
1 tsp. granulated onion
  (preferred) or onion
  powder
1 tsp. dried thyme leaves
11 cups chicken stock
  (preferred) or water
about 3 cups hot Basic
  Cooked Rice

SEASONING MIX
(or substitute Louisiana Cajun Magic Poultry Magic)

1 tbsp. salt
1½ tsp. granulated onion
  (preferred) or onion
  powder
1½ tsp. granulated garlic
  (preferred) or garlic
  powder

1 tsp. white pepper
1 tsp. dry mustard
1 tsp. rubbed sage
½ tsp. dried thyme leaves

Thoroughly combine the seasoning mix ingredients in a small bowl, breaking up any lumps. Sprinkle about 1 tablespoon of the mix on the chicken pieces, patting it in by hand. Combine the remaining mix with the flour in a plastic or paper bag, mixing well. Set aside.

In a large skillet heat ½ inch oil to 350° over high heat. Just before frying, dredge the chicken pieces in the seasoned flour, shaking off excess. Fry the hen in the hot oil (large pieces and skin side down first) until golden brown, about five minutes per side. (Adjust heat as needed to maintain the oil's temperature at about 350°.) Drain on paper towels and set aside.

In a 5½-quart saucepan or large Dutch oven, melt the fat over the high heat. Add the bacon and cook just until it starts to get crisp, about 3 to 4 minutes, stirring often. Stir in the onions, celery, bay leaves, and 1 teaspoon of the Tabasco; cook until vegetables start to get tender, about 3 to 5 minutes, stirring frequently. Add the peas, garlic, sage, granulated onion, and thyme, stirring well; cook until all the oil and juice is absorbed and mixture starts sticking excessively, about 2 to 4 minutes, stirring often. Add the stock, chicken pieces, and the remaining tablespoon Tabasco; bring to a boil, then reduce heat and let simmer until chicken and peas are tender, about 1½ to 2 hours, stirring occasionally. (*Note*: Cooking time will vary according to toughness of hen.) Adjust salt to taste toward the end of cooking time. Meanwhile, heat the serving plates in a 250-degree oven.

To serve, place 1 to 2 pieces of chicken on each heated serving plate. Mound about ½ cup rice to the side, then top the rice with about ½ cup peas. Spoon extra sauce over the peas and chicken.

Serves 4 to 6.   – PP

DUCKLING WITH CHERRIES

3 3½-lb. ducklings
salt and pepper
rosemary
¼ cup orange cognac

¼ cup port wine
2 cups rich brown sauce
1 14-oz. can bing cherries

Roast ducklings seasoned with salt and pepper and rosemary at 400° for about 2 hours.

Make a sauce with orange cognac, port wine, and rich brown sauce. Combine and cook 15 minutes.

Remove duck and split in half with French knife.

Sauté bing cherries. Serve over half of each duckling.

Serve with duck sauce.   – GP

CHICKEN ETOUFFÉE

½ cup plus 1 tbsp.
  vegetable oil
¾ cup flour
3½ cups (approximately)
  chicken stock
1 cup unsalted butter
½ cup chopped celery (in
  ⅛-inch pieces)
½ cup chopped green bell
  pepper (in ⅛-inch pieces)
½ cup chopped onions (in
  ⅛-inch pieces)

1½ tsp. salt
1½ tsp. ground red pepper
¾ tsp. black pepper
½ tsp. white pepper
½ tsp. granulated garlic
¾ cup finely minced green
  onions (with tops)
4 cups boned and skinned
  cooked chicken, cut in
  bite-size pieces
6 cups Uncle Ben's
  Converted Rice, cooked

Note: Roux reaches an extremely hot temperature, and can seriously burn your skin. Take care not to splash any on you as you proceed through the recipe.

In a 9-inch cast-iron skillet heat the oil over high heat until it's at the smoking point (about 5 minutes). Remove the skillet from the heat and add the flour. Using a metal whisk, blend until all the flour is dissipated into the oil. Return the skillet to a medium-high heat and whisk continuously until the roux is red-brown in color (about 3½ to 4 minutes), being sure not to allow the roux to burn. Immediately remove the roux from heat and quickly whisk in ¼ cup each of the chopped celery, bell pepper, and onions. Continue whisking 2 to 3 minutes or until roux no longer is cooking or turning darker. Set aside. (If you see black specks in the roux or if it smells like burned popcorn instead of a nutty smell, the roux is burned. Allow it to cool, discard, and start over. If you do not have a cast-iron skillet you may need to allow more cooking time to achieve the red-brown color of the roux.)

Bring the chicken stock to a rolling boil in a 2-quart saucepan. Using a metal whisk, whip in the roux. Bring the mixture to a rolling boil again, and boil uncovered over low heat for 15 minutes, stirring fairly constantly. Your sauce should be the consistency of very thick gravy. Reserve.

Meanwhile melt ⅓ cup of butter in a 9-inch skillet. Add ¼ cup each of the celery, bell pepper, and onions. Sauté over very low heat, stirring occasionally, 10 to 12 minutes or until the vegetables are completely wilted. Add the reserved sauce, salt, red pepper, black pepper, white pepper, and garlic. Simmer uncovered 15 minutes, stirring frequently.

Melt the remaining ⅔ cup butter in a 4-quart saucepan over medium heat. Add the green onions and sauté 2 minutes. Then add the chicken and etouffé sauce and gently bring to a boil uncovered. Remove pan from heat, and allow to sit 15 minutes. Skim oil off the surface with a ladle. Reheat sauce just until thoroughly heated. You may need to thin the sauce with additional chicken stock. The end result should be a thick brown gravy. Serve immediately.

For each person, allow ½ cup of sauce. Pour the sauce over a scant cup of cooked rice. This dish is excellent served with potato salad on the side.

Serves 6.   – PP

POULET RÔTIE AUX HERBES DE PROVENCE

1 3-lb. chicken
½ tsp. thyme leaves
2 bay leaves
1 head whole unpeeled
  garlic
1 doz. whole black
  peppercorns
1 tsp. salt

½ tsp. rosemary
½ cup dry white wine
½ lemon
1 chicken bouillon cube
½ cup water
olive oil
butter

Season inside of whole chicken by sprinkling with thyme, bayleaf, and crushed whole garlic, black peppercorns, salt, and rosemary. Tie legs and wings. Sauté chicken on top of stove, until light golden brown, in equal parts of olive oil and butter. Place pan in oven at 475° for approximately 45 minutes to 1 hour. When done, remove grease from pan, remove seasoning from inside of chicken into pan, and add white wine, lemon juice, bouillon cube, and water. Reduce by approximately half and strain. Disjoint chicken and serve with sauce.

I recommend serving this with fresh green beans sautéed in butter with the white of green onions.

Serves 2.   – CK

CORNISH HEN GRILLED DIABLE

6 Rock Cornish game hens
Madagascar green
  peppercorns

salt
black pepper
6 tbsp. fresh butter

Split hens down back, open up, and remove back bone and rib cage. Trim wings off. Place hen flat with skin side up. Make incisions around breasts and thighs, inserting some crushed green peppercorns. Place hens on flat roasting pan, season with salt and black pepper, adding a little fresh butter on each hen. Place in a preheated 450-degree oven, immediately turning oven down to 350°. Roast about 25 to 30 minutes, basting hens twice throughout with their own juices. — GP

LEMON CHICKEN

3 pieces boneless chicken
  breast
juice of 1 lemon (save peel)
1 tsp. custard powder
1 tbsp. dry sherry
1½ tbsp. sugar
¼ tsp. salt

1 tbsp. vinegar
½ cup water
2 tsp. cornstarch, mixed
  with 2 tbsp. water
½ tbsp. oil
½ tsp. minced garlic
½ tsp. hot pepper oil

MARINADE:

1 tsp. sherry
1 tsp. light soy sauce
¼ tsp. salt

1 tbsp. cornstarch
½ egg, beaten

Season chicken with marinade ingredients for 20 minutes. Dip chicken in flour. Mix in a separate bowl lemon juice, custard powder, sherry, sugar, salt, vinegar, water, and oils.

Heat wok or heavy skillet. Add ½ cup oil. Pan-fry chicken until both sides are golden brown. Remove from skillet and chop into bite-size pieces. Reheat skillet, add garlic, and cook for a few seconds. Add sauce and lemon peel.

When sauce comes to boil, thicken with cornstarch. Remove lemon peel. Pour sauce over chicken. — TW

LES AIGUILLETTES DE CANARD RÉVOLUTION

8 half duck breasts, boned
¼ cup finely chopped
  onions

2 oz. brandy
1 cup cream
1 tbsp. green peppercorns

MARINADE:

5 bottles red wine
1 cup salad oil
6 bay leaves
2 tbsp. coriander
1 tbsp. thyme leaves
1 tbsp. juniper berries

2 sprigs parsley, chopped
1 tbsp. whole black pepper
1 cup each celery, onions,
  and carrots, roughly
chopped

Put oil in saucepan. Add all spices and cook on medium heat for 3 minutes. Add red wine and cook until reduced by a third, about 15 to 20 minutes. Let marinade cool in refrigerator. Put duck breast in marinade and let stand in refrigerator for 4 days minimum. Will keep for 3 weeks.

Take duck from marinade and dry wipe. Put salt and fresh cracked black pepper on breast and pound slightly to flatten. Heat small amount of cooking oil in heavy sauté pan. Add duck breast and sauté 2 minutes on each side until medium-rare to medium. Remove duck breast from pan and pour off excess oil. Add ¼ cup finely chopped onions and sauté; add 2 ounces brandy and flame; add 1 cup strained marinade. Reduce on high heat until ¼ cup remains. Add 1 cup cream and 1 tablespoon crushed green peppercorn; continue to reduce until sauce will coat spoon. Serve over duck breasts that have been kept warm in 160-degree oven.

– LED

Serves 8.

KUN BOW CHICKEN

½ chicken breast, about ½
 lb. when boned
3 dried red peppers
1 tsp. finely chopped fresh
 ginger

1 green onion
¼ cup cashews or peanuts or
 almonds

MARINADE:

2 tsp. cornstarch
2 tsp. soy sauce
1 tbsp. rice wine or dry
 sherry

½ egg white
½ tsp. salt

SEASONING:

1 tsp. cornstarch
2 tsp. rice wine or dry
 sherry
1 to 2 tbsp. soy sauce
1 tsp. vinegar

½ tsp. salt (omit if using
 salted nuts)
1 to 2 tsp. sugar
1 tsp. sesame oil

Bone the chicken breast and cut the meat into pieces 1 inch or slightly smaller.

Make the marinade by mixing cornstarch with soy sauce and wine, then adding the salt and egg white. Mix the marinade with the chicken and marinate at least 15 minutes.

Cut off the ends of the dried red pepper and shake out the seeds. Chop the ginger very finely and cut the green onions into pieces ¾-inch long.

In a small bowl, make the seasoning by first mixing the cornstarch with the soy sauce and wine and then mixing in the other ingredients.

Heat about 4 tablespoons cooking oil in a wok or large frying pan. Add the red peppers, cooking over a medium flame until they start to char. Turn the fire up as high as possible and as soon as the peppers are black, add the chicken pieces and reduce the flame to medium.

Stir-fry until the chicken is white, then add the ginger and green onions. Cook, stirring for a few more seconds, then add the cashews or other nuts and the seasoning (give it a quick stir first). When the sauce has thickened slightly and is glazelike, remove to a serving dish and serve hot.   – TW

MOO GOO GUY PAN
(Chicken with Mushrooms)

½ lb. chicken breast, sliced
¼ lb. fresh mushrooms,
  sliced
2 green onions, each 3
  inches long
1 tsp. cornstarch
1 tsp. soy sauce

½ egg white
¼ tsp. salt
1 tbsp. oil
2 tbsp. rice wine or dry
  sherry
oil for frying

GRAVY

Mix together:
2 tsp. oyster sauce
¼ cup chicken broth
1½ tsp. cornstarch
1 tbsp. soy sauce

½ tsp. sesame oil
1 tsp. oil
dash of white pepper

Bone the chicken breast and cut the meat into small pieces, 1 inch or slightly smaller.

Make the marinade by mixing cornstarch with soy sauce; add egg white, salt, and oil; mix together, add chicken, and marinate for 15 minutes.

Heat the wok or a heavy iron skillet with ½ cup of oil till hot. Throw chicken in and stir until about 80 percent done; take out the chicken and drain the oil.

Put 3 tablespoons of oil back in wok; after it is hot, put the green onions in and add the mushrooms; cook for about 15 to 30 seconds. Then put the chicken in and add rice wine or dry sherry; stir about 15 seconds and add gravy mix. Stir until gravy is done, about 1 minute.

                                                                   – TW

STEWED CHICKEN

1 5- to 6-lb. stewing hen,
  cut into 12 pieces
salt
pepper
2 cups peanut oil
2 cups flour

1 rib celery, chopped
1 medium onion, chopped
4 sprigs parsley, chopped
1 gal. chicken stock (or
  water)

Season hen with salt and pepper. Heat oil in Dutch oven or heavy skillet and brown chicken pieces on all sides. Remove and set aside. Add celery, parsley, and onion to pot containing chicken drippings. Stir in flour and sauté gently for 15 to 20 minutes until browned. Add stock to pot and stir to prevent sticking. Return chicken pieces to pot, being sure that the stock covers the chicken. Cover pot and cook over medium heat for 1½ to 2 hours. Season to taste.
Serves 6.

– AL

FRIED CHICKEN

1¼ cups peanut oil for
  frying
1 3- to 3½-lb. fryer, cut up
salt
pepper

1 egg, lightly beaten
1 cup light cream or half-
  and-half
1 cup water
½ cup flour

Preheat oil in frying pan to about 350°. Wash chicken pieces under cold running water and pat dry. Sprinkle with salt and pepper. Make egg batter by combining egg, cream, water, salt, and pepper. Dip pieces of chicken first in egg batter to coat and then in flour. Add chicken pieces to skillet, meatiest parts first. Do not crowd. Turn to brown on all sides. If oil pops, reduce flame. Cook until meat is tender and skin crisp, about 10 to 12 minutes.
Serves 6.

– AL

CHICKEN CLEMENCEAU

8 chicken breasts, poached
  in white wine
½ cup butter
4 tbsp. finely minced garlic
1½ cups finely chopped
  green onion
1½ cups sliced mushrooms

1 cup cooked green peas
4 tsp. finely chopped parsley
1½ cups deep-fried diced
  potatoes
½ cup dry white wine
1½ tsp. salt (or to taste)
¾ tsp. pepper (or to taste)

Melt the butter in a large heavy skillet or sauté pan. Add garlic, green onion, and mushrooms. Sauté until lightly browned, stirring frequently but gently. Add the remaining ingredients and mix well. Cook for about 4 to 6 minutes longer. Place the chicken on heated plates and cover with the sauce.
Serves 8.

– MR

BOUDIN BLANC (French Style)

1 lb. chicken breast
1 pt. whipping cream
¼ lb. pork fat
1 tbsp. cooked French
  shallots

2 tbsp. port wine
3 yards pig casing
green peppercorns, salt,
  pepper

Puree the chicken until smooth and hold in the refrigerator. Puree the fat, salt, pepper, shallots, and green peppercorns until the fat is smooth. Add the chicken and puree until blended. Add ½ pint cream and blend. Remove from the food processor and stir in the port wine and the rest of the whipping cream with a wooden spoon.

Stuff this into casings, tie into links, and poach in simmering water until done (about 6 to 10 minutes). Don't overheat them or let the water boil because they will burst.

To serve, sauté the boudin lightly in a small frying pan and place in a 350-degree oven for 12 to 15 minutes.
Serve immediately.

– RH

POULET A LA BELLE-MEUNIÈRE

Stuff a fryer chicken with 4 sliced chicken livers and 3 ounces of raw quartered mushrooms slightly coated in butter.

Slip 5 or 6 fine slices of truffle under the skin of the breast. Truss the chicken and brown it in butter.

Place it in a covered casserole with 2 ounces of butter, 4 rectangles of blanched salt pork and 3 ounces of raw quartered mushrooms. Season to taste with salt and pepper. Cook in 350-degree oven about 1 to 1½ hours.

When done, add a few tablespoons of veal velouté, bring to a boil, and serve.
— RH

DEMI POULET SAUTÉ
VALLÉE D'AUGE
(Chicken Breasts in Calvados)

2 5-oz. boneless chicken breasts
½ cup Calvados (apple brandy)
¼ cup apple vinegar (optional)
1 tbsp. chopped green onions
¼ tsp. chopped garlic
1 tsp. leaf thyme
¾ cup fresh quartered mushrooms
½ cup heavy cream (whipping cream)

Salt and pepper chicken breasts and dredge in flour. In a sizable skillet with 2 tablespoons oil sauté until brown both sides of the chicken breasts. Remove skillet from fire and deglaze pan with Calvados and apple vinegar.

Then add green onions, garlic, thyme, mushrooms and cream and mix well.

Return whole to heat and cook until sauce begins to tighten (5 to 6 minutes). Adjust salt and pepper to taste.

Serve with egg noodles, rice, or barley and garnish generously with fresh chopped parsley.

Serves 2.
— GP

CHICKEN CURRY

2 2½- to 3-lb. fryer
    chickens, cut up
3½ oz. butter
1 tbsp. salt
10 oz. onion, chopped
4 apples, sliced
2 small bell peppers, diced
2 tomatoes, skinned and
    diced

1 small toe garlic, minced
2 tbsp. curry powder
1¾ pts. chicken stock
1½ tbsp. cornstarch
2 tbsp. lemon juice
1½ cups cream

Sauté the chicken pieces in butter (use bones and skin for stock). Add the chopped onions and sliced apples and continue sautéing. Dust with curry powder, add garlic, and deglaze with the chicken stock, just covering the chicken. Braise 25 to 40 minutes until meat is tender. Remove chicken pieces from stock; thicken stock with cornstarch dissolved in water. Sauté peppers and tomatoes lightly and add to sauce. Add the cream and lemon juice; reduce the liquid to a smooth sauce. Put chicken back in the sauce and keep it warm. Serve with rice.

Serves approximately 10.   – WC

TURKEY WINGS LOUIS

6 turkey wings
2 cups flour
1½ qts. chicken stock
½ white onion
2 pieces celery

salt
pepper
thyme
2 bay leaves
2 cups shortening

Cut turkey wings in half and wash in cold water, then dry with a cloth. Salt and pepper. Dust them in the flour. In a roasting pan, add the 2 cups shortening. Place the turkey wings in the pan. Cook until brown. Chop the onion and celery, add to the turkey wings, along with bay leaves, thyme, and chicken stock. Cover and cook 1 hour and 45 minutes, or until tender.

Serves 6.   – LE

BLANC DE POULET A LA TOMATE ET HUÎTRES
(Chicken Breast Fraccaro)

4 4-oz. chicken breasts
olive oil and butter, mixed,
  enough to cover bottom
  of a small sauté pan
4 tbsp. minced white of
  green onion
4 tbsp. parsley and garlic
  minced together fine
24 oz. tomatoes, seeded
  and diced fine

12 oz. chicken stock
16 oz. tomato sauce
dash of fresh lemon juice
salt and pepper to taste
12 oz. cooked vermicelli,
  heated and mixed with a
  small amount of butter
3 oysters per person

Salt and pepper chicken breasts and sauté in oil in small sauté pan until skin browns; turn and place in a 400-degree oven for 8 to 10 minutes. Remove breasts from pan and place in a warm place.

Pour off excess grease from pan and add onion, parsley and garlic; sauté quickly. Add oysters, sauté quickly, and add tomatoes. After edges curl remove oysters and add chicken stock and tomato sauce, reduce slightly. Replace oysters and add a small amount of cold butter and swirl pan until melted.

Remove skin from breasts and arrange on a serving plate. Place a small amount of pasta on plate also. Spoon sauce over breasts and pasta and garnish with oysters. — CK

POULET AUX FONDS D'ARTICHAUTS

Brown the cut-up chicken in butter, and put it in a covered casserole with 5 raw, sliced artichoke bottoms dredged in butter. Complete its cooking gently in a 300-degree oven. Chicken is done when thigh juices run clear when pierced with a fork. When about to serve, add some veal velouté and a few drops of lemon juice. Add salt and pepper to taste. — RH

BREAST OF CHICKEN AU POIVRE VERT

8 oz. boneless, skinned
   breast of chicken
2 serving spoons cooking
   oil
1 small can Madagascar
   green peppercorns
½ cup dry white wine

1 oz. brandy
1 cup heavy cream
1 cup brown chicken stock
salt
1 serving spoon flour
1 tsp. butter

Preheat skillet. Add cooking oil. Flour the breast of chicken. On slow fire, sauté chicken lightly. When the chicken is done, flambé with brandy. Then add white wine, chicken stock, and cream as well as 1 soup spoon of green Madagascar pepper. Remove chicken onto service platter. Reduce the sauce and finish with 1 teaspoon butter. Add salt to taste.

– LED

CHICKEN FLORENTINE

2 cups seasoned mashed
   potatoes
1 cup warm creamed
   spinach
6 slices chicken breast
2 tbsp. butter
2 tbsp. flour

½ tsp. salt
dash cayenne
1 cup milk
2 tbsp. grated Parmesan
   cheese
1 tsp. paprika
butter

On two small platters, make a wall around extreme edge with potatoes in pastry bag. Make a bed in the center of each with creamed spinach with sliced chicken. In a small heavy saucepan, melt 2 tablespoons butter. Stir in flour, salt, and pepper. Add milk gradually and stir constantly until thickened. Reduce heat and cook one or two minutes more. Pour this sauce over chicken. Sprinkle sauce with cheese. Sprinkle potatoes with paprika. Dot with butter and broil until sauce and potatoes brown lightly.
Serves 2.

– MR

POLLO ALLA BIRRA
(Chicken Cooked in Beer)

1 chicken, about 3¼ lbs.
2 large onions, sliced
¼ cup olive oil
6 tbsp. butter
¼ cup flour

salt and pepper
2 cups beer
1 cup heavy cream
mashed potatoes

Clean and wash the chicken. Sauté the onions lightly in the oil and butter in a large saucepan. Sprinkle the chicken with flour and place it in the saucepan. Sauté it, turning to brown evenly, for about 10 minutes. Put the chicken in a casserole, season with salt and pepper, and pour the beer over it. Cover and cook in a preheated 350-degree oven for 1¼ hours. If necessary, moisten with a few spoonfuls of water during cooking. When the chicken is cooked, puree the onions in an electric blender. Return the puree to the casserole and heat, mixing with the cream. Add salt to taste. Serve the chicken and sauce on a warm dish accompanied with mashed potatoes.

Serves 6.   – GF

FRICASSÉ DE POULET NORMANDE

2 3-lb. chickens cut into 6
   pieces each
3 cups sliced mushrooms
1 soup spoon chopped
   shallots
1 bay leaf
1½ tsp. thyme
1 cup dry white wine

3 apples, cut into wedges
3 cups chicken stock
3 cups heavy cream
2 oz. Calvados
1 soup spoon fresh chopped
   parsley
salt and pepper

Preheat skillet to 350°. Sauté the chicken to nice light color. Add shallots, mushrooms, apples, thyme, bay leaf, salt, and pepper. Add wine, chicken stock, and cream. Cover and cook for 20 minutes, then flame with Calvados. Serve with rice pilaf or noodles and sprinkle with parsley.   – LED

ÉMINCÉ OF CAPON BREAST
TROUVILLOISE

2 double capon breasts,
  boneless and skinless
  (cut into 2-inch long
  strips)
1 tbsp. chopped white
  onions
1 cup heavy cream
1 cup chicken stock or
  consommé
1 cup sliced fresh
  mushrooms
1 doz. shucked oysters
1½ cups gumbo-size
  shrimp, peeled and
  deveined

1 tbsp. chopped green onion
1½ tbsp. chopped parsley
1 cup all-purpose flour
3 oz. vegetable oil
3 tbsp. butter
½ cup dry white wine
2 oz. Calvados brandy
1½ tsp. fresh chopped basil
juice of one lemon
salt and pepper to taste

In skillet, sauté the capon strips in 3 ounces oil and 2 tablespoons butter with salt and pepper, until light brown. Flame with Calvados brandy. Add the onion and stir. Add shrimp, oysters, and mushrooms. Add white wine and chicken stock. Bring to a boil, then simmer. Add the cream; reduce the heat. Make "beurre manie," a combination of equal parts of flour and soft butter. Strain the remaining juices into another skillet. Bring to boil and thicken with "beurre manie" progressively till correct consistency (keep sauce light).

Finish sauce with 1 tablespoon butter, green onion, parsley, basil, and a touch of lemon juice.

Correct seasoning to your taste. Serve with noodles, steamed rice, or boiled potatoes.   – LED

OUR FRIED CHICKEN

3 2½-lb. chickens, cut up
  at joints
3 tbsp. salt
1 tbsp. black pepper

2 tsp. celery salt
1 tsp. Accent
flour
oil

Mix spices together and sprinkle over chicken and toss thoroughly. Mix in two handfuls of crushed ice and refrigerate for 3 to 4 hours to marinate. Stir chicken well, dredge in flour and fry at 340° for 10 to 15 minutes, depending on size of pieces.   – WL

BLANC DE VOLAILLES AU
VINAIGRE DE JEREZ
(Chicken Breast with Vinegar)

1 chicken breast per person
6 pieces of garlic
2 tbsp. white mustard
2 tbsp. tomato paste
2 tomatoes, seeded and
  diced

1 stick butter
½ cup sherry vinegar
1 cup white wine
2 oz. cognac or brandy
½ cup cream, optional
salt and pepper

Salt and pepper chicken. Heat butter and sauté chicken skin side first, slowly without coloring too much. Add garlic without cleaning. Cook for 15 minutes. If there is too much grease in pan, remove excess. Set aside.

Removing all residue, place pan back on fire with vinegar. In a separate bowl, whip mustard, cognac, wine, and tomato paste (add cream, if desired). Add to the pot and cook 5 minutes on high fire. Strain through fine chinacap over chicken breast; finish with butter. Garnish chicken with diced tomatoes and chives or parsley.

Serves 6.   – CK

POULET AU BROUILLY

chicken, cut into pieces
red wine
¼ cup chopped shallots
½ tsp. black pepper
½ tsp. thyme

2 bay leaves
2 tbsp. butter
pearl onions and sliced fresh
   mushrooms

Preheat oven to 350°F.

Sauté chicken, but *do not brown!* Add red wine to cover. Add shallots, black pepper, thyme, and bay leaves. Cover pan and bake in oven for 15 minutes. Remove chicken (keep warm). Reduce liquid. Whip in butter and pour over chicken. Place pearl onions and sautéed fresh mushrooms on top.

      – CK

CAILLES PORTO ROGER SAVERAIN

8 quail, deboned, except
   for leg bones
1 tbsp. rosemary
1 doz. whole black
   peppercorns
1 whole onion, chopped
vegetable oil (enough to
   cover quail for marinade)

½ cup ruby port
½ cup Burgundy
1/5 cup red wine vinegar
olive oil (enough to coat
   saucepan)
6 tbsp. unsalted butter
salt and pepper

Marinate boned quail in refrigerator with rosemary, peppercorns, onion, and oil for 3 to 4 days. Blend in a sauté pan port, Burgundy, and vinegar. Reduce over high heat for about 7 minutes to a dark ruby color. Place aside. Coat a very hot saucepan with olive oil and seal marinated quail 10 seconds per side (brown skin side first). Then transfer quail to broiler (also high heat) and cook (pink-to-the-bone), turning frequently, for 2 minutes. Remove from heat and place aside. To the still-warm wine reduction add cold butter and stir to syrupy consistency over high heat. Pour sauce into oval plate, place quail on plate, add salt and pepper to taste.

Leek vegetable dish should be served with the quail at both ends of the oval plate.

      – CK

STEWED CHICKEN

1 large fryer
1 stick butter
salt and pepper to taste
2 tbsp. shortening
2 tbsp. flour
2 medium onions, chopped
   fine

2 ribs celery, chopped fine
½ bell pepper, chopped
½ bunch green onions,
   chopped fine
1 bay leaf
3 cups water

Cut chicken into serving pieces, sprinkle with salt and pepper to taste, and place in a large saucepan containing 1 stick melted butter. Sauté until browned on all sides. Melt shortening in skillet, add flour and brown well. Add onions and bell pepper and cook for 5 minutes. Add water, stir well, then add celery, green onions, bay leaf. Pour this mixture over the chicken, which you have browned. Cook for 45 minutes or until tender. Stir from bottom frequently to prevent sticking. Serve with steamed rice.   – LE

PRESIDENTIAL CHICKEN

½ lb. boneless chicken
½ cup shredded bell
   peppers
½ cup shredded carrots
3 green onions, cut in half
2 cloves garlic, crushed

2 quarter-size slices ginger,
   crushed
3 chili peppers, cut in half
½ cup unsalted peanuts
2 tsp. sesame seed oil
1 tbsp. sherry

MARINADE:

½ egg white
½ tsp. cornstarch

1 tbsp. vegetable oil
1½ tsp. light soy sauce

SAUCE:

1 tbsp. red rice vinegar
2 tsp. sugar

3 tbsp. light soy sauce
½ tsp. cornstarch

Mix all ingredients for the marinade. Slice chicken into ½-inch strips and marinate.

Mix all ingredients for the sauce.

Heat 2 cups oil in wok to 300°. Add chicken; stir to separate. When chicken is about 70 percent done, remove and drain oil. Reheat wok with 2 tablespoons vegetable oil, add chili peppers, and cook until brown. Add ginger and garlic, stir, add vegetables (except green onions) and chicken, and stir for 30 seconds. Sprinkle in sherry and stir in sauce until it thickens, then add sesame seed oil, green onions, and peanuts.

– TW

WALNUT CHICKEN

10 oz. deboned chicken,
  cut in cubes
2 medium green peppers,
  cubed
1 medium red hot pepper,
  cubed

4 scallions, cut 1-inch
  lengths, white part only
1 cup walnuts
1 tsp. chopped ginger

MARINADE:

½ egg white (beaten)
1 tbsp. light soy sauce

1½ tsp. cornstarch
pinch of salt and pepper

GRAVY:

1½ tbsp. soy sauce
½ tbsp. vinegar
1 tbsp. rice wine or sherry

1 tsp. cornstarch
½ tsp. salt
1 tsp. sugar

Marinate chicken in marinade ingredients listed above for ½ hour. Cut all vegetables. Mix all ingredients for gravy, ready to use. Deep-fry walnuts until golden brown. Put aside and drain.

Heat 2 to 3 cups oil, scatter chicken in, and stir until 80 percent cooked. Pick up chicken and drain oil. Reheat wok with 3 tablespoons oil. Add ginger, scallions, red hot pepper, and bell peppers. Stir-fry for 30 seconds; put chicken back in for 15 seconds. Add gravy. Mix until thickens, shower in walnuts, and serve.　　– TW

CHICKEN MACINTOSH

3 8-oz chicken breasts
  (boned but reserve bones)
1 tsp. thyme
1 bay leaf
½ tsp. salt
¼ tsp. pepper
¼ cup shortening
8 oz. water chestnuts
1 white onion (one half
  chopped, one half sliced)
1 rib celery, chopped
1 carrot, chopped
½ bell pepper, chopped
6 oz. flour
1½ qts. chicken stock
2 cups white wine
1 large red apple, unpeeled
  and quartered
1 tbsp. butter

Salt and pepper chicken (save remaining salt and pepper). Dust in flour. Place in shortening with skin toward bottom of pan and brown on both sides.

Remove chicken from sauté pan. Add 4 ounces flour and stir into shortening left in pan. Cook until browned. Add chopped onion, celery, bell pepper, carrot, thyme, bay leaf, balance of salt and pepper, and bones from chicken. Cook for about 15 minutes on slow heat (reduce by half).

Add chicken stock and cook for about 30 minutes. Remove bones.

In another pan, place sliced onion and 1 tablespoon of butter. Cook for about 5 minutes. Place chicken breasts in this pan. Add water chestnuts and apple quarters. Add 2 cups white wine and cook for another 5 minutes.

Add stock and strain over chicken breasts. Place in oven for about 15 to 20 minutes at 350° and serve with rice.

Serves 3.   – LE

POULET AU FROMAGE

½ deboned chicken
1 tbsp. clarified butter
1 tsp. shallots
½ cup vermouth
¾ cup cream
1 tbsp. grated Swiss cheese
1 tbsp. blue cheese butter
  (equal parts blue cheese
  and butter mixed until
  uniform)
1 tbsp. Dijon mustard

Preheat oven to 350°F. Sauté chicken in clarified butter – do not brown.

Add shallots and vermouth. Reduce by half. Add cream.

Place in oven, covered with oiled wax paper; cook 15 minutes or until done. Remove chicken, strain sauce to another pan, and reduce until thickened.

Whip in Swiss cheese and blue cheese butter; add mustard.

Pour sauce over chicken.   – CK

CHICKEN AU POIVRE

8 pieces chicken breast
about ½ cup cracked black
   peppercorns
1 lb. butter

1 tsp. salt
1 tbsp. lemon juice
3 tbsp. finely minced parsley

Pound the cracked peppercorns into both sides of the pieces of chicken with the back of a saucer or the flat side of a pounding mallet. Set aside while you turn on the broiler to preheat. Prepare the butter sauce by melting the butter in a saucepan, then adding the salt, lemon juice, and parsley. Prepare a broiling rack or baking sheet by brushing the rack with some of the butter sauce, then place the chicken breasts bottom side up on the rack. Baste with some of the butter sauce and set to broil, about 5 inches from the heat, for 15 minutes. Remove the pan from the broiler, turn the chicken on preheated plates, then spoon the pan drippings from the broiling pan over them. Top with the remaining butter sauce.
Serves 8. – MR

CHICKEN DOROTHY

24 pieces chicken (legs and
   thighs)
2 cups flour
½ lb. butter
salt and pepper
2 tbsp. garlic salt
4 green peppers, chopped

1 celery heart, chopped
2 onions, chopped
3 tbsp. tomato paste
3 bay leaves
5 cloves
2 tbsp. chicken base
juice of 2 lemons

Season chicken pieces with salt and pepper. Dust with flour then brown in butter. In sauté pan, brown lightly in butter the peppers, celery, and onions. Add the tomato paste, bay leaves, cloves, chicken base, and lemon juice. Add the browned chicken pieces and enough water to cover. Add garlic salt. Stir and let cook for 15 to 20 minutes.
Serve with steamed rice and green vegetables such as peas or beans.
Serves 8. – JLA

CHICKEN LIVER BROCHETTE

½ lb. bacon
3 doz. chicken livers
3 doz. mushrooms
2 cups flour
2 eggs

1 cup milk
1 tsp. salt
1 tsp. pepper
vegetable oil for frying

Cut bacon strips in half and cook lightly. Alternating livers, bacon, and mushrooms, place close together on 6 skewers. Season the flour with salt and pepper. Combine eggs and milk in a shallow bowl. Dip skewers in egg wash, then in seasoned flour. Fry in a 3-quart deep fryer at 360° for 4 minutes. Remove skewers.
Serves 6.

– AL

POULET AUX CREVETTES OU ÉCREVISSES

1 3-lb. chicken
16 large fresh shrimp,
   peeled and deveined or
   24 fresh crawfish, peeled
   and deveined
2 tbsp. butter
2 tbsp. tomato puree
1 cup chicken stock

1 tbsp. shrimp paste or 1
   cup of shrimp stock
fresh shallots or the white of
   a green onion
1 clove garlic
1 bay leaf
pinch of thyme
½ cup white wine

Separate chicken into four pieces. Sauté the chicken in butter in a shallow pan about 3 minutes on each side (do not brown). Then add fresh shallots or white of green onion. Add 1 clove of garlic; deglaze the pan with ½ cup of white wine. Then add 2 tablespoons of tomato puree, bay leaf, thyme, chicken stock, and then shrimp paste or stock. Cover chicken with buttery paper or a couple of lettuce leaves. Cook for about 18 minutes at 475°. Remove pan from oven and remove chicken. Strain the sauce through a fine china cap (or fine sieve). Return to fire, add shrimp and chicken and cook for another 2 minutes.
Serves 4.

– CK

ROASTED TURKEY BREAST

1 8- to 10-lb. turkey breast
  (bone in) at room
  temperature

½ cup coconut oil
¼ cup soy sauce
½ tsp. white pepper

Heat oven to 350°. Dry turkey breast well with paper towel. Brush turkey every 20 minutes with basting sauce. Stir sauce well when using. When all the basting sauce is used, baste with drippings that accumulate in bottom of pan.

CHICKEN CLEMENCEAU

1 2-lb spring chicken,
  disjointed
1 large potato, diced
butter

garlic
sliced mushrooms
green peas
chopped parsley

Fry potato in deep fat. Sauté chicken in butter until brown. Drain chicken of excess butter, then place chicken, diced potatoes, and a little mashed garlic in a slow oven for 20 minutes.

Add to the chicken some sliced mushrooms and some small green peas; warm them slightly for a few minutes. Serve with chopped parsley. Serves 2. – JGF

POULET RÔTI A L'AIL
(Roast Chicken with Garlic Cloves)

1 3-lb. chicken, washed and
  dried in and out
salt and white pepper
1 head garlic, crushed with
  skins left on

1 bay leaf
1 tbsp. dried thyme
1 24-inch piece of string
1 tbsp. butter
1 tbsp. oil

Salt and pepper the inside of the chicken. Place garlic, bay leaf, and thyme in the cavity. Truss the chicken with the string. In an oven-proof pan, heat butter and oil. Place chicken in pan, breast side down first. Cook until chicken has a golden brown color. Turn breast up and put into a 475-degree oven for 50 minutes, or until done. Let settle for 10 minutes. When done, remove chicken from pan, pouring off excess grease. Remove seasonings, and set aside. Debone chicken, keeping chicken warm.

SAUCE

seasoning from the chicken
   and bones
1 bottle white wine

8 oz. water
½ stick butter
salt and white pepper

Put seasonings, chicken bones, white wine, and water in pan the chicken was cooked in. Reduce until almost all of it has evaporated. Strain. Return to a clean pan, and reduce until the sauce has small tight bubbles, and finish with butter.

Correct salt and pepper if necessary. Spoon over the cut-up chicken.

– CK

BREAST OF CHICKEN A L'ORANGE

8 chicken breasts
½ cup flour
2 tbsp. salt
1 tbsp. paprika

½ cup butter
2 cups orange juice
1 cup white wine

Dust chicken with a mixture of flour, salt, and paprika. Sauté in butter at medium heat until golden brown. Discard fat.

Add orange juice and wine and cover and simmer for 15 minutes. Baste the breasts once in a while. Uncover, take the breasts out and reduce the liquid to a slightly thickened sauce. Season to taste.

Can be served with rice, noodles, and green vegetables. With the sauce over the chicken, garnish with fruit sections such as orange, grapefruit, and papayas or with mushrooms, avocado slices, and chopped nuts.

– JLA

QUAILS IN CRANBERRY SAUCE

1½ tbsp. butter
½ tsp. French shallots, chopped fine
½ tsp. green onions, chopped fine
¼ tsp. tarragon
3 tbsp. bread crumbs
salt to taste
white pepper to taste

2 2½-oz. quails, boneless
2 slices bacon
½ tbsp. cranberries, whole (fresh or frozen)
1 oz. brandy
¼ cup red wine
½ cup brown sauce
½ tbsp. French shallots, chopped fine

Make the stuffing: In a sauté pan, melt 1 tablespoon butter. Add the shallots, green onion, and tarragon. Sauté for 1 minute. Incorporate the bread crumbs into the mixture, taking care to distribute the butter and bread crumbs evenly. Season to taste with salt and white pepper. Transfer the stuffing to another container and cool in the refrigerator.

Prepare the quail: Preheat the oven to 350°. The boneless quails should already be split down the back; if not, do so. Spread the quails out, flesh side down. Spread the chilled stuffing onto the interior of the boneless quails. Roll up and shape the quails into their original shape. With the legs sticking upward, wrap the quails with bacon, secure with toothpicks. Roast in pan at 350° for 25 to 30 minutes.

Make the sauce in the pan: Remove the quails from the oven. Pour the excess oil out of the pan. Add the cranberries and stir into the pan drippings. Deglaze and flambé with brandy. Extinguish the flame with red wine. Add the brown sauce and shallots. Simmer for an additional 5 minutes. Finish the sauce by swirling in ½ tablespoon butter. Arrange the quail, legs up, on a plate. Sauce the quails.

Serves 1.   – GP

Pasta

RAVIOLI

PASTA:

4 cups all-purpose flour	**1 cup water**
1 pinch salt	**2 eggs**

Put the flour on a large pastry board. Make a well in the middle and add the eggs, water, and salt. Work the eggs and water into the flour, then knead to a smooth elastic dough about 10 minutes.

Roll the dough out as thinly as possible into two sheets. On one sheet arrange teaspoons of the stuffing (see recipe below) in little heaps at regular intervals 1½ inches apart. Cover with the second sheet of dough and press with the finger round the heaps of stuffing. Cut the ravioli square with a pastry wheel and make quite sure the edges are firmly sealed.

Sprinkle lightly with flour and let them rest for 30 minutes, turning them after 15 minutes.

Bring a large pan of salt water to boil, add the ravioli, and cook for 12 minutes. Lift out with a slotted spoon and transfer to a heated serving dish.

Add your favorite tomato sauce. Toss gently and serve with additional Parmesan cheese.

MEAT FILLING:

1 medium onion, chopped	**¼ cup grated Romano**
2 tbsp. olive oil	**cheese**
1 lb. ground pork	**2 cloves garlic**
1 lb. ground meat	**½ tsp. nutmeg**

Sauté meat and onions and garlic for 5 minutes until brown. Let cool. Add cheese, and season with salt, pepper, and nutmeg, mixing thoroughly. Put the mixture through the fine blade of a meat grinder.

Serves 6 to 8.   – GF

CRAWFISH OR SHRIMP BORDELAISE WITH PASTA

3 cups pasta, cooked
  according to package
  directions and kept warm
½ cup butter

1 lb. crawfish or shrimp
6 tbsp. minced garlic
6 tbsp. minced parsley

Over medium heat in 9-inch skillet, melt butter and sauté crawfish or shrimp until tender. Add garlic; cook for 3 minutes. Stir in pasta and parsley; serve hot.

          – MR

SPAGHETTI WITH WHITE CLAM SAUCE

1 lb. spaghetti
¾ cup olive oil
2 cloves garlic
¼ dried red pepper
8-oz. can chopped shelled
  clams
1 tbsp. flour

½ cup white wine
2 tbsp. fresh chopped
  parsley
1 tbsp. chopped chives
4 tbsp. butter
salt and white pepper to
  taste

Peel the garlic and chop it finely. Put it into a small saucepan with the oil and the piece of red pepper and sauté over a low flame. When the garlic is almost golden in color, add the clams, salt, and pepper, and continue to sauté for a few minutes. Add the flour and stir well. Add the white wine, stir, and allow half of it to evaporate. Add ½ cup of hot water (more if needed) and continue to cook over a low fire for 15 minutes.

In the meantime, the water for the spaghetti will have come to a boil. Cook the spaghetti for 8 minutes. While spaghetti is cooking, add the butter and the chopped parsley and the chives to the sauce. Add a little more hot water if necessary and continue to cook until the spaghetti is ready. Drain the spaghetti and put into a serving bowl. Add all of the sauce and toss until well mixed.

Serves 4.

          – GF

CRAWFISH AND PASTA

1 lb. crawfish
4 large mushrooms, sliced
½ bunch green onions,
  chopped
1 clove garlic, chopped fine
¼ lb. butter
1 qt. crawfish stock
½ tsp. basil
½ tsp. oregano

½ tsp. pepper
1 tsp. salt
1 cup white vermouth
1 pt. half-and-half
2 tbsp. grated Parmesan
  cheese
2 tbsp. flour
2 lbs. flat pasta

Sauté green onions, garlic, and mushrooms in butter for 5 minutes. Add flour; cook for 3 minutes more. Add crawfish and crawfish stock; mix well. Add oregano, basil, salt, pepper, and vermouth, and cook for 10 minutes on slow heat.

Add grated cheese and half-and-half. Cook for another 3 minutes and pour over pasta, prepared as follows: Place pasta in 1 quart boiling water with ½ teaspoon salt. Boil for 5 minutes and drain. Rinse with hot water and place on serving plate. Top with sauce.

Serves 8 to 10.   – LE

FETTUCCINE ALLA GOFFREDO

1 lb. fettuccine
½ cup melted butter
½ cup heavy cream

1 cup grated Parmesan
  cheese

Start cooking the fettuccine in 2 quarts boiling salted water. Boil for 5 minutes. Put an oval serving dish in a hot oven to heat. Partly drain the cooled fettuccine, turn into the hot serving dish (put combined butter and heavy cream in dish first). Add the cheese and mix with fork and spoon until all the ingredients are well blended. The result should be a real creamy sauce. Serve immediately.

Serves 4.   – GF

CANNELLONI RIVIERA

½ cup olive oil
1 onion, chopped
½ lb. lean veal meat, cut in
small pieces
½ lb. pork, cut in small
pieces
½ lb. Italian sausage, cut
in small pieces
1 sprig rosemary
salt

½ cup dry white wine
½ cup stock
½ cup veal sweetbreads, cut
in small pieces
2 eggs
a pinch of nutmeg
1 cup grated Parmesan
cheese
1 lb. manicotti tubes
1½ cups Bechamel sauce

Heat the oil in a skillet and sauté the onion until browned. Discard the onion and add the veal, pork, and sausage with rosemary; sauté until meat is browned. Season with salt and add the wine. When the wine has evaporated, add stock and transfer the meat to a preheated 350° oven to continue cooking until dry. Add the sweetbreads to the meat shortly before taking from the oven. Discard the rosemary and put all the meat through a grinder. Add the eggs, nutmeg, and grated Parmesan cheese to the mixture. Cook the tubes according to package directions. Use pastry bag for the mixture, closing the edges by pressing together with the fingers. Cover the bottom of an oven-proof gratin dish with a layer of Bechamel sauce. Put the cannelloni in the dish in rows and cover them with the remaining Bechamel sauce. Sprinkle additional Parmesan cheese over the top and put the dish in a preheated 350-degree oven for 30 minutes. Serve immediately.

Serves 6.

– GF

SHRIMP AND PERNOD WITH PASTA

1½ lbs. peeled raw shrimp
   (21 to 25 count)
4 large mushrooms
2 oz. grated Parmesan
   cheese
½ qt. shrimp stock
1 clove garlic, chopped fine
1 cup Pernod
½ bunch green onions,
   chopped fine
1 tbsp. fresh sweet basil,
   chopped fine

½ lb. butter
½ tbsp. fresh oregano,
   chopped fine
3 bay leaves
1 tsp. chicken base
1 pt. half-and-half
1 tbsp. green pepper sauce
4 oz. all-purpose flour
2 lbs. fresh cooked pasta

In sauté pan, place chopped onion, garlic, sliced mushrooms, and butter. Cook for about 3 minutes. Add shrimp. Cook for about 5 minutes. Add flour, cook for another 3 minutes. Pour Pernod over this mixture (it will flame), then add shrimp stock, bay leaves, oregano, basil, and green pepper sauce.

Add Parmesan cheese, half-and-half, and chicken base, and keep stirring. Cook for another 5 to 10 minutes and serve over pasta.   – LE

PASTA WITH EGGPLANT, SHRIMP & BASIL

1 lb. pasta
8-12 shrimp per person,
   peeled and de-veined
2 large tomatoes, peeled,
   seeded, and diced
1 large eggplant

2 cloves garlic, chopped fine
1 pt. whipping cream
2 green onions, sliced thin
½ cup olive oil
4 sprigs fresh basil

Peel and cube the eggplant. Place it in a colander. Sprinkle salt over it and let stand for 2 hours.

Sauté the eggplant in the olive oil and drain. Save the oil and use it to sauté the shrimp. Drain the shrimp.

Cook the pasta, rinse and drain.

In a large skillet over medium heat, add the cream, tomatoes, garlic, eggplant, and bring to a boil. Then add the shrimp, pasta, and green onions. Bring to a boil and, if the sauce is thin, cook for a minute or two. Add basil, salt, pepper, and cayenne to taste.

Serve immediately.

Grated Romano cheese is optional.

Serves 4-6.

– RH

SPAGHETTI ALLE OSTRICHE
(Spaghetti with Oysters)

1 lb. spaghetti
¾ cup olive oil
2 cloves garlic
piece dried red pepper,
   approx. ¼ tsp. in volume
1 pt. oysters
1 tbsp. flour

½ cup white wine
2 tbsp. fresh chopped
   parsley
1 tbsp. chopped chives
4 tbsp. butter
salt and white pepper to
   taste

Peel the garlic and chop it finely. Put it into a small saucepan with the oil and the piece of red pepper and sauté over a low flame. When the garlic is almost golden in color, add the oysters, salt, and pepper and continue to sauté for a few minutes. Add the flour and stir well. Add white wine, stir, and allow half of it to evaporate. Pour in half cup of hot water (more if needed) and continue to cook over a low fire for 15 minutes. In the meantime, the water for the spaghetti has come to a boil. Cook the spaghetti for 8 minutes. While spaghetti is cooking, add the butter and the chopped parsley and the chives to the sauce. Add a little more hot water if necessary and continue to cook until the spaghetti is ready. Drain the spaghetti and put into a serving bowl. Add all the sauce and toss until well mixed.

Serves 4.

– GF

OYSTERS AND ARTICHOKES
WITH FRESH HERBS

2 chopped dill leaves
2 chopped basil leaves
3 chopped rosemary sprigs
2 bay leaves
½ lb. butter
4 oz. flour
1 cup vermouth
2 oz. green pepper sauce
8 medium sliced
  mushrooms

½ bunch chopped green
  onions
⅓ cup chopped parsley
2 cups heavy cream
½ qt. chicken stock
8 hearts of artichokes, cut
  up
½ gal. oysters
2 oz. salt

Place ½ gallon of oysters with chicken stock, bay leaves, dill, rosemary, and basil in a pot and let come to a boil. Skim off the top.

In another pot, melt butter and add green onions and mushrooms. Cook for 3 to 4 minutes, then add flour and cook for additional 5 minutes. Add oysters and liquid and mix well. Add vermouth, heavy cream, green pepper sauce, salt, and cut-up artichoke hearts. Cook for 15 minutes.

Suggested Serving: Sprinkle with parsley and serve over pasta. – LE

GASSE ALLA GENOESE
(Bowties with Meat and Tomato
Sauce)

1 16-oz. pkg. bowties
6 oz. canned mushrooms
  (drained)
¼ cup butter
¾ lb. lean veal (cut into
  small pieces)
1 clove chopped garlic

1 chopped onion
4 ripe or 1 can peeled
  tomatoes
1 tbsp. flour
⅔ cup grated Parmesan
  cheese

Melt the butter in a pan and brown the pieces of veal on all sides with the chopped onion and garlic, stirring continually. Peel tomatoes, squeeze out the seeds and chop coarsely (put canned tomatoes through a food mill) and add to the meat, together with the chopped mushrooms. Season with salt and freshly ground pepper and simmer covered for 15 minutes. Put 1 tablespoon of flour in a pan and stir continually over a moderate heat until brown, then stir into the meat sauce, adding some boiling stock if it seems too dry. Cook covered until the meat is tender.

Cook bowties in plenty of boiling salted water, drain while still firm and mix in a serving dish with the meat sauce and grated Parmesan cheese.

Serves 4 to 6.   – GF

SPAGHETTI PRIMAVERA
(Springtime Spaghetti)

1 medium onion	3 small ripe tomatoes
4 tbsp. oil	¾ cup shelled peas (or
⅛ lb. fresh mushrooms	frozen)
1 medium carrot	2 thin slices cooked ham
1 stalk celery	salt and pepper to taste
2 basil leaves (or ⅛ tsp.	1 lb. spaghetti
dried)	¾ cup Parmesan cheese

Cut the onion into very thin strips and allow to soften (do not brown) in the oil. Wash the mushrooms and cut into very thin slices. Add to the onion mixture and cook 2 minutes on low flame. In the meantime, cut up the carrot, the celery, the basil leaves and the tomatoes into very thin strips, and add all at once. Add the peas, which have been boiled in salted water and drained. Next add the ham, also cut up into very thin strips, and salt and pepper. Simmer slowly for 15 minutes.

Cook the spaghetti in abundant water for 8 minutes and drain.

Turn onto preheated serving dish. Pour the above sauce over the spaghetti, add the Parmesan, mix well and serve.

Serves 4.   – GF

MAUDE'S SPAGHETTI AND
MEATBALLS

MEATBALLS:

2 lbs. ground veal (veal
  round, boned and
  trimmed)
1 medium white onion,
  finely chopped
2 stalks celery, finely
  chopped
½ small green pepper, finely
  chopped
4 cloves garlic, very finely
  chopped

3 tbsp. grated Parmesan
  cheese
3 large eggs, well beaten
2 tsp. salt
¾ tsp. black pepper (or to
  taste)
1 cup Italian bread crumbs
¼ cup vegetable oil
  (approximately)

GRAVY:

oil and meat juices left in
  skillet
1 medium white onion,
  finely chopped
2 stalks celery, finely
  chopped
½ small green pepper
6 cloves garlic, finely
  chopped
4 sprigs fresh parsley, finely
  chopped

1 green onion, finely
  chopped
1 6-oz. can tomato paste
¼ tsp. sugar
2 8-oz. cans tomato sauce
2 cups plus 6 tbsp. water
1½ tsp. salt (or to taste)
¾ tsp. black pepper (or to
  taste)
2 bay leaves, broken up fine
spaghetti

To make the meatballs, put the veal in a large mixing bowl with the chopped vegetables. Sprinkle in Parmesan cheese. Add the beaten eggs, salt, and pepper. Mix gently with your fingers with a kneading motion. (This will mix the ingredients thoroughly without beating the air out of them.) On a separate plate sprinkle the Italian bread crumbs in an even layer. Dampen your hands and pick up about ½ cup of the mixture. Shape it into a ball by rolling it gently between your hands. Roll each meatball in the bread crumbs right after shaping and set aside on another platter. Heat vegetable oil to a depth of ½ inch in a large deep skillet or sauté pan over medium heat until quite hot (about 340° if your skillet has a thermostat). Put the meatballs into the hot oil in a single layer. If necessary, cook the meatballs in 2 batches, but don't overcrowd the skillet. When the bottom sides of the meatballs are nicely browned, turn them over carefully and brown on the other side. When cooked, remove them from the skillet with a long fork or a slotted spoon, allowing the oil to drain back into the pan. Reserve on a platter.

To make the gravy, place the skillet in which the meatballs were cooked over low heat. Add the chopped vegetables and cook just a few minutes, then add the tomato paste. Stir well. Simmer for about 2 minutes more, then add the sugar, tomato sauce, water, salt, pepper, and bay leaves. Mix thoroughly. Put the meatballs into the gravy and cook over very low heat for 1 to 1¼ hours. Stir gently from time to time, being careful not to break up the meatballs. Turn off the heat.

Cook the spaghetti and drain well. Serve with about ⅔ cup gravy and 2 meatballs over each portion of spaghetti. Provide a shaker of grated Romano cheese to be added at the table to taste.

Maude, Mrs. Owen Brennan, prefers ground veal in this dish, veal of good quality. You can substitute ground beef if you prefer. She suggests you use #4 spaghetti, cooked chewy. If you plan to serve four, prepare the entire amount and freeze half the gravy and meatballs for another meal.

Serves 8.   – MR

AGNOLOTTI PASTA

4 cups all-purpose flour   **1 cup water**
1 pinch salt   **2 eggs**

Put the flour on a large pastry board. Make a well in the middle and add the eggs, water, and salt. Work the eggs and water into the flour, then knead to a smooth elastic dough (about 10 minutes).

Roll the dough out as thinly as possible into two sheets. On one sheet arrange teaspoons of the stuffing in little heaps at regular intervals, 1½ inches apart.

Cover with the second sheet of dough and press with the finger round the heaps of stuffing. Cut the Agnolotti square with a pastry wheel and make quite sure the edges are firmly sealed.

Sprinkle lightly with flour and let them rest for 30 minutes, turning them after 15 minutes.

Bring a large pan of salted water to boil. Add the Agnolotti and cook for 12 minutes. Lift out with a perforated spoon and transfer to a heated serving dish.

Add sauce and top with additional Parmesan cheese.   – GF

RAVIOLI
Agnolotti alla Fraccaro

This recipe won first prize at the 1980 San Francisco Crab-cooking Olympics.

THICK BECHAMEL

½ cup milk   **¼ tsp. salt**
1 tbsp. butter   **pinch of white and red**
1 tbsp. flour   **pepper**
          1 egg yolk

Cook together, then let cool.

STUFFING

½ cup chopped green onion	**1 tbsp. butter**

Sauté and let cool.

ADD TO ABOVE:

1 egg white	**1 lb. crabmeat**
2 tbsp. parsley	**4 tbsp. cracker crumbs**

After completed stuffing and Bechamel sauce have lost their heat, fold stuffing into Bechamel and blend thoroughly. This becomes the stuffing for the agnolotti. Use as directed in the following recipe.

SAUCE

1 cup whipping cream	**salt and red and white**
(reduce by ½)	**pepper to taste**
1 stick butter	

When cream is reduced by half by boiling, melt butter in and season to taste. Reserve and reheat if necessary to top agnolotti.　　　– GF

ST. MICHAEL'S PASTA

1 lb. fresh broccoli, cleaned	**salt and pepper to taste**
and cut into flowerettes	**Parmesan cheese to taste**
1 lb. priggatoni	**fresh black pepper**
½ cup cream	**4 cloves garlic, minced**
1 stick butter	

Place broccoli in salted boiling water and cook until tender. Retaining water, remove broccoli and cool in ice water. Replace water on heat, add a small amount of oil, and let it return to a boil. Add pasta to the boiling water and cook until tender. Drain and cool. Place broccoli in food processor and process with garlic and cream until smooth. Place the broccoli cream and butter in a medium sauté pan and heat slowly only until the butter is melted. Add salt and pepper and add pasta to the broccoli cream. Reduce until nice and thick.

Place finished pasta on a serving plate, sprinkle with cheese, and grind some fresh black pepper on top. – CK

GNOCCHI WITH PESTO GENOVESE

1 lb. potatoes, freshly
  boiled
1½ cups all-purpose flour

1 egg, beaten
salt, pepper, and nutmeg

Drain the potatoes well and shake over the heat to dry thoroughly. Mash very finely (there must be no lumps) and add the flour, egg, salt, pepper, and nutmeg to taste. Mix to a dough and turn onto a floured board. With floured hands, roll pieces of the dough into long sausages, about ½ inch in diameter. Cut into 1-inch lengths and, using your little finger, make a dent in the center of each one to make them curl slightly. Drop the gnocchi, a few at a time, into a large pan of gently boiling salted water. Cook until they rise to the surface, about 3 to 5 minutes. Lift out with a slotted spoon. Drain, put into a buttered dish, and keep hot until all are cooked. Dot with butter and sprinkle with cheese. Thin the pesto with a spoonful of the cooking water, then pour it over the gnocchi and serve at once.

Serves 4. – GF

GNOCCHI WITH MEAT SAUCE

3 tbsp. salad oil
1 medium onion, finely
  chopped
1 stalk celery, finely
  chopped
1 carrot, finely chopped
2 cloves garlic, finely
  chopped
⅓ cup chopped mushrooms
½ lb. ground beef

¼ lb. cooked ham, ground
¼ lb. chicken livers, finely
  chopped
1 tbsp. flour
1 8-oz. can tomato sauce
1 tsp. salt
½ tsp. chopped rosemary
½ tsp. sugar
1 bay leaf
½ cup dry red wine

Heat oil in large, heavy saucepan. Sauté onions, celery, carrot, garlic, rosemary, and mushrooms in hot oil until onion is transparent. Add beef, ham, and chicken livers. Cook until meat is lightly browned. Drain off excess fat. Stir in flour until well blended. Add wine. Cook 3 to 5 minutes. Add remaining ingredients. Cook over medium heat, stirring occasionally, about 30 minutes. Serve over gnocchi (see recipe above).
Serves 4.   – GF

RAVIOLI WITH RICOTTA CHEESE

1 lb. ricotta cheese
2 eggs, well beaten
2 tbsp. minced parsley
2 tbsp. olive oil

¼ cup grated Parmesan
  cheese
salt and white pepper
nutmeg to taste

Mix all ingredients together until smooth. Use 1 heaping teaspoon for each ravioli.

SAUCE:

1 cup heavy cream

5 tbsp. butter

Melt butter and cream in a saucepan on low heat. Add to the ravioli, mixing thoroughly and gently. Sprinkle with Parmesan cheese.
Serve immediately.   – GF

SPAGHETTI ALLA PUTANESCA
(Untranslatable)

10 to 15 black olives
1 lb. (3 medium) very ripe
   tomatoes
1 tbsp. capers
1 tsp. crushed red pepper
3 anchovy fillets
4 tbsp. olive oil

2 cloves garlic, finely
   chopped
3 tbsp. finely chopped
   parsley
salt to taste
1 lb. spaghetti

Remove the pits from the olives and cut olives into small pieces. Peel the tomatoes and cut them into very thin slices. Wash the capers and chop extremely fine. Mash the anchovies with a fork. Put the oil into saucepan. Add the garlic. When it begins to color, add the red pepper, capers, anchovies, olives, parsley, and tomatoes. Add salt to taste. Cook for 15 minutes. Cook the spaghetti in abundant salted water for 8 minutes. Pour sauce over the drained spaghetti and serve.
Serves 4.

– GF

FETTUCCINE WITH RICOTTA

½ medium onion
2 tbsp. olive oil
4 tbsp. butter
1 8-oz. can peas, drained
salt to taste
⅛ tsp. sage (dried)

7 tbsp. ricotta cheese
2 egg yolks
1 lb. fettuccine
½ cup grated Parmesan
   cheese

Sauté the chopped onion in the oil and 2 tablespoons of butter in a suacepan until barely golden. Add the peas, salt, and sage and cook for 8 or 10 minutes. In a serving bowl mix together the ricotta with the egg yolks. Cook the fettuccine in abundant boiling salted water for 6 minutes if fresh (8 minutes if dry). Put drained fettuccine in the bowl with the egg yolk-ricotta mixture. Add 1 tablespoon of the boiling water in which the pasta was cooked and the grated Parmesan cheese. Toss until well mixed. Add the sauce and the rest of the butter in dabs. Mix again and serve.
Serves 4.

– GF

Vegetables

CAJUN CABBAGE WITH SMOKED SAUSAGE

SEASONING MIX (or substitute Cajun Magic Vegetable Magic)

2¼ tsp. salt
1½ tsp. sweet paprika
1 tsp. white pepper
½ tsp. onion powder
½ tsp. garlic powder
½ tsp. ground red pepper (preferably cayenne)

½ tsp. black pepper
½ tsp. dried thyme leaves
¼ tsp. dried sweet basil leaves

4 tbsp. unsalted butter
2 cups julienned onions (see Note)
10 packed cups shredded cabbage
1 cup Basic Chicken Stock (recipe follows)
2 bay leaves, halved
3 cups unpeeled, julienned apples (see Note)

3 tbsp. dark brown sugar
½ lb. andouille smoked sausage (preferred) or any other good pure smoked pork sausage as Polish sausage (kielbasa), cut into ½-inch pieces

Note: Julienned strips should be ⅛-inch by ⅛-inch by 2 inches.

In a small bowl, combine the seasoning mix ingredients; mix well. Set aside.

Melt the butter in a 4-quart saucepan over high heat. Add the onions and sauté about 2 minutes, stirring occasionally. Add the cabbage, then ½ cup of the stock, the bay leaves, and the seasoning mix; stir well. Cook 5 minutes, stirring occasionally. Stir in the apples and cook 15 minutes, stirring occasionally. Stir in the sugar and the remaining ½ cup stock; mix well. Cook about 2 minutes, stirring occasionally. Add the andouille and cook and stir for 5 minutes more. Remove from heat, discard bay leaves, and serve immediately.

Serves 8 as an appetizer. — PP

BASIC CHICKEN STOCK

10 cups cold water (see
  Note)
1½ to 2 lbs. chicken backs,
  necks, giblets (excluding
  liver) and/or bones

1 medium onion, unpeeled
  and quartered
1 rib celery
1 large clove garlic,
  unpeeled and quartered

Note: Always start with cold water, enough to cover the other stock ingredients.

Place all the ingredients in a large saucepan; bring to a boil over high heat, then gently simmer at least 4 hours, preferably 8, replenishing the water as needed to keep about 1 quart of liquid in the pan. Strain, cool, and refrigerate until ready to use. (Note: Remember, if you are short on time, that using a stock simmered 20 or 30 minutes is far better than using just water in any recipe.)

Makes about 1 quart.   – PP

MA-PO BEAN CURD

1 lb. bean curd (in 1″
  cubes)
6 oz. ground pork
1 tsp. minced garlic
2 scallions, finely chopped
½ tsp. ground Szechuan
  peppercorns
2 tbsp. soy sauce
1 tsp. Szechuan hot bean
  paste

1 tsp. sesame seed oil
⅔ cup chicken broth
dash of vinegar
1 tbsp. sherry
pinch of cayenne
2 tsp. cornstarch mixed with
  4 tsp. water

Heat 4 to 6 tablespoons oil in wok until hot. Add ground pork and stir fry for 30 seconds. Toss in garlic and sherry, add Szechuan hot bean paste and dash of vinegar, and stir briefly. Then add bean curd, chicken broth, soy sauce, and cayenne. Stir gently and bring to a boil. 30 seconds after boiling begins, thicken with cornstarch mix. Garnish with peppercorns, scallions, and sesame seed oil and serve.   – TW

RATATOUILLE

4 medium onions, sliced
1½ cups olive oil
1 small unpeeled eggplant,
  cubed
1 zucchini, cubed
4 tomatoes, peeled,
  seeded, and coarsely
  chopped

4 green peppers, seeded and
  cubed
½ tsp. thyme
½ cup minced parsley
3 garlic cloves, finely
  chopped
salt and pepper to taste

Sauté sliced onions and green peppers in ½ cup of olive oil in a casserole dish until golden brown. Add vegetables and herbs. Mix gently. Bring remaining olive oil to a boil and pour over vegetables. Cover casserole tightly and simmer at a low heat for 30 minutes. Season with salt and pepper.

Serve hot or cold.   – WC

DIRTY RICE

1 lb. chicken livers,
  chopped fine
4 tbsp. vegetable oil
1 cup finely chopped
  onions
½ cup finely chopped
  celery
½ cup finely chopped green
  pepper

1 tsp. finely chopped garlic
¼ cup thinly sliced green
  onion
¼ cup finely chopped
  parsley
½ tsp. salt
¼ tsp. black pepper
pinch cayenne pepper
8 cups cooked rice

Sauté chicken livers, onions, celery, green pepper, and garlic in vegetable oil until lightly browned. Add salt and peppers, then combine liver mixture and cooked rice in bowl. Add green onions and parsley and toss well with fork. Place rice in casserole dish and bake at 350° until heated through.

Serves 4.   – AL

FRENCH-FRIED EGGPLANT

1 large, long eggplant	salt and white pepper to
1 egg	taste
¾ cup milk	oil for deep frying
flour	powdered sugar

Peel eggplant and cut to size of large French fries. Soak 30 minutes in salted water. Rinse and pat dry. Make a batter with egg and milk and season well with salt and pepper. Dip eggplant into batter, roll in flour and deep fry until golden. Sprinkle with additional salt and serve with powdered sugar.

Serves 4 as hors d'oeuvre with cocktails or as vegetable with entrée.

– JGF

GAMBAS AUX PETITS LÉGUMES CHRISTIAN EYRAUD

10 medium shrimp per person	5 oz. whipping cream
salt	dash lemon juice
cayenne pepper	2 oz. fish stock
powdered thyme	½ zucchini
3 oz. butter	½ carrot
1 tbsp. chopped shallots	½ stalk celery
½ oz. Pernod, Ricard or Herbsaint	½ fresh tomato, peeled

Clean and devein shrimp, leaving tail on. Sauté shrimp lightly in butter for 1 or 2 minutes. Season with salt, cayenne, and thyme; add shallots. Flame with Pernod. Add fish stock and immediately remove shrimp. Reduce liquid to half its volume; add whipping cream and lemon juice. Let sauce reduce to desired thickness. Replace shrimp into sauce just long enough to reheat (do not boil shrimp). Remove shrimp and display on plates, cover with sauce. Sprinkle with Petits Légumes.

Petits Légumes (celery, carrots, zucchini and tomato) – remove juice from tomato; dice all vegetables. Poach for 1 minute.   – CK

EGGPLANT A LA BAYOU TECHE

3 each medium eggplants
1 lb. lump crabmeat
6 buster or soft-shell crabs
¼ cup chopped green
   onions
¼ cup oil

2 oz. butter
oil for deep-frying eggplants
2 cups seasoned bread
   crumbs
shrimp etouffée

Peel and cut eggplants in half lengthwise. Scoop out center to form a boat. Bread with seasoned bread crumbs and fry. Sauté green onions in butter, add crabmeat, stir for 1 minute, and set aside. Salt and pepper cleaned crabs, dredge in flour, and sauté in oil. Divide sautéed crabmeat among the eggplant boats. Place buster crab on top. Pour generous amount of shrimp etouffée on top. Serve with rice pilaf.　　　　　– GP

SAUERKRAUT

3 lbs. fresh or canned
   sauerkraut, well drained
5 tbsp. butter and/or finely
   minced bacon or chicken
   fat
2 sour apples, peeled,
   cored, and chopped
1 large onion, chopped

3 to 4 cups dry white wine or
   as needed
8 to 10 juniper berries or 1½
   tbsp. caraway seeds
1 to 2 tbsp. flour or 1 small
   potato, grated
salt and pepper to taste

If sauerkraut is very sour, rinse in a colander under cold running water and drain thoroughly, pressing out as much water as possible. Heat butter or fat in an enameled Dutch oven and sauté apple and onion for 10 minutes or until golden brown. Add sauerkraut; stir with apple and onion. Cover and braise slowly for 8 to 10 minutes. Add water to half cover, along with juniper berries or caraway seeds. Cover and simmer slowly for about 1½ hours or until sauerkraut is soft. Add water if needed during cooking. To thicken juices, dissolve flour in 1 or 2 tablespoons water, stir in, and simmer gently for 5 minutes; or add grated raw potato, stir, and simmer for 10 minutes. Season to taste.

Serves 6 to 8.　　　　　– WC

SAUTÉED VEGETABLES

½ head cauliflower   **COOKING TIME:**

½ head cauliflower	4 minutes
½ lb. string beans or	6 minutes
½ lb. snow peas	No blanching
2 carrots	3 minutes
2 zucchini	No blanching
1 bunch broccoli	3 minutes
2 turnips	No blanching
2 dry shallots	4 4-qt. pots water
fresh parsley	2 tbsp. salt per pot
1 stick butter	ice to chill vegetables

Remove cauliflower flowerettes by hand, *not knife*. Wash zucchini, dry, and cut in slices. Peel turnips and slice thin. Slice carrots into thin slices. Use only flower of broccoli. Heat water with salt. Start beans, carrots, cauliflower, and broccoli, each in a separate pot. Blanch, strain, and chill. Mix all vegetables, including those you do not blanch. Refrigerate with wet cloth on top. When ready to use, prepare hot water with salt. With a strainer, dip vegetables into hot water, and strain immediately. Sauté with butter and chopped shallots (or white of green onion). Sprinkle with parsley. Serve at once.

Note: Vegetable preparation may be done in morning for evening.

– CK

CANDIED SWEET POTATOES

6 lbs. sweet potatoes	2 cups sugar
boiled until tender,	¼ tsp. nutmeg
cooled in ice water, then	⅛ tsp. cinnamon
cut into thick slices	4 oz. Southern Comfort
½ lb. butter	chopped parsley

Boil all ingredients except potatoes 2 minutes and pour over cut potatoes in baking dish. Bake at 350° for 20 minutes. Garnish with chopped parsley.

– LLL

GEORGIA RED RICE WITH HAM

½ lb. butter
2 cups rice
1 bunch green onions
10 toes garlic
¼ tsp. black pepper
¼ tsp. red pepper
2 tbsp. paprika

1½ tsp. thyme
6 bay leaves
1 lb. boiled ham, diced
1 lb. hot smoked sausage
3¾ cups water
¼ cup chopped parsley
1 chopped tomato

Sauté all vegetables and spices in butter well. Add ham, sausage, rice, and water. Bring to boil on stove, then cover and bake at 400° for 25 minutes. Garnish with chopped parsley and enjoy.　　　　　－ LLL

DRY FRY STRING BEANS
SZECHUAN STYLE

1½ lbs. fresh "four season
　beans" or green beans
4 oz. ground pork
½ tsp. chopped garlic

½ tsp. chopped ginger
1 tsp. dry shrimp
1 tbsp. scallion

SEASONING:

2½ tbsp. soy sauce
2 tsp. dry sherry
1 tsp. salt

1 tsp. sugar
1 tsp. sesame seed oil
2 tbsp. water

Soak dry shrimp in warm water for 2 to 3 minutes and chop very fine. Wash green beans, drain and cut off both ends; remove strings. Cut into 3-inch lengths.

Heat 2 cups oil in wok, deep-fry beans at 375° until they start to wrinkle. Drain all but 2 to 3 tablespoons of oil. Put beans aside. Heat these 3 tablespoons oil and add ground pork along with all seasoning (except dry sherry, soy sauce, and water) and garlic and ginger. Continue to stir-fry for another minute, add string beans. Shower in dry sherry, soy sauce, and water. Cover and cook until all liquid is absorbed. Top with scallions and serve.　　　　　－ TW

AUNT HELEN'S STEWED OKRA

2 lbs. fresh okra, sliced
   crosswise to ½ inch
   thickness
4 large tomatoes, peeled,
   seeded, and diced
1 large onion, chopped
1 large bell pepper,
   chopped
1 tbsp. garlic, finely
   chopped
½ lb. bacon (fried,
   crumbled, and drippings
   reserved)

½ cup vegetable oil
½ lb. seasoning ham, diced
½ lb. smoked sausage,
   sliced ¼ inch thick
½ lb. small shrimp
1 tsp. thyme
1 bay leaf
salt, pepper, and cayenne to
   taste

In enameled Dutch oven, heat bacon drippings and vegetable oil over moderate heat. Brown ham and smoked sausage. After they are browned, remove them. Next add okra and onions, bell peppers, and garlic and gently sauté them, covered, until okra is no longer slimy. Stir often and pour off any excess fat from pot. Add reserved ham, sausage, crumbled bacon, thyme, and bay leaf. Cook, covered, until okra is tender. Stir frequently. Finally add diced tomatoes, shrimp, salt, pepper, and cayenne and cook 10 minutes more. Serve with fresh rice.

Serves 8 to 10. — AL

STUFFED EGGPLANT

2 medium eggplants
1 medium white onion
½ bunch green onions
bacon drippings
2 tbsp. minced parsley
3 to 4 small French loaves,
  soaked in water

1 lb. shrimp
1 small piece chopped ham
2 eggs
½ tsp. sugar
salt and pepper to taste
dash thyme
bread crumbs

Preheat oven to 375°. Boil eggplant until tender. Let cool. Chop onion and the green onion finely. Sauté in bacon drippings (do not brown). Then add shrimp and ham. Scoop out eggplant pulp carefully so as not to damage skin, then add pulp to the onion mixture. Simmer for 20 minutes and then remove from heat. Add the eggs and soaked bread and mix well. Add salt, pepper, sugar and thyme. Put the mix in eggplant shell and sprinkle with bread crumbs and parsley. Bake in oven for 20 minutes.
         – LE

RED-COOKED CHINESE
BLACK MUSHROOMS

¼ lb. medium dry Chinese
  black mushrooms
1 tbsp. sherry
5 tbsp. oil
2 tbsp. soy sauce
1 tbsp. oyster sauce
1 cup rich chicken broth

1 tbsp. sesame seed oil
1 tbsp. sugar
2 pieces ginger, each the
  size of a quarter
dash white pepper
2 green onions (cut into 2½″
  lengths)

Soak black mushrooms in warm water for 30 seconds. Squeeze dry and discard the stems. Heat saucepan. Add oil, toss in ginger, then black mushrooms and sherry. Stir rapidly for about 2 minutes. Pour in all ingredients and spices except green onions and sesame seed oil. When mixture begins to boil, turn heat to low to maintain a very gentle simmer until most of the liquid has been reduced. Add sesame seed oil and green onions and serve.
         – TW

ENDIVES FLAMANDE

6 whole Belgium endives,
  cleaned and washed
2 tbsp. granulated sugar
2 tbsp. butter
juice of 1 lemon

dash of salt
2 cups cold water
6 slices (approximately 6
  oz.) canned ham
12 slices Swiss cheese

In small braising pan, set endives, salt, sugar, butter, lemon juice, and add the cold water. Bring to a boil.

Cover and bake in 375-degree oven for 20 minutes.

Once endives have cooled, drain and press lightly to remove excess water.

Sauté each endive in hot pan with butter. Roll each endive in 1 slice of cooked ham and Swiss cheese. Set in buttered baking dish. Bake in 375-degree oven for 15 to 20 minutes. Serve very hot.

Serves 6.

– LED

STUFFED BELL PEPPERS

6 bell peppers, cleaned and
  cut in half
2 lbs. ground beef
2 lbs. shrimp, peeled and
  deveined
2 loaves stale French bread
6 eggs

¼ cup fresh parsley
1 large onion
1 stalk celery
½ lb. margarine
1 tsp. thyme
salt and pepper to taste
bread crumbs

Melt margarine in large skillet, add seasonings (parsley, onion, and celery), simmer 20 minutes. Add beef and shrimp; cook 20 minutes, stirring constantly. Wet stale bread in large baking pan; add eggs whole and mix thoroughly. Add beef and shrimp (from skillet) to the mixture, stir well together. Add thyme, salt, and pepper. Place pan containing mixture into 350-degree oven. Stir well every half hour. Bake 2 hours. Cool in refrigerator, then stuff bell pepper halves. Top with bread crumbs and melted margarine and brown under broiler. Makes 12 servings.

– AL

YAMS

1 lb. yams (sweet potatoes)   ¾ cup sugar
½ cup lemon juice (about 3
  lemons)

Preheat oven to 350°. Wash yams and place in baking pan. Bake for
1 hour. After the first 15 minutes, puncture the yams once on top and
bottom. After 1 hour of baking take the yams out of the oven and peel
while hot. Cut into 1½-inch cubes. Place in Pyrex baking dish and
sprinkle with lemon juice and sugar. Return to oven for 30 minutes and
serve.
Serves 6.   – AL

VEGETABLE JAMBALAYA

½ onion   1 carrot
1 bunch green onions   3 tbsp. chopped pimento
½ bell pepper   1 jalapeño pepper
½ eggplant   1 cup chicken stock
1 zucchini   olive oil
1 stalk celery   butter
4 toes garlic   ½ cup Uncle Ben's
3 tbsp. parsley   Converted Rice
1 banana pepper   ½ cup long grain rice
½ head cauliflower   1 cup water
½ tomato   salt and pepper
1 turnip

    Clean and wash all vegetables. Dice all very fine. Heat olive oil and
small amount of butter in a sauté pan. Add carrot, onion, green onion,
bell pepper, eggplant, celery, garlic, banana pepper, turnip, and jalapeño. Sauté for a few minutes and add rice. Stir in and sauté for a few
minutes, stirring constantly. Add chicken stock and water to mixture and
cauliflower. Place in a 500° oven for 18 to 20 minutes, covered with
butter paper. Take rice from oven and stir in remaining vegetables. Stir
well. Salt and pepper to taste.   – CK

ROTKOHL MIT APFELN
(Red Cabbage with Apples)

2 to 2½ lbs. red cabbage
⅔ cup red wine vinegar
2 tbsp. sugar
2 tsp. salt
2 tbsp. lard
4 small apples

½ cup finely chopped onions
2 whole cloves
2 bay leaves
4 cups chicken stock, plus
   ½ cup water
3 tbsp. dry red wine

Drop shredded cabbage into a large mixing bowl and sprinkle it with the vinegar, sugar, and salt. Toss the cabbage to moisten it evenly with the mixture. In a 5-quart casserole, melt the lard (or use grease from 3 or 4 slices of bacon) over moderate heat.

Add apples (cored, peeled, and cut into wedges) and chopped onions. Cook for 5 minutes until apples are lightly browned. Add cabbage, cloves, and bay leaves. Stir thoroughly; pour in boiling chicken stock and water.

Bring to a boil over high heat, stirring occasionally. Reduce heat to lowest point. Cover and simmer 1½ to 2 hours until cabbage is tender. Check cabbage at intervals. If it seems dry, add a tablespoon or two of boiling water.

When cabbage is done, there should be almost no liquid left in the casserole. Remove bay leaf before serving. Stir in wine. If a sweeter taste is desired, add a couple of teaspoons of currant jelly.   – WC

SMOTHERED CABBAGE

1 large or 2 small heads of
   cabbage, quartered and
   cored
2 onions, chopped
4 cloves garlic, minced

3 tbsp. bacon drippings or
   vegetable oil
1 lb. pickled rib tips
1 tsp. salt
½ tsp. black pepper

Soak cabbage in water. Shake off excess water and place in pot with heated bacon drippings or vegetable oil. Add other ingredients and simmer for 1 hour, stirring occasionally.   – AL

HUEVOS RANCHEROS

3 tbsp. bacon fat or lard
8 tortillas (canned)
1 medium onion, minced
4 small hot red peppers,
   minced, or ½ tsp.
   crushed dried red
   peppers

1 small clove garlic, minced
1 small can tomato sauce
salt and pepper
8 eggs
2 to 3 tbsp. butter

Heat fat and fry tortillas until golden. Keep them warm. Fry the onion, peppers, and garlic in the same oil until soft but not brown. Add tomato sauce; season to taste. Fry the eggs in butter; season to taste. Place an egg on each tortilla and cover with tomato sauce. For a milder sauce, use less red pepper.

Serves 4. — WC

STEAMED WHITE RICE

½ cup long grain rice per
person

Wash rice two to three times, rubbing it gently between your hands and drain well.

Place the washed rice in a heavy saucepan. Add water until about one inch over the rice level. Cook over high heat until water comes to a boil. Stir with a spoon or chopstick two to three turns. Place cover over pan and lower heat to simmer. Let rice steam for about 20 minutes. Do not peek. Fluff the cooked rice with chopstick or fork. Keep cover on saucepan until ready to serve. Turn off heat. — TW

MUSTARD GREENS

4 bunches (about 4 lbs.)
  mustard greens
1 cup water
1 lb. pickled rib tips,
  chopped
1 onion, diced
1 rib celery, finely chopped

1 clove garlic, finely
  chopped
4 sprigs parsley, finely
  chopped
salt
pepper

Wash and clean greens and pull leaves off stems. Put meat in bottom of pot first with the cup of water; add seasonings (onion, celery, garlic, parsley) and fill pot with greens. Cover. Cook over medium heat for 2 hours, stirring every 15 minutes. When done, add salt and pepper to taste. This recipe may also be used to prepare collards, turnips, cabbage, or string beans.

Serves 4 to 6.   – AL

RED BEANS

1 lb. red beans
2 medium onions, diced
1 lb. pickled pork rib tips
  or smoked shoulder of
  ham or cubed or smoked
  ham hocks

1 rib celery, diced
1 clove garlic, finely
  chopped
4 sprigs parsley, chopped
salt and pepper to taste
4 cups cooked rice

Pick over beans before cleaning and remove any bruised or spotted ones. Soak in water overnight in a covered pot. Add diced onion to beans while they are soaking. The following day, strain and pour off water. Return beans and onions to pot; fill three-fourths full of water. Add celery, garlic, parsley, and pickled meat. Cook over a medium flame. Reduce flame as necessary to simmer for 2½ to 3 hours. Serve over boiled rice.

Serves 6.   – AL

STUFFED MIRLITON

12 large mirlitons
½ bunch green onions
½ white onion
1 stalk celery
2 oz. ham
2 oz. butter

1 doz. shrimp
2 bay leaves
1½ cups bread crumbs
⅛ tsp. thyme
salt and pepper to taste

Boil mirlitons until soft; cut in half. Scoop out insides and place in pan. In another pan, sauté the onions, celery, butter, ham, shrimp until tender. Add reserved mirliton and cook for 20 minutes. Add salt and pepper, bay leaves, 1 cup bread crumbs and mix together. Stuff mirlitons with mixture and sprinkle with rest of bread crumbs. Bake at 375° for 20 minutes and serve.

Serves 12.   – LE

NEW ORLEANS COLESLAW

1½ cups mayonnaise
¼ cup Brennan's Creole
   Mustard
3 tbsp. white wine vinegar

2 tsp. Brennan's Seasoning
   for Vegetables
10 cups green cabbage,
   shredded

In a large bowl, combine the mayonnaise, mustard, vinegar, and seasoning. Add the cabbage to the dressing and mix until all the cabbage is evenly coated. Cover and refrigerate briefly before serving.

How to buy cabbage: Cabbage heads should feel solid and heavy in relation to their size. They should be closely trimmed, with stems cut close to the head and only 3 or 4 outer or wrapper leaves. The cabbage should show no discolored veins and the outer leaves should have a fresh appearance, with no signs of puffiness or wormholes. Undamaged, unwashed heads can be stored in a plastic bag in the refrigerator for a week to 10 days.

Raw cabbage is rich in vitamin C and has a fair amount of vitamin B. Cabbage also has significant amounts of calcium, phosphorus, and potassium. One cup of finely shredded cabbage contains 24 calories.

Serves 10.   – MR

ARTICHOKE PRUDHOMME

4 doz. oysters
1 can sliced artichoke
  bottoms
4 oz. butter
2 tbsp. flour
1 bunch green onions,
  chopped

1½ pts. oyster liquid
salt and pepper to taste
6-8 fresh whole artichokes
Parmesan cheese to taste

Sauté onions in butter and stir in flour; add oysters, artichoke slices, oyster liquid, salt, and pepper. Simmer for ten minutes; sauce will thicken.

Steam 6 to 8 fresh whole artichokes. Remove center leaves and thistles. Spoon mixture into artichoke center and on leaves. Sprinkle with Parmesan cheese. Run under the broiler for 2 to 3 minutes. Top with heavy serving of Béarnaise sauce.   – PP

DIRTY RICE

½ cup chicken livers,
  coarsely ground
½ cup chicken gizzards,
  coarsely ground
½ cup pork, coarsely
  ground
¾ cup yellow onions,
  chopped
½ cup chopped celery

½ cup chopped bell pepper
½ cup chopped green onions
2 tbsp. minced garlic
1 tbsp. Cajun meat
  seasoning
1½ cups chicken stock
¼ cup (½ stick) butter
4 cups cooked rice

Sauté chicken livers, gizzards, and pork in butter. When brown, add all other ingredients except stock and rice. Cook for 20 minutes and then add stock. Boil rapidly for 15 minutes.

Add to cooked rice; rice is best when cooked in chicken stock rather than water.   – PP

STIR-FRY EGGPLANT
IN MEAT SAUCE

2 medium to small
  eggplants
2 tbsp. peanut oil
½ cup finely minced pork
½ tbsp. minced ginger
1 tbsp. minced garlic
1-1½ tbsp. Szechuan hot
  bean sauce
1½-2 tbsp. soy sauce

¼ cup chicken stock
1½ tbsp. rice wine or dry
  sherry
2 tbsp. sliced scallions
1 tsp. sesame seed oil
1 tsp. vinegar
salt and white pepper to
  taste

Peel and cut eggplant into ½-inch-thick by 2-inch-long pieces.

Heat wok over high heat. Put in peanut oil. When oil begins to smoke, place in minced pork, spreading pork out so it can cook evenly on both sides. When pork is about 80 percent cooked, remove pork from wok leaving the oil to reheat.

Put minced ginger, garlic, and eggplant into wok and stir-fry over medium heat. Shower in rice wine. Add hot bean sauce, pork, soy sauce and chicken stock into wok and cover for one minute or until stock comes to a boil. Add remaining ingredients. Reduce the stock to desired consistency. If it is too thin, add a little corn starch that has been mixed with water to thicken.

Serve with steamed rice.   – TW

FRIED RICE

3 cups cooked rice (cooked
  the night before,
  preferably; do not use
  instant rice)
1 cup shrimp, pork,
  chicken, beef, ham, or a
  combination of all these
¼ cup chopped green
  onions

1 egg, beaten
1 cup bean sprouts or diced
  mushrooms
cooking oil (approximately
  ¼ cup each time oil is
  called for below)
salt, white pepper to taste,
  and a pinch of Accent
2 tbsp. soy sauce

Heat large skillet or wok until very hot. Add oil and heat until it too becomes very hot.

Add beaten egg to hot oil and stir. When done the egg will be in rather small pieces. Add type of meat preferred and cook until brown. Remove egg and cooked meat and reserve.

Again add oil and bring to high temperature. Add rice and fry until grains are fairly dry and each grain separate. There should be no lumps. Rice should be constantly stirred while frying.

Add bean sprouts and meat and egg mixture previously reserved and mix together while adding seasoning. Sprinkle soy sauce over rice and mix into the fried rice by stirring briskly. Add onions and cook while continuing to stir briskly for about a minute.   – TW

FRESH GREEN ASPARAGUS WITH ALMOND BUTTER

2 lbs. fresh asparagus
4 cups water
2 tsp. salt

¾ cup clarified butter
½ cup toasted almonds

Clean asparagus with vegetable peeler. Tie into 3 to 4 bunches.

In skillet bring water and salt to boil. Cover and simmer asparagus until tender (4 to 5 minutes). Drain well, untie and place on serving platter. Heat butter and almonds until butter begins to brown. Pour over asparagus and serve with peppermill on side.

Serves 3.   – GP

STUFFED TOMATOES

6 whole tomatoes
¼ tsp. white pepper
1 oz. cream sauce

1 tsp. salt
1 lb. cooked spinach,
   chopped

Mix chopped spinach with cream sauce. Add salt and pepper. Slice the bottom off the tomatoes. Take soup spoon and scoop out a hole in the tomatoes. Stuff with creamed spinach. Bake at 350° for 15 minutes.

Serves 6.   – LE

ASPARAGUS ELLEN

4 bunches fresh asparagus
about 2 cups cold water
1½ tsp. salt

1½ lbs. lump crabmeat
4 tbsp. butter

MOUSSELINE SAUCE:

8 egg yolks
4 tbsp. lemon juice
1½ tbsp. dry white wine
1 tsp. salt
a dash of cayenne

2 lbs. hot melted butter
2 tbsp. finely chopped
  parsley
2 tbsp. heavy cream

Rinse the asparagus thoroughly under cold running water, then break off the hard ends of the stems. Place flat in the bottom of a large skillet. Add the water and salt, turn the heat to high, and bring to a boil. Then turn the heat to very low and cover the skillet. Cook just until the asparagus are tender when pierced with a fork, about 8 to 12 minutes, depending on size. Remove the asparagus gently from the skillet with a large slotted spatula, allowing the liquid to drain back into the pan. Place the asparagus on a large platter, then cool to room temperature. Cover the platter with plastic wrap and refrigerate. About half an hour before you plan to serve, remove the asparagus from the refrigerator and prepare the other elements.

To sauté the lump crabmeat, melt the butter over low heat in a large heavy skillet, then add the crabmeat. Cook over low heat, stirring very gently so as not to break up the lumps, until the crabmeat is warmed through. Set the skillet in a 175-degree oven while you prepare the sauce.

To prepare the Mousseline sauce put the egg yolks, lemon juice, wine, salt, and cayenne in a mixing bowl. (All the preceding ingredients should be at room temperature.) Pour in the hot melted butter very gradually, beating constantly and quickly with a wire whisk. When the sauce is thick, beat in the parsley, then the cream. The finished sauce should have the texture of a good Hollandaise.

To serve, place the asparagus on each plate. Top with sautéed lump crabmeat, then spoon Mousseline sauce generously over each portion. Serve immediately.

Serves 8.

– MR

ROESTI
(Swiss Potato Cake)

8 large very firm potatoes,
  boiled in their skins
⅓ cup butter

salt
2 tbsp. water or milk

If possible, boil potatoes a day in advance. Peel, slice, and cut into julienne strips. Heat the butter in a large frying pan. Add the potatoes, season with salt, and toss them with a spatula until they have absorbed the butter. Spread potatoes in a round cake pan; sprinkle with water or milk. Cover with a flat lid or plate that fits inside the pan, and cook over low heat for 15 to 20 minutes to form a golden crust on the bottom. Shake the pan occasionally so the potato cake does not stick. When done, invert the pan onto the lid, crusty side up. Slide onto a heated platter and cut like a pie.

Serves 6 to 8.   – WC

BLACK-EYED PEAS

1 lb. black-eyed peas
2 medium onions, diced
1 lb. pickled pork rib tips,
  smoked shoulder of ham,
  or cubed or smoked ham
  hocks

1 rib celery
1 clove garlic, finely
  chopped
4 sprigs parsley, chopped
salt and pepper to taste
4 cups cooked rice

Pick over peas before cleaning and remove any bruised or spotted ones. Soak in water overnight in a covered pot. Add diced onion to peas while they are soaking. The following day, strain and pour off water. Return peas and onions to pot. Fill three-fourths full of water. Add celery, garlic, parsley, and pickled meat. Cook over a medium flame. Reduce flame as necessary to simmer for 2½ to 3 hours. Serve over boiled rice.

Serves 6.   – AL

EGGPLANT SZECHUAN STYLE

1 small (1 lb.) eggplant
¼ lb. pork
2 green onions, finely
  chopped
1 tsp. finely chopped fresh
  ginger

1 tsp. finely chopped garlic
1 tbsp. hot bean sauce
1 tsp. cornstarch, mixed
  with 1 tbsp. water

SEASONING:

2 tbsp. soy sauce
¾ tsp. salt
1 tsp. sugar
1 tbsp. hot chili oil

1 tsp. sesame seed oil
½ cup soup stock
1 tbsp. vinegar
1 tbsp. dry sherry

Cut eggplant into 3-inch-long pieces. Chop pork into ¼-inch pieces. Mix seasoning in bowl.

Heat about ½ cup of cooking oil in wok or frying pan until hot. Put eggplant in and stir-fry until soft, about 3 minutes. Remove eggplant to dish and drain oil.

Heat 3 tablespoons of oil in wok until very hot. Add meat pieces and stir-fry until pork changes color, then add ginger, garlic, and hot bean sauce, stirring until meat begins to turn red color from the hot bean sauce.

Add the seasoning, then add the precooked eggplant. Cook until liquid starts thinning down.

Add green onion and sesame seed oil and add cornstarch mixed with water until the sauce gets thick.   – TW

SWEET AND SOUR CABBAGE

2-lb. round cabbage or
  Chinese cabbage
6 dried hot red peppers
  (remove seeds and cut in
  1-inch strips)
½ tbsp. peppercorns

3 tbsp. soy sauce
2 tbsp. vinegar
2 tbsp. sugar
2 tsp. salt
½ tbsp. sesame seed oil
5 tbsp. oil

Remove and wash cabbage leaves. Tear into pieces about 2 inches long and 1½ inches wide. Spine of leaf is to be cut into smaller pieces.

Heat oil in frying pan; fry red pepper until dark. Then add peppercorns and cabbage, stirring quickly over high heat for 3 minutes. Add salt, sugar, and soy sauce; stir briefly before adding vinegar and sesame seed oil. Mix well and serve. (May be served cold.)   – TW

SPINACH MOLD

2 envelopes Knox plain
  gelatin
1 10-oz. can condensed
  beef broth
¼ cup cold water
½ tsp. salt
2 tbsp. lemon juice

1 cup Miracle Whip salad
  dressing
1 10-oz. package frozen
  chopped spinach
½ cup chopped green onions
4 hard-boiled eggs, chopped
½ cup crisp bacon bits

Mix gelatin and beef broth over low fire until dissolved. Add lemon juice, salt, Miracle Whip, and cold water. Put in refrigerator until chilled but not firm.

Add spinach (uncooked), eggs, green onions, bacon bits and mix. Pour ingredients in mold and let it set in refrigerator.

Put pimento strips on top for decoration.   – LE

RICE AND ALMOND STUFFING

1 lb. bacon, cut into 1"
  pieces
1½ cups chopped onions
1 cup chopped parsley
4 cups cooked rice
4 cups dry bread crumbs
2 cups slivered blanched
  almonds, toasted

½ tsp. thyme
½ tsp. crushed red pepper
  flakes
⅛ tsp. black pepper
1⅓ cups beef consommé

Cook bacon until crisp. Drain, reserving 1 cup drippings. Cook onions in bacon drippings until tender. Add parsley, rice, bread crumbs, bacon, almonds, thyme, and peppers. Moisten with consommé, tossing to mix thoroughly.
— WL

TURNIP GREENS

8 bunches of turnip greens
1 lb. pickle tips, cut in
  chunks
1 large onion

1 garlic
¼ lb. margarine
salt and pepper to taste

Wash the turnip greens under cold running water. Trim off any bruised or blemished spots, and strip the leaves away from their stems. Scrub turnips with a brush; scrape or pare. Leave small white turnips whole if desired. Slice or dice large ones.

Melt margarine in 3- to 4-quart saucepan. Add seasonings and meat, and sauté for about 10 minutes. Add greens and turnips, cover the pan, and cook for 2 hours, stirring every half hour – being sure to get to the bottom of the pot. Taste for seasoning and serve.
— AL

BULB FENNEL OR ANISE

Bulb fennel or anise is a licorice-flavored vegetable. It resembles celery in its texture and can be eaten raw as well as cooked. Fennel is an excellent condiment. It is available from November through February. The stalks of fennel should be cut and used for seasoning and stocks as you would celery. The bulbs should be washed, drained, and kept refrigerated.

Fennel can be served raw in a salad; slice the fennel very thin and toss with the salad in a vinaigrette dressing. It can also be used as a crudité for dipping. Cut the bulb into strips easy enough to handle with your fingers and dip as you would other raw vegetables (cauliflower, broccoli, carrots). The bulbs can be braised by placing them in a sauté pan or skillet, filling with chicken or veal stock and cooking, covered, in a 325-degree oven until the bulb is tender when pricked. Remove the fennel and reduce the liquid until it starts to thicken. Add 2 tablespoons butter and reduce until the liquid coats the fennel with a glaze.

Fennel can be julienned and blanched and used as a garnish for a sauce with chicken or fish. It can also be cooked "à la grecque" just as you would mushrooms, and served as an hors d'oeuvre.　　　　– RH

LEEKS
("L'Asperge du Pauvre")

Leeks are a delicious vegetable that can be used in many different ways. They are native to Europe but are generally grown in California and are available all year long. They are a relative to the onion but not as strong in flavor. Leek bouillon is claimed to be a diuretic.

Leeks can be braised like the fennel in the previous recipe. They can also be blanched and served warm or cold with a vinaigrette. Leeks make a delicious cream soup as well as the classic vichyssoise. Leeks must be cleaned carefully before using; cut off the beard and the top green leaves. Split the top of the leek and immerse in cold water. Inspect all leaves and be sure to clean all the dirt from the leaves. The tops of the leeks can be used in stocks for soups.　　　　– RH

CELERY ROOT
(Celeriac)

Celery root is a variety of celery that has a large edible root. It is available in the fall and spring. The celery root must be peeled and rinsed. After it is peeled, the celery root must be handled as you would cut apples. You must keep them submerged in water. A little lemon should be squeezed in the water to keep them from oxidizing.

To blanch the celery root you must cook it in a "blanc," which is a mixture of water, flour, and lemon juice. This keeps the celery root white. It can be served as an appetizer; celery root remoulade is a classic way: Make some mayonnaise, grate the celery root into a bowl, squeeze a little lemon on it, add the mayonnaise and season with English mustard, salt, and pepper. Serve this over shredded lettuce or on top of a salad.

Celery root can be used in place of any recipe that calls for potatoes. It has the texture of a potato but the flavor of celery. It can be sautéed, made into a puree or served cold on a salad. —RH

Breads

CROISSANTS A LA SS *JOAN D'ARC*

5 lbs. flour
3 cups warm milk
3 cups warm water
3 oz. dry yeast

1½ oz. salt
9 oz. sugar
1½ cups flour
3 lbs. unsalted butter

Dissolve yeast in warm water with a little sugar. Stir in the flour and milk. Add salt last. Mix 4 to 5 minutes by hand or 3 minutes on mixer. Ferment the dough for 45 minutes to 1 hour in refrigerator.

Use 3 pounds unsalted butter for this amount of dough. With your hands, mix 1½ cups of flour in butter to absorb the water in butter. Butter should be cold. Roll butter into a 10-inch by 10-inch piece and fold into dough which is rolled to 20 inches by 10 inches. Roll to ¼-inch thickness. Fold dough as you would a letter, folding up one-third of the dough, then covering it with remaining third of the dough. Allow dough to rest in refrigerator 1 hour. Roll dough into another 10-inch by 20-inch rectangle (original folds should be perpendicular to you) and fold again. Repeat this a total of 3 or 4 times, allowing dough to rest in refrigerator 1 hour between folds. Rest dough overnight in refrigerator. Cover with plastic bag.

Cut into 5-inch strips and then into triangles. Starting at the wide end, roll each triangle towards you, stretching slightly. Tuck the end of the dough piece almost underneath the croissant. Bend to form crescent shape. Proof for 1 hour at about 80°. Egg wash twice and bake at 375° for 20 minutes. The croissants can be filled with fillings such as almond, fruit, meats or vegetables.

     – WL

BISCUITS

12 lbs. flour
8 lbs. shortening
2 cups baking powder
2 cups sugar

½ cup salt
2 qts. buttermilk
1 qt. milk

Mix all ingredients together and let stand 4 hours. Roll the dough out about ⅛ inch thick and cut with biscuit cutter. Place on greased baking sheet and bake at 350° for 35 minutes.

     – LE

JALAPEÑO CORNBREAD

1 cup cornmeal
¼ cup flour
2 tsp. salt
1 tsp. soda
¼ cup salad oil
2 eggs

1 cup cream-style corn
2 or more chopped jalapeño
  peppers
1 cup grated sharp Cheddar
  cheese

Mix all ingredients together. Bake at 400° for 20 to 30 minutes.

– WL

ARMY BISCUITS

2 pkgs. dry yeast
¼ cup warm water
pinch sugar
5 cups all-purpose flour
3 tsp. baking powder

¼ cup sugar
1 tsp. soda
⅔ cup lard
2 cups buttermilk

Dissolve yeast in warm water. Sift dry ingredients. Cut lard into flour until it looks like coarse meal. Add buttermilk and work to nice dough. Roll dough ¼ inch thick and wash with melted butter. Lay half of dough on other half and cut. Rest 15 minutes. Bake at 425° for 12 to 15 minutes.

– LLL

GARLIC BREAD

1 medium loaf French
  bread
1 stick butter, melted
garlic powder to taste

¼ cup chopped parsley
¼ cup freshly grated
  Parmesan cheese

Slice French bread lengthwise. Add garlic powder to melted butter and brush onto French bread. Sprinkle parsley and Parmesan cheese on bread and cut crosswise into 1-inch pieces. Heat in oven and serve immediately.

– PP

CARROT MUFFINS

1⅓ cups salad oil
5 eggs
3½ cups all-purpose flour
3 tsp. baking powder
1¼ tsp. soda

½ tsp. salt
¼ tsp. nutmeg
2 tsp. cinnamon
2½ cups shredded carrots
½ cup white raisins

Mix all ingredients together. Fill muffin cups two-thirds full. Bake at 360° for 20 to 25 minutes.

Makes 3 to 4 dozen muffins.

– LLL

COVINGTON PEAR BREAD

1⅓ cups sugar
4 eggs
¾ cup salad oil
1 tsp. salt
1 tsp. grated orange rind
2¼ cups grated cooking
  pears

2¼ cups all-purpose flour
½ tsp. soda
1½ tsp. baking powder
1 tsp. vanilla
1 cup chopped pecans

Mix eggs and sugar. Add oil, salt, orange rind, and pears. Stir in vanilla and dry ingredients and then pecans. Divide equally into 2 small bread pans and bake at 350° until an inserted toothpick comes out clean.

Makes 2 loaves.

– WL

FRENCH BREAD

3 pkgs. dry yeast
1 cup warm water
pinch sugar
5½ to 6½ cups strong
  bread flour
2½ tsp. salt

2 tsp. sugar
½ tsp. Arkady yeast food
  (can be purchased from
  your baker)
1 tbsp. shortening
1 cup water

Dissolve yeast in water and sugar. Add other ingredients and knead dough 10 to 12 minutes. Let dough rise for 1¼ hours and punch down. Divide into 5 pieces and round up. Rest for 15 minutes and mold into loaves. Proof loaves for 1 to 1¼ hours. Bake at 450° for about 20 minutes.

Makes 5 loaves.   – LLL

PANETTONE
(Fruited Easter Bread)

⅔ cup warm water	2 tsp. vanilla
5 pkgs. dry yeast	¾ cup butter (soft)
pinch of sugar	½ cup sugar
3 eggs	4 to 5 cups flour
6 egg yolks	⅔ cup raisins
2 tsp. grated lemon rind	⅔ cup diced citron
¾ tsp. salt	¼ cup white raisins

Dissolve yeast in water with pinch of sugar. Add all other ingredients except fruit. Knead 5 to 7 minutes. Add fruit mix and knead another 3 minutes. Let rise for 1 hour. Punch down and rest 15 minutes. Divide into 3 pieces and round up. Let rest for 15 minutes. Place each dough ball in greased 8-inch round cake pan and press dough to fit in pan. Let rise for 1 hour and bake at 375° for 30 minutes. Brush with hot butter when out of oven.

Makes 3 loaves.   – WL

TABASCO CRACKLIN BREAD

2 lbs. pork fatback
(preferably with some
meat in it), cut into 1-
inch squares
water
1⅓ cups all-purpose flour
½ cup corn flour (available
at many health food
stores)

½ cup cornmeal
2 tbsp. baking powder
½ tsp. salt
2 eggs
1½ cups milk
⅔ cup sugar
2 tbsp. Tabasco sauce

Place the pork in a large skillet. Add just enough water to cover the bottom of the skillet. Turn heat to high and cook until cracklins are golden brown, crispy, and crunchy, about 20 to 25 minutes, stirring occasionally. (If pork grease pops excessively, cover skillet with a screen or lid, leaving the skillet open a crack.) Drain on paper towels and let cool about 10 minutes, then process a few seconds in a food processor or blender until coarsely chopped (make sure no large pieces remain). Set aside.

In a medium-sized bowl, combine the flours, cornmeal, baking powder, and salt, mixing well and breaking up any lumps.

In a large bowl of an electric mixer, beat the eggs and milk together a few seconds until frothy. Add the sugar and continue beating a few seconds more until the sugar is dissolved. Add the flour mixture and Tabasco and beat until smooth, about 1 to 2 minutes. Add the cracklins and continue beating until thoroughly mixed, about 1 minute more. Pour mixture into a 9- to 10-inch heavy, oven-proof skillet (preferably cast iron) which is ungreased. Bake at 350° until done and golden brown on top, about 35 minutes. Remove from oven and serve immediately.

Makes 1 9- to 10-inch round loaf.   – PP

CHALLAH
(Jewish Holiday Bread)

2 cups warm water
3 pkgs. dry yeast
10 cups all-purpose flour
   (approximately)
⅓ cup sugar

⅔ cup salad oil
1 tbsp. salt
5 large eggs
5 egg yolks

Dissolve yeast in 1 cup of water with a little of the sugar. Add all other ingredients. Knead dough for 10 minutes. Rest for 1 hour and punch down. Divide into 12 pieces and form each piece into 13-inch string. Braid 3 strings to each loaf. Proof for 1 hour (until double in size). Brush with egg wash twice and sprinkle with poppy seeds. Bake at 400° for 35 minutes.

Makes 4 large twisted loaves.

– LLL

REFRIGERATED DOUGH FOR
BREAD AND ROLLS

4 pkgs. dry yeast
1¼ cups warm water
pinch sugar
1 13½-oz. can evaporated
   milk

¼ cup sugar
⅓ cup shortening
2½ tsp. salt
2 eggs
11 to 12 cups bread flour

Dissolve yeast in water and pinch of sugar. Add other ingredients and knead for 10 to 12 minutes. Rest dough for 15 minutes then refrigerate for at least 4 hours (overnight is O.K.).

Make up into loaves or dinner rolls. Proof for 1 hour and bake at 400° for 20 to 25 minutes.

This dough can be used for cinnamon rolls and doughnuts.

Makes 4 loaves or 48 rolls.

– LLL

CORNBREAD

1 cup flour
3½ tsp. baking powder
1 tsp. salt
3 tbsp. sugar

1 cup yellow cornmeal
1 egg, slightly beaten
1 cup milk
¼ cup melted shortening

Sift flour, measure, and add baking powder, salt, and sugar. Sift again and add cornmeal; mix thoroughly.

Combine egg, milk, and melted shortening; pour into flour mixture and stir just enough to blend. Do not beat.

Pour into greased square pan (8 inches by 8 inches by 2 inches) and bake in a hot oven (425°F) about 40 minutes. Cut into squares and serve. — AL

Desserts

MILE HIGH ICE CREAM PIE

1½ cups sifted flour
½ tsp. salt
½ cup shortening
4 to 5 tbsp. cold water
1 pt. vanilla ice cream

1 pt. chocolate ice cream
8 egg whites
½ tsp. vanilla
¼ tsp. cream of tartar
½ cup sugar

To make crust: Sift together flour and salt. Cut in shortening until pieces are the size of small peas. Sprinkle 1 tablespoon cold water over flour mixture and gently toss with fork. Repeat until all is moistened. Form into a ball with fingers and roll out to ⅛-inch thickness on lightly floured surface. Fit loosely into a 9-inch pie pan, pricking well. Bake 10 to 12 minutes at 450°. Cool.

Layer ice cream in pie shell. Beat egg whites with vanilla and cream of tartar until soft peaks form. Gradually add sugar, beating until stiff and glossy and sugar is dissolved. Spread meringue over ice cream to edges of pastry. Broil 30 seconds to 1 minute to brown meringue. Freeze at least several hours. Drizzle chocolate sauce over each serving.

Serves 8 to 12.   – LE

TEA PLEASURES

⅔ cup heavy cream
2 tbsp. water
5 tbsp. butter

1½ tbsp. tea
10 oz. semi-sweet chocolate
   (in pieces)

Bring cream to a boil then add water and butter. While liquids are boiling, stir in tea.

Remove from heat and leave to allow infusion of tea for about 3 minutes (up to 5 minutes for stronger taste). Strain out tea leaves. Return liquids to heat and reboil. Once boiling, remove from heat and add chocolate. Stir with wooden spoon till a smooth cream develops. Leave to cool about 1 hour.

Once mixture is cooled, beat lightly with a wire whisk (avoid over-mixing). Pipe rosettes with a star tube onto wax paper. Refrigerate to harden. Can be dipped or served as is.

Makes 45 truffles.   – GP

PECAN PIE

1 egg
5 oz. sugar
1 cup dark Karo syrup
1 tbsp. vanilla

1 cup pecans
1 cup butter
pinch of salt
1 8-inch unbaked pie shell

Blend all ingredients except pie shell together in a mixing bowl. Pour into unbaked pie shell, and bake for 1½ hours at 350°.　　　　　– LE

CHARLOTTE RUSSE

10 egg yolks
9 oz. fresh orange juice
  (preferably frozen
  concentrate)
4 oz. white wine
5 oz. Grand Marnier (or
  other orange flavored
  liqueur)

1 heaping tbsp. unflavored
  gelatin
1 good shot of brandy
4 cups whipping cream
lady fingers

Combine ingredients except lady fingers and cream in a large metal bowl. Cook over (not in) boiling water, rotating bowl and whisking constantly. When mixture holds a thorough pattern on the surface, it is cooked (10 to 15 minutes). Place in refrigerator and stir occasionally until well cooled.

Meanwhile whip cream until thick. Fold and mix the Bavarian cream and 3 cups of the whipped cream (reserve 1 cup for decoration) thoroughly.

Lightly butter (preferably using almond oil) a 2½-quart soufflé dish; fill with orange Bavarian cream and chill.

To decorate and serve, unmold Bavarian cream onto a silver tray (or such) and stand lady fingers along the sides, all the way around.

Seal the top edge (between lady fingers and top of Russe) with some whipped cream by using a pastry bag.

Fill in the top with some raspberry sauce (recipe follows), decorate with whipped cream, and serve, passing raspberry sauce.　　　　　– GP

APRICOT SOUFFLÉ GLACE

1 cup egg whites
2 cups granulated sugar
4 cups whipping cream

½ tsp. almond extract
2 cups fresh apricot puree

First heat egg whites and sugar in hot water to 115°, stirring all the time. Beat to stiff meringue. Combine whipping cream and almond extract and beat to stiff consistency. Begin to fold apricot puree and whipped cream into meringue. Place in 8 cup mold and freeze overnight. Serve with raspberry or strawberry sauce.   — WL

CALAS
(Rice Cakes)

1 egg
¼ tsp. salt
2½ tbsp. sugar
1½ tsp. baking powder
1 tbsp. vanilla extract
½ cup flour

1 cup cooked rice, converted
   or similar type
4 cups vegetable oil, for
   frying
powdered sugar to taste

In a medium-size mixing bowl, whisk the egg vigorously with a metal whisk until it is frothy and until bubbles are the size of pin-heads (about 1½ to 2 minutes). Add the salt, sugar, and baking powder, and whisk until well mixed. Whisk in the vanilla extract, then the flour. With a spoon, fold in the cooked rice. Let the batter stand for 20 minutes at room temperature, covered with a tea towel.

In a deep skillet, heat the vegetable oil to 350°. Place rounded tablespoons of the calas batter into the hot oil, slipping the batter into the oil so it maintains a relatively flat shape. Fry, turning at least once, until both sides are golden brown and middles are cooked (3 to 4 minutes total frying time). Drain the calas on paper towels. (You may keep the fried calas warm in a low oven, about 275°, while completing the entire frying procedure.)

Serve the calas warm, sprinkled with powdered sugar.

Yields about 1 dozen (serves 4).   — PP

TARTE TATIN

6¼ oz. flaky pastry dough
½ cup butter
1¼ cups scant, granulated
sugar

2¾ lbs. tart cooking apples,
peeled, cored, and halved

On a floured table, roll out the dough 1/16-inch thick into a 10-inch circle. Place dough on a plate and prick with a fork. Store in refrigerator while you prepare apples.

Preheat the oven to 400°.

Use a cake pan or preferably a round, cast-iron enameled dish, 9½ inches wide and 2 inches high. In the pie pan or dish, melt the butter and sugar on the top of stove, then place the apples in the dish very close together. Continue cooking very slowly until the sugar begins to caramelize. This should take about 20 minutes and the apples should soften considerably. The caramel should be very light in color.

Put the dish in the oven for 5 minutes, then cover the apples with the rolled out flaky dough. Raise the oven temperature to 450° and continue cooking for 20 minutes or until the pie crust looks done.

Once cooked, turn the dish over on a serving platter and serve tart warm.

– LED

PESCHE ALLA PIEMONTESE
(Peaches Piedmont Style)

7 medium-size peaches
2 tbsp. sugar
1¼ tbsp. butter

5 macaroons, crushed
1 egg yolk

Cut 6 peaches in halves. Remove pits and scoop out a little of pulp from each half. Remove all pulp from extra peach and mash together with pulp removed from peach halves. Add sugar, butter, macaroons, and egg yolk and mix well. Fill each peach half with pulp mixture. Place in well buttered baking dish and bake in moderate oven (375°) 1 hour. Serve hot or cold.

Serves 6.

– GF

CHOCOLATE PECAN PRALINES

The trickiest part about making pralines is judging the precise moment they are done (see Note), and then spooning them out quickly so they will harden with just the right texture.

Note: To judge doneness, use one or more of the following guides:

Candy thermometer will read 240°.

When done the batter will begin forming distinct threads on the sides or bottom of the pan.

Near the end of cooking time, make a test praline every few seconds. The early test pralines will be somewhat runny, very shiny, and somewhat translucent. The ideal praline will have progressed past that stage – it will not be runny and will be less shiny; when cooled it will be opaque, lusterless, and crumbly instead of chewy.

Near the end of the cooking time drizzle spoonfuls of the mixture across the pan's surface. When ready the mixture will form a neat thread across the surface.

⅜ lb. (1½ sticks) unsalted
butter
1 cup sugar
1 cup packed light brown
sugar
1 cup milk
½ cup heavy cream

1 cup coarsely chopped
pecans
2 cups whole pecan halves
2 tbsp. vanilla extract
1½ cups semisweet
chocolate chips, chilled

Assemble all the ingredients and utensils before starting to cook. (Measure out the chocolate chips and leave them refrigerated until just before needed.) You will need a large, heavy-bottomed aluminum pot or skillet with deep sides, a long-handled metal whisk or spoon, 2 large spoons (or an ice cream scoop with a manual release), and a very lightly greased cookie sheet.

Melt the butter in the pot over high heat; add the sugars, milk, cream, and chopped pecans. Cook 5 minutes, whisking constantly. Reduce heat to medium, and continue cooking and whisking 10 minutes. Add the pecan halves and continue whisking and cooking until done, about 8 to 10 minutes. (If the mixture smokes excessively toward end of cooking time, lower the heat.)

Stir in vanilla. Then immediately drop about ¼ cup of chocolate chips onto about one sixth of the batter. Stir quickly and just enough to cover some of the chips with batter but not enough to allow the chips to melt. Quickly drop the chocolate mixture onto the cookie sheet by spoonsful, using the second spoon to push the batter off the first (or use ice cream scoop); each praline should be about 2 inches in diameter. Repeat with remaining mixture, stirring briefly before adding more chocolate chips. The cooled pralines should be light brown, opaque, somewhat chunky, and crumbly.

Cool pralines and store at room temperature in an airtight container or wrapped individually in plastic wrap or foil.

Makes about 2 dozen. — PP

PIÑA COLADA TORTE

1½ cups coconut, toasted
and flaked
½ cup bread crumbs,
toasted
½ cup butter or margarine,
melted
1⅓ cups (1 14-oz. can)
sweetened condensed
milk

1 cup crushed canned
pineapple, well drained
¼ cup dark rum
1 tsp. coconut extract
1 qt. whipping cream,
whipped
½ cup crushed canned
pineapple, drained
2 tbsp. coconut, toasted

In a bowl, gently toss together coconut and bread crumbs. Reserve ½ cup coconut mixture; set aside. Add margarine to remaining coconut mixture; gently toss to combine. Press 1¾ cups mixture on bottom of 9-inch springform pan. Chill. Combine sweetened condensed milk, pineapple, rum, and extract; mix well. On low speed of blender, fold half the whipped cream into sweetened condensed milk mixture; fold in remaining whipped cream. Pour 3¾ cups filling into prepared pan. Sprinkle with ½ cup reserved coconut mixture. Top with additional 3 cups filling. Freeze 6 hours or until firm and remove 30 minutes before serving; remove pan rim. Cut into 12 portions. Use ½ cup pineapple and 2 tablespoons coconut as garnish.

Makes 1 9-inch torte (12 portions). — WC

CHOCOLATE SOUFFLÉ

5 egg yolks
½ cup sugar
¼ tsp. vanilla
¾ cup flour
2 cups milk
2 1-oz. squares
  unsweetened chocolate
  (melted and cooled)

2 tbsp. Kahlua coffee liqueur
  (I particularly like to use
  coffee liqueur to increase
  the chocolate flavor)
8 egg whites
¼ cup sugar
powdered sugar
sweetened whipping cream

In small mixing bowl beat yolks until thick. Gradually beat in sugar and vanilla. Then beat in flour, gradually. Add milk, beating until smooth. Transfer to saucepan. Cook and stir for 10 minutes. Remove from heat then stir in chocolate. Add coffee liqueur. Add stiffly beaten egg whites. Turn into 8 greased and sugared individual souffle dishes. Bake in oven at 350° for 30 to 35 minutes. Sprinkle with powdered sugar. Serve with sweetened whipped cream.
Serves 8.

– LED

KAHLUA CAKE

3 sticks butter (at room
  temperature)
5 large eggs (at room
  temperature)
3 cups sugar

3 cups cake flour, sifted
  twice
3 tbsp. almond or vanilla
  extract
¾ cup Kahlua

Preheat oven to 325°. Grease and flour bundt pan (use shortening and cake flour). Beat butter by hand in a mixing bowl for several minutes. Add sugar to butter, one cup at a time. Beat well after each addition. Continue beating butter and sugar until creamy. Add 5 raw eggs, one at a time, until each disappears in the mixture. Next, fold flour, one cup at a time, into the above mixture. Add extract of choice and Kahlua. Beat in lightly. Pour into prepared bundt pan and bake in middle of oven for approximately 1½ hours or until a straw inserted into the center comes out clean. Cool on cake rack for 1 hour, then unmold.

– AL

PROFITEROLES AU CHOCOLAT
(Pâte à Chou)

7 oz. butter　　　　　　　**9 oz. flour**
2 cups hot water　　　　　**8 eggs**

Combine first 2 ingredients in a saucepan and bring to a rolling boil. Turn off heat and add the flour all at once. Beat well with a wooden spoon. Turn on burner and continue to beat the mixture in order to dry it out. Pour mixture into a stainless steel bowl and let rest for 5 minutes. Add eggs, one at a time, and incorporate each well with a wooden spoon before adding the next. With a pastry bag, pipe out the profiteroles on a greased cookie sheet and bake at 400° for 20 minutes. Lower the oven to 325° and bake until they are done in the center, about 30 more minutes.

Cut profiteroles in half. Scoop ice cream onto the bottom half. Place the top half on the ice cream and cover with your favorite chocolate sauce.

Serve immediately.
　　　　　　　　　　　　　　　　　　　　　　　　　　– RH

LEMON TEQUILA SOUFFLÉ

2½ oz. lemon juice　　　　**1½ oz. tequila**
6 egg yolks　　　　　　　　**⅔ cup sugar**
3 oz. white wine　　　　　**1½ cups whipped cream**

Combine sugar with 1 cup water in a saucepan and boil gently until mixture begins to thicken (syrup stage). Remove and let cool thoroughly. When above mixture is cold, combine with the egg yolks, wine, lemon juice, and tequila. Now cook this mixture over a low flame, whisking constantly until the foam goes down (taste to be sure eggs are cooked). Now place in refrigerator and stir occasionally to cool. When cool, fold in 1½ cups whipped cream and place in freezer.

To serve, place soufflé in hollowed out lemons, put on a bed of shaved ice and freeze. When about to serve, garnish with whipped cream from a tube and a mint leaf.

Serves 6.
　　　　　　　　　　　　　　　　　　　　　　　　　　– GP

TIRAMISU
(Lift me up)

8 oz. bittersweet chocolate
24 lady fingers (Stella
  D'Oro cookies)
2 cups strong espresso
  coffee, cooled
1 oz. brandy

6 eggs, separated
6 tbsp. granulated sugar
1 lb. Philadelphia cream
  cheese
¼ cup whipping cream

Chop the chocolate coarsely or cut into small pieces. Put the lady fingers in a plate and lightly soak them with the cold coffee mixed with the brandy. Arrange half of the lady fingers in one layer on a rectangular serving dish with sides at least 2 inches high.

While the lady fingers are soaking, use a wooden spoon to mix the egg yolks together with the sugar in a crockery bowl. Mix until the sugar is completely incorporated and the egg yolks turn a lighter color. Add the cream to the cream cheese mixed well with wooden spoon until softened. Then add to the egg yolks and stir gently. In copper bowl beat the egg whites with a wire whisk until they are stiff. Gently fold the whites into the cream cheese-egg-sugar mixture. Use half of this mixture to make a layer on top of the lady fingers in the serving dish. Sprinkle with half of the chopped chocolate. Repeat the procedure, to make another layer of soaked lady fingers, cream cheese mixture, and the chopped chocolate.

Cover with aluminum foil and refrigerate for at least 3 hours before serving.

Note: All of the above may done in an electric mixer.

Serves 12.

– GF

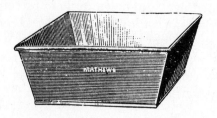

FLORENTINE COOKIES

4 oz. unsalted butter
1 cup granulated sugar
1 tbsp. honey
½ cup heavy cream
   (whipping cream)
1½ cups chopped pecans

4 tbsp. all-purpose flour
4 oz. semi-sweet chocolate
   morsels
2 oz. unsweetened baking
   chocolate

Preheat oven to 350°. Combine butter, sugar, honey, and cream and boil until golden (8 to 10 minutes). Remove from heat and add pecans and flour.

Drop mixture by teaspoonful (3 inches apart) onto a cookie sheet covered with foil, buttered lightly and dusted with flour. Bake until edges are brown (8-10 mins.). Remove from oven and place entire cookie sheet in the freezer. When cookies are set they will remove easily.

For chocolate coating gently melt chocolate morsels and baking chocolate. Coat the bottom of each cookie with chocolate and store in freezer.

Makes 4 to 5 dozen.   – GP

DESSERT CRÊPES

2 cups flour
2 tbsp. sugar
½ tsp. salt

2 eggs, well beaten
2 cups milk
4 tbsp. butter, melted

Mix the dry ingredients together. Combine the liquid ingredients with the dry and beat until smooth. The batter should be the consistency of thin cream. Grease an 8-inch (overall diameter) crêpe pan or frying pan lightly with butter and heat until the butter is quite hot, but not burned. Pour or ladle about ⅓ cup or a bit less of the batter into the pan and rotate the pan to spread the batter evenly. Cook the crêpe until it looks firm and is lightly browned at the edges, about 1 minute, then turn over with a thin spatula or your fingers and cook on the other side for about 30 seconds. Repeat until the batter is all used up. Grease the pan with a bit more butter about every other crêpe or when the crêpes begin to stick. Stack the finished crêpes one on top of the other on a platter.

Makes 24 6-inch crêpes.   – MR

CANNOLI

7 tbsp. confectioners'
sugar, sifted
1 tbsp. butter
1 egg
½ cup all-purpose flour,
sifted
1½ tbsp. cream sherry
½ tbsp. wine vinegar
fat for deep frying

½ lb. ricotta cheese
2 oz. mixed candied fruit,
diced
½ tsp. vanilla extract
¼ tsp. ground cinnamon
½ tbsp. or more heavy cream
pistachio nuts or
maraschino cherries for
garnish

Mix together 1 tablespoon sugar, butter, egg, flour, sherry, and vinegar. If too stiff, add a little water. Let dough stand at room temperature for about 30 minutes. Cut dough into pieces about the size of a walnut. Roll out each piece to an oval shape. Wrap each around an oiled wooden stick about 1 inch in diameter and 6 inches long. Seal the edge with a drop of cold water.

Heat the fat to 365° on a frying thermometer.

Gently remove the stick and drop each rolled wafer into fat. Fry until golden brown, lift out carefully, drain, and place on a cake rack to cool.

Drain the ricotta cheese. Be sure it is cold and dry, but not iced. Mix with the remaining 6 tablespoons confectioners' sugar, the candied fruits, vanilla, cinnamon, and cream. If the mixture is too thick, add a little more cream. Mix well. Use to fill the cooled wafers.

Garnish each end with chopped pistachio nuts or halved maraschino cherries. Sprinkle with confectioners' sugar when ready to serve.

This is a traditional Italian pastry.   – GF

BANANA ALL' AMARETTO
(Sweet Fried Bananas)

4 large bananas
2 tbsp. sugar
2 tsp. lemon juice
½ tsp. grated orange reel
2 jiggers Amaretto

2 tbsp. flour
½ cup water
1 egg white, beaten stiff
½ cup plus 1 tbsp. olive oil

Cut bananas into halves lengthwise. Sprinkle with sugar, lemon juice, orange peel, and Amaretto and let stand 2 hours.

Make a batter of flour, water, and 1 tablespoon oil, mixing well, and blend in stiff egg white.

Drain bananas, dip into batter, and fry in hot olive oil only until golden in color. Sprinkle with sugar and serve hot.

Serves 2 or 4.   – GF

CHOCOLATE MOUSSE

2 egg whites
2 cups sugar
6 oz. vanilla sweet
   chocolate

2 tbsp. water
½ pt. whipping cream

Mix the egg whites and sugar together and make a meringue.

Melt the chocolate and the water over a bain-marie with water that is not yet boiling. Fold the meringue into the chocolate and let cool. Meanwhile place the cream in the mixer bowl and place in the freezer. After 15 minutes whip the cream and fold into the chocolate mixture. Keep refrigerated until serving.

Serves 4.   – RH

TUILES AUX AMANDES
(Cookie Tiles with Almonds)

4 eggs
1 cup granulated sugar

1 cup chopped almonds
¼ cup all-purpose flour

Preheat oven to 400°. Combine ingredients. On a greased cookie sheet, 4 inches apart, drop by spoonsful this mixture. Bake until edges are thoroughly brown (8 to 10 minutes). Quickly remove cookies with a spatula and "drape" over a rolling pin or cup to give the tuile a cup-like shape. Store in a dry, airtight container. Tuiles can be used as a dessert cup for fresh fruit, ice creams, mousses, etc.

Makes 2 dozen.   – GP

CRÊPES MAISON

8 6-inch dessert crêpes
8 tbsp. grape jelly
6 tbsp. toasted, sliced
   almonds

peel of one orange and one
   lemon, slivered
powdered sugar
4 jiggers Grand Marnier

Roll 1 tablespoon grape jelly in each crêpe. Place 2 crêpes on each of 4 oven-proof plates. Top with sliced almonds and orange and lemon peel and sprinkle with powdered sugar. Pass under broiler until hot. Pour 1 jigger of Grand Marnier over each serving.
Serves 4.
          – JGF

RUBY'S BREAD PUDDING WITH RUM SAUCE

1 loaf stale French bread
¼ lb. butter
¼ lb. raisins
3 eggs, beaten
¼ cup light brown sugar
1 can evaporated milk

1¼ cups sugar
1 small can crushed
   pineapple
3 tbsp. vanilla extract
½ tsp. nutmeg

Preheat oven to 350°. Wet the bread and squeeze the water out of it. Melt the butter and mix with all other ingredients. Pour mixture into a well-buttered 8-inch × 11-inch baking pan. Bake for 40 to 50 minutes or until a knife inserted in the center comes out clean.
          – AL

RUM SAUCE

¾ cup butter (at room
   temperature)

1½ cups sugar
2 oz. white rum

Whip butter until light and gradually add the sugar until the mixture is fluffy. Next, add the rum and beat several more minutes. Refrigerate. Serve over warm pudding.
Serves 8.
          – AL

ENGLISH CUSTARD CREAM

1½ cups milk
5 egg yolks
½ cup sugar

½ tsp. pure vanilla extract
¼ cup Grand Marnier

Bring milk to a boil. Set aside. Place the yolks, sugar, and vanilla in a bowl and beat with wire whip for 3 to 4 minutes until it forms a pale yellow color. Combine the hot milk and the yolk mixture in a saucepan. Cook for a few minutes on low until the mixture coats the spatula. (Do not let the mixture boil or it will curdle.) Once you draw a line with your finger on the spatula and the custard does not drip, it is ready. Strain into a cold bowl. Add Grand Marnier, then stir and refrigerate.　– AL

STRAWBERRY SABAYON (COLD)

4 egg yolks
¾ cup sugar
1 cup Kirsch or strawberry
　liqueur

⅓ cup water
1 cup cream

Combine egg yolks, sugar, Kirsch, and water; beat and cook over hot water. Cook until thick (approximately 20 minutes) then place over cracked ice and whisk until thoroughly cool.

Add cream. Serve over marinated strawberries and garnish with fresh whipped cream.

Makes about 2 cups.　– GP

MOCHA FILLING

½ lb. butter
½ lb. powdered sugar
½ cup cream

coffee to taste
chopped pecans
3 egg yolks

Beat butter until creamy. Add sugar, then add egg yolks one at a time. Add cream and coffee to taste. Sprinkle chopped pecans on top and sides.　– RH

PRALINE PARFAIT

1 pt. Karo syrup
1½ lbs. shelled pecans
1 oz. caramel color
½ gal. vanilla ice cream

1 cup heavy cream for
  whipping
8 maraschino cherries

Mix the Karo syrup, pecans, and caramel color together in a bowl, using a long spoon or spatula, with a circular motion. When the mixture is even and soft enough to use easily, spoon 1 tablespoon into a 6-ounce parfait glass for each serving, then fill each glass with vanilla ice cream not quite to the top. As you fill each glass, push the ice cream down with the back of a spoon so that the syrup is forced up around the inside of the glass. Top with about ½ tablespoon of the syrup mixture, a generous dollop of whipped cream, and a maraschino cherry. If desired, set to chill briefly on the top shelf of the refrigerator before serving.
Serves 8.

— MR

FLORENTINE PETITS FOUR
MONSIEUR JACQUES

½ cup plus 2 tbsp. (1¼
  sticks) unsalted butter
½ cup sugar
2 tbsp. whipping cream
1¼ cups sliced almonds

⅓ cup golden raisins
1 tbsp. candied cherries
1 tbsp. mixed candied citrus
  peel
4 oz. semi-sweet chocolate

Preheat oven to 450°. Line 15½-inch by 10½-inch baking pan with heavy-duty foil. Coat surface completely with vegetable oil. Melt butter in small saucepan over medium heat, stirring in sugar and mixing until well blended. Stir in the cream; add almonds, raisins, cherries, and citrus peel. Bring to boil, reduce heat, and simmer 2 minutes. Turn mixture into prepared pan, spreading evenly to edges; bake until mixture is light caramel color, about 10 minutes. Remove from oven and let stand until cool enough to handle, turn out onto another sheet of oiled heavy-duty foil. Chill thoroughly. Melt chocolate in top of double boiler, set over hot water, and spread over top of candy. Return to refrigerator and chill until chocolate is set. Break florentine into small pieces. — LED

BREAD PUDDING WITH
RUM SAUCE

1 loaf stale French bread
¼ lb. butter
¼ lb. raisins
3 eggs, beaten
¼ cup brown sugar

3 oz. evaporated milk
1¼ cups sugar
1 small can crushed
   pineapple
3 tbsp. vanilla

Preheat oven to 350°. Wet the bread and squeeze the water out of it. Melt the butter and mix with all other ingredients. Pour mixture into a well-greased 4-inch by 10-inch baking pan. Bake for 2½ hours. The pudding will rise in the first hour. After an hour, remove pan from oven and stir the mixture to tighten it. Return to the oven for the second hour of cooking.   – AL

RUM SAUCE

¼ stick butter, melted
1 cup flour

1 cup sugar
½ cup rum

Place all ingredients in double boiler and cook for 10 minutes. Beat until fluffy.
Serves 10.   – AL

PECAN TORTE

8 oz. brown sugar, sifted
8 oz. powdered sugar, sifted
2 eggs
8 oz. butter, softened

½ tsp. vanilla
1 cup pecans, chopped
8 oz. coconut macaroons,
   crumbled

Mix all ingredients well with a wooden spoon in a bowl and refrigerate. When firm, roll in heavy aluminum foil to desired diameter and freeze.

When ready to serve, unwrap and slice the roll. Place a scoop of vanilla ice cream on top of each slice. Serve immediately. If desired, put hot chocolate sauce on top.   – RH

STRAWBERRY SHERBET

1½ qts. fresh strawberries
2 cups sugar

3 tbsp. lemon juice

Puree strawberries (stemmed and washed) in a food processor; there should be 3 cups. Pour puree into a metal bowl, add sugar and lemon juice. Set on a bowl of ice and whip puree while it chills.

Freeze in freezing compartment and beat puree every 10 to 15 minutes to break up any ice crystals. When puree has set, it is ready to serve. Serves 6 to 8.
— GP

APPLE STRUDEL

DOUGH:

2½ cups flour
½ tsp. salt
2 eggs, beaten

3 tbsp. cooking oil
½ cup lukewarm water
2 tbsp. butter or margarine

Mix flour, salt, and butter (or margarine) together. Add water and oil, constantly mixing together so that there are no lumps in the dough. Add the eggs and mix to keep dough smooth (resembles noodle dough). Let rest 1 hour before using.

FILLING:

¼ cup melted butter
¼ cup butter
1½ cups fine bread crumbs
1½ cups nuts
5 cups coarsely grated
   peeled apples

2 lemon peels, grated
½ cup sugar
⅛ tsp. cinnamon

Roll out dough about ⅛ inch thick. Cut into squares of 4 to 5 inches. Combine filling ingredients and stuff squares, folding them over into triangles, and sealing edges. For golden brown crust, paint dough with egg yolk before baking. Bake in 375- to 400-degree oven for 25 to 30 minutes.
— WC

DESSERT CRÊPES

1 cup all-purpose flour
¼ tsp. salt
¼ tsp. vanilla extract
1 tbsp. sugar

4 tbsp. melted butter
2 eggs
1 cup milk
vegetable oil

Combine flour, salt, vanilla, sugar, milk, eggs, and melted butter in food processor. Process at high speed for 1 minute, then turn off. Scrape down sides of bowl with a rubber spatula and process for 1 more minute. Pour batter in bowl and cover and let rest 1 hour. To fry crêpes, lightly oil 7-inch crêpe pan and place on high flame. With 2-ounce ladle pour batter in center of the pan and quickly tilt pan from side to side until bottom is covered evenly. When edges of crêpe turn brown, flip crêpe with hand and cook 30 seconds longer. When crêpe is finished, place on plate. Repeat process and stack crêpes on top of another. Oil crêpe pan when necessary.

Makes about 20 crêpes.   – AL

GLENN'S CARAMEL CUSTARD

6 egg yolks
1 cup sugar (reserve ½ cup)
1 tsp. vanilla extract

2½ cups milk
nutmeg
½ cup water

In a mixing bowl, beat the eggs, sugar, and vanilla until the yolks are thick. Scald the milk and add to yolk mixture, stirring constantly. Next, place reserved ½ cup of sugar and ½ cup water in heavy skillet. Boil over low heat until it attains a deep amber color. Pour caramel into 6 custard cups. Swirl the caramel around to coat the sides and bottoms of the cups evenly. Pour custard mixture into cups. Place cup in roasting pan and pour hot water into the pan until it reaches half up the sides of the cups. Bake in preheated 350-degree oven for 30 to 40 minutes or until toothpick inserted in center can be drawn clean. To serve, run knife around the sides of cups to loosen the custard and unmold onto serving dishes.

(Caution must be taken with the caramel or a severe burn may occur.)
Serves 6.   – AL

SPONGE CAKE

6 eggs, separated
1½ cups Swans Down flour
1½ cups sugar

1 tsp. cream of tartar
1 tsp. vanilla
½ tsp. salt

Combine egg whites and cream of tartar in large bowl and beat until soft mounds form. Add sugar gradually and continue beating until stiff peaks form. Beat yolks until creamy, add vanilla, then fold into stiffly beaten egg whites (do not stir or beat – fold). Lastly, fold in flour which has been sifted three times with salt (do not beat or stir – fold). Pour batter into ungreased 10-inch tube pan and gently cut into batter to remove large bubbles.

Bake about 50 minutes at 325° or until cake springs back when pressed lightly with fingers. Cool upside down 1 or 2 hours, then loosen from side and center tube of pan with knife. Remove from pan.   – RH

LEMON ICE

This recipe was obtained from the pastry chef at the Gritti Palace Hotel in Venice in 1968 by my son, Larry. I remember he used Maître d'Scivini as his interpreter.

2 liters water
24 lemons, peels only
1.2 kilograms sugar

24 lemons, juice only
2 egg whites

Peel lemons with potato peeler and soak in water overnight in refrigerator. This procedure allows oil from skin to flavor water. Strain out lemon peels. Add sugar and lemon juice. Mix very well to dissolve sugar. The mix should register 19° on sugar hydrometer.

Pour into shallow baking pan or similar type pan and place in freezer. When sherbet is almost frozen fold in whipped egg whites and allow to harden well before serving.

In New Orleans most of the lemon ice is extra sour. This can be accomplished by adding ½ ounce citric acid solution (which is by weight equal parts citric acid crystals and water).   – WL

CRÊPES FITZGERALD

16 dessert crêpes,
 preferably warmed
 slightly (to prepare, see
 following recipe)
2 cups Creole cream
 cheese (or 4 parts
 Philadelphia cream
 cheese to 1 part heavy
 sour cream)

3 cups fresh strawberries
3 to 4 tbsp. sugar
²/₃ cup Maraschino liqueur

Have the crêpes and Creole cream cheese ready. Place a flambé pan or attractive skillet over an alcohol burner and mash the strawberries in the pan with a fork. Add the sugar and cook for about 3 to 4 minutes, until the strawberries are beginning to get soft. On each of 8 preheated plates place 2 crêpes. Fill each crêpe with ¼ cup Creole cream cheese and roll up. Add the Maraschino liqueur to the sautéed strawberries and heat until quite hot. Tip the pan to ignite and flame until the flame dies out. Tip the pan with a rolling motion to prolong the flaming, if desired. Ladle the syrup from the pan evenly over the portions of filled crêpes and serve immediately.
Serves 8.

– MR

GERMAN POTATO PANCAKES

2 lbs. large potatoes,
 peeled
½ lb. onions, peeled
2 eggs

1 cup flour
pinch nutmeg
oil
salt and pepper to taste

Finely grate potatoes and onions. Drain well. Combine all ingredients. Heat ½ inch of oil in skillet over moderate heat. (Add more oil as needed.) For each pancake, spoon a heaping tablespoon of potato mixture into skillet (to make a cake 4 inches wide). Brown on both sides. Drain on paper towels. Serve piping hot with applesauce and sour cream. Enjoy!

– WC

CRÊPES KAHLUA

1¼ cups butter
½ cup sugar
½ cup macaroon crumbs
½ cup Kahlua or other
  coffee-flavored liqueur

24 French crêpes (5 or 6
  inches in diameter)
½ cup butter
1 pt. heavy cream, whipped
additional Kahlua

Make filling by creaming together ¾ cup butter, sugar, macaroon crumbs, and Kahlua. Spread mixture on pancakes and roll. When it's time to serve, heat crêpes in the remaining ½ cup butter in a chafing dish or electric frying pan. Serve with whipped cream and a drizzle of Kahlua.

Serves 12 (2 crêpes per serving). – LE

CRÊPES BARBARA

2 lbs. lump crabmeat
1 lb. boiled shrimp, cut up
  if large
¼ cup butter

¾ tsp. salt
¼ tsp. white pepper
8 7- to 8-inch main dish
  crêpes

LEMON BUTTER SAUCE:

½ cup brown sauce (rich
  beef stock and flour
  cooked together to a
  medium-thick
  consistency)

2 tbsp. lemon juice
1½ lbs. melted butter

MORNAY SAUCE FOR GLAZING THE FILLED CRÊPES:

½ cup butter
½ cup flour
2 cups hot milk
1 tsp. salt
about ⅛ tsp. white pepper
a pinch of nutmeg

2 egg yolks
½ cup grated Parmesan or
  French Gruyère cheese
1 tbsp. butter
heavy cream for thinning out
  sauce, if desired

To sauté the crabmeat, melt the butter over low heat in a heavy skillet, then add the crabmeat and sprinkle with the salt and pepper. Stir very gently and cook over low heat just until the crabmeat is warmed through, about 5 minutes. Add the shrimp and set the skillet in 175-degree oven to keep warm while you prepare the lemon butter sauce. Combine the ingredients for the lemon butter sauce in a small heavy saucepan and cook, stirring, over low heat until well blended. Set the saucepan in the oven along with the crabmeat. If you are using crêpes prepared in advance and frozen, remove 8 of them from the freezer and set on the kitchen counter to defrost while you prepare the Mornay sauce. Also begin preheating the broiler for glazing the crêpes.

To prepare the Mornay sauce, melt the butter in a saucepan and mix in the flour, stirring. Cook over low heat for about 3 minutes, then gradually pour in the hot milk, stirring. Sprinkle in the salt, pepper, and nutmeg. Cook over low-medium heat until the sauce thickens. Stir almost continually to keep the sauce smooth. Remove the pan from the heat and mix in the egg yolks, stirring constantly to keep them from curdling. When the yolks are thoroughly blended in, return the pan to very low heat for a few minutes while you add the grated cheese and butter, and mix them in thoroughly. Be careful not to let the sauce get too hot or come to a boil. Remove the pan from the heat again and check the consistency of the sauce. If it appears a bit too thick to make a nice thin and even coating for the crêpes you will be filling, thin the sauce out a bit with heavy cream. Add about 2 teaspoons at a time and mix in until you get the desired thickness.

To assemble the crêpes, fill the center of each one with ⅛ of the crabmeat and shrimp, then top with ⅛ of the lemon butter sauce. Roll up the crêpes and place them on a lightly buttered heavy baking sheet or cookie pan. Smooth about 3 to 4 tablespoons of the Mornay sauce over each crêpe and place the pan under the broiler for a minute or so, just long enough for the Mornay to begin to brown a bit. Remove the pan from the broiler and carefully lift the crêpes, sauce and all, onto preheated dinner plates for serving. If you wish, spoon any sauce which remains on the baking sheet decoratively around the crêpes.

Serves 8.   – MR

SCHWARZWALDER KIRSCHTORTE
(Black Forest Cake)

1 9-inch chocolate sponge
  cake
1 can pitted dark sweet
  cherries
3 pts. whipping cream
1 tsp. vanilla extract

1½ cups sugar
3 oz. Kirschwasser (Cherry
  Brandy)
1 big bar of semi-sweet
  chocolate
12 maraschino cherriess

Slice sponge cake into three equally thick slices. Drain can of cherries well. Add ½ cup of sugar to juice and bring to boil. Simmer for 5 minutes until thick like syrup. Let cool.

Add vanilla extract and one cup of sugar to heavy cream and whip until stiff. Sprinkle first layer of cake with syrup and one ounce of Kirschwasser. Put all drained cherries on same layer. Cover cherries generously with whipped cream.

Add next layer of cake. Sprinkle with syrup and Kirschwasser; add whipping cream. Repeat with third layer. Cover whole cake with rest of whipping cream and decorate with chocolate shavings. Garnish with maraschino cherries.

Ready to serve.

– WC

CHOCOLATE TRUFFLES A LA
LEE R. LERUTH

1 cup cream
2½ sticks butter
12 oz. powdered sugar,
  sifted 3 times
24 oz. semi-sweet
  chocolate chips

1 oz. Grand Marnier
½ tsp. LeRuth's Vanilla Bean
  Marinade

Melt chocolate in double boiler. Set aside. Reduce cream by one third and add butter and bring to boil. Stir in powdered sugar then melted chocolate. Add Grand Marnier and LeRuth's Vanilla. Leave for 24 hours at 60°F. Spoon truffle mix into little shapes like truffles, then roll in sifted powdered sugar or cocoa. Store at 60°F.

– LLL

LEMON TART

6 lemons (juice and grated
   rind)
6 oz. butter

12 oz. sugar
5 eggs

Bring lemon juice and butter to boil. Whip eggs and sugar and pour over hot lemon and butter and add grated rind. Pour into tart pan that has been lined with tart dough. Bake for 20 to 25 minutes at 375°F. Makes 1 9-inch tart.   – WL

ESTELLE'S BROWNIES

3 squares bitter chocolate
½ stick butter
2 eggs
1¼ cups sugar
1 cup cake flour

½ tsp. baking powder
¼ tsp. salt
1 tsp. vanilla
1 cup pecan pieces

Place chocolate and butter to melt in double boiler. Mix eggs, sugar, salt, and vanilla for 5 minutes. Add chocolate and butter. Add 1 cup flour, baking powder, and, last, pecans. In a 9-inch by 9-inch pan (greased) bake at 350° for 25 minutes.   – WL

ESTELLE'S PECAN PIE

3 eggs
¾ cup sugar
1 tsp. vanilla
1 cup white Karo syrup

½ stick butter
1 cup pecans
1 9-inch unbaked pie shell

Mix eggs, sugar, and syrup; add melted butter and vanilla. Add pecans. Pour into unbaked shell. Bake at 350° for 45 to 50 minutes. Cool and serve.

Tip: For maximum flavor always shell your own pecans – practically all commercially packed pecans are washed before packaging.   – WL

COCONUT MOUSSE

1 14-oz. can sweetened
 condensed milk
1 cup water
1 cup Lopez coconut cream
5 egg yolks

1 tbsp. plain gelatin
3 tbsp. Grand Marnier
2 cups whipping cream
1 cup (3½ oz.) Angel
 coconut

Bring sweetened condensed milk, water, and coconut cream to boil.
Whip egg yolks till light and yellow. Pour hot milk mixture over beaten yolks, stir well.
Dissolve gelatin in Grand Marnier and stir into milk mixture and eggs. Cool until it begins to thicken to a soft custard consistency.
Beat whipping cream and fold into chilled milk, egg, and gelatin mixture. Fold in Angel coconut. Chill for 3 hours before serving.
Serves 6.

– WL

CHEESE CAKE

4 eggs
3 8-oz. pkgs. Philadelphia
 cream cheese
sugar
12 pieces unsweetened
 Zwieback

½ tsp. cinnamon
1 pt. sour cream
1 tsp. vanilla

Blend eggs, cheese, and 1 cup sugar in mixer at high speed for about 3 minutes until light.
Roll out Zwieback; add cinnamon and 2 tablespoons sugar. Grease pan with Crisco, put Zwieback crumbs on bottom of pan, and sprinkle lightly on sides.
Pour in batter and place in 350-degree oven. Cook for 40 minutes. Remove and set aside.
Mix sour cream, vanilla, and 3 tablespoons sugar. Pour onto cheesecake and bake for 10 minutes.
Serve cold.

– LE

ZABAGLIONE

6 egg yolks
4 tbsp. sugar
½ cup Marsala wine

whipped cream (optional)
shaved chocolate
4 crisp sugar cookies

Place egg yolks and sugar in top of double boiler. Beat with egg beater or electric mixer until light and creamy. Gradually beat in wine. Set into bottom of double boiler over simmering water. Beat until mixture becomes thick, about 3 to 5 minutes. When beater is lifted, mixture should hold its shape. Do not overbeat. Remove from heat, pour into sherbet glasses. Top with whipped cream; garnish with shaved chocolate. Serve with a crisp sugar cookie.
Serves 4.

– GF

BANANAS FOSTER

4 tbsp. butter
1 cup brown sugar
½ tsp. cinnamon
4 tbsp. banana liqueur

4 bananas, cut in half
  lengthwise, then halved
¼ cup rum
4 scoops vanilla ice cream

Melt the butter over an alcohol burner in a flambé pan or attractive skillet. Add the sugar, cinnamon, and banana liqueur and stir to mix. Heat for a few minutes, then place the halved bananas in the sauce and sauté until soft and slightly browned. Add the rum and allow it to heat well, then tip the pan so that the flame from the burner causes the sauce to light. Allow the sauce to flame until it dies out, tipping the pan with a circular motion to prolong the flaming. Serve over vanilla ice cream. First lift the bananas carefully out of the pan and place 4 pieces over each portion of ice cream, then spoon the hot sauce from the pan over the top.

This is one of Brennan's most famous and most popular desserts. It's really quite simple to prepare. Wait until the rum gets hot, so that you get a good flame when it's ignited. This can also be prepared over a stove burner, then brought to the dinner table and flamed.
Serves 4.

– MR

CHOCOLATE PECAN PIE

1 cup pecans
3 oz. Southern Comfort
4 eggs
½ cup chocolate chips
1¼ cups light corn syrup

1¼ cups brown sugar
1 tsp. LeRuth's Vanilla
4 oz. melted butter
1 10-inch unbaked pie shell

Mix corn syrup, eggs, sugar, chocolate chips, pecans, Southern Comfort and vanilla. Stir well and add hot melted butter.

Pour filling into 10-inch unbaked pie shell. Bake at 350° for 1 hour or until pie rises and then dips in center. This pie is great in the morning with coffee and Grand Marnier with whipped cream. — LLL

FRERES LERUTH EGG NOG

24 eggs
2 cups sugar
3 cups Southern Comfort

2 qts. cream
fresh ground nutmeg

Separate egg yolks from whites. Mix yolks, sugar, and Southern Comfort and chill overnight. Next day whip 2 quarts cream and fold into yolks. Then whip egg whites until they peak; fold into cream and yolks. Serve in large bowl or small cups garnished with fresh nutmeg.

Serves 24.

— LLL

COCONUT TART

12 oz. sugar
12 oz. coconut
10 egg whites

½ cup water
½ tsp. vanilla
½ tsp. almond extract

Heat oven to 375°.

Line tart pan with short crust. Mix all ingredients well and pour in short crust. Bake for 20 to 25 minutes at 375°. Cool and serve with pineapple sauce.

Makes 1 9-inch tart.

— WL

LOTUS BANANA

**2 bananas cut into quarter
  sections
8 oz. lotus nut paste**

**8 spring roll wrappers
paste with 1 tsp. flour and
water**

Cut firm bananas lengthwise in half. Take halved pieces and cut in half crosswise. You should have 4 pieces of banana about 3½ to 4 inches long.

Spread lotus nut paste on the cut side.

Position the spring roll wrapper in a diamond shape in front of you with the south side toward you.

Place the banana with the lotus paste just below the center line of east and west.

Fold the south side flap over the banana and fold once again.

Tuck the east and west sides in and keep rolling firmly. Make a paste with flour and water. Place the paste on the tip of the north flap to seal the banana in place.

Deep fry Lotus Banana roll until golden brown in oil that has been pre-heated to 300-325°.

Top with powdered sugar and garnish with ½ cherry slice. Serve by itself or with ice cream.   – TW

SWISS MERINGUE

**5 egg whites
1¼ tsp. cream of tartar
¼ tsp. salt**

**2 tsp. vanilla extract
1¼ cups sugar**

Combine all the ingredients except sugar in a large bowl and beat until eggs form soft peaks. Add ¾ cup sugar, 2 tablespoons at a time, until meringue is very thick, stiff, and dull. Fold in the remaining sugar. Shape 3-inch ovals of meringue with a pastry bag on a buttered and floured cookie sheet, 2 inches apart, and bake in a preheated 250-degree oven for 25 to 30 minutes. Cool, put a scoop of ice cream or other desired filling between 2 meringues; top with whipped cream.

Serves 6.   – WC

LEMON SOUFFLÉ

1 lb. sugar
7 egg yolks
juice and rind of 4 lemons

4 oz. tequila
4 oz. white wine
1½ pts. whipped cream

Take sugar and make a simple syrup.

Combine egg yolks, the lemon juice and rind, tequila, white wine, and the simple syrup.

Whip over a double boiler until it reaches a smooth, heavy consistency, about 15 minutes.

Remove from the fire and let cool in ice box for 15 to 20 minutes.

Now fold in whipped cream.

Place in the freezer until good and firm.   – GP

BUDINO
(Cup Custard)

3 eggs
¼ cup sugar
2 cups milk, scalded

½ tsp. vanilla
salt

In the top part of a double boiler beat eggs until frothy; stir in sugar and a pinch of salt; add milk gradually, stirring constantly. Cook over hot (not boiling) water until mixture is smooth and coats the spoon. Stir in vanilla. Let cool.

Makes about 2 cups.   – GF

BIGNÉ DI SAN GIUSEPPE
(St. Joseph's Fritters)

6 tbsp. butter
1 cup cold water
1½ cups all-purpose flour
4 eggs
2 egg yolks

1 tbsp. sugar
2 tsp. grated lemon rind
olive oil and lard for deep
    frying
vanilla-sugar

Place the butter, a pinch of salt, and the water in a saucepan. Over low heat, bring to a boil. Remove from the heat and, all at once, add the flour. Blend together thoroughly with a wooden spoon, then replace over the heat, and stir until the paste comes away from the side of the pan to form a ball. When this begins to sizzle, remove from the heat, allow to cool slightly, and beat in the eggs and egg yolk one at a time, thoroughly after each addition.

When tiny bubbles appear, add the sugar and lemon rind and mix thoroughly until blended. Form into a ball. Remove from the pan and let stand, wrapped in a cloth, in a cool place for about 30 minutes.

Roll pieces of the dough into walnut-size balls. Heat the olive oil and lard in a large saucepan over moderate heat and drop in several of balls. The puffs will turn over automatically in the hot oil. When they begin to swell, increase heat. Fry for about 5 to 10 minutes, or until golden brown; then remove and drain. Let the oil cool slightly; then repeat the procedure with several more balls. (It is best to fry only a few puffs at a time.) Arrange on a serving plate covered with a paper and sprinkle with vanilla sugar.

Serve very hot.

To make vanilla sugar, cut a whole vanilla bean crosswise into 3 equal parts. Then cut each piece in half lengthwise and with the point of small knife, loosen the central seeds in each half. Bury the pieces in two pounds of sugar. Keep the jar tightly closed for one week and the sugar will be permeated with vanilla flavor. As the sugar is used, add more to the jar. The bean will give off flavor for 6 to 9 months.

Serves 6.

    – GF

FLO'S COFFEE CAKE

1 cup sugar
½ cup butter
2 eggs
½ cup milk
1½ cups flour, sifted
  several times

1 tsp. vanilla
1 heaping tsp. baking
  powder

Preheat oven to 325°F.

Cream butter and sugar well together. In mixer bowl combine eggs, milk, and vanilla and mix on medium speed. Then add butter-sugar mixture and mix until well blended. Gradually add flour and baking powder, waiting until each addition is absorbed into batter before adding more. When all of flour and baking powder have been added and batter is smooth, pour into 15-inch by 18-inch baking pan and bake until done.

When cake is done put on following icing:

5 tbsp. melted butter
5 tbsp. brown sugar

3 tbsp. cream
1½ cups nuts

Cook butter, sugar, and cream together for a while and then add nuts. Spread over cake and put under medium flame a few seconds. Cut in squares and serve while hot.

– LE

ORANGE MOUSSE

7 egg yolks
juice and rind of 4 oranges
juice of 2 lemons
4 oz. Grand Marnier

4 oz. white wine
1 oz. sugar
1½ pts. heavy whipped
  cream

Mix together all ingredients except cream. Stir combined ingredients over a double boiler with a wire whip until it reaches a smooth, heavy consistency, about 15 minutes.

Remove from fire and let cool in ice box for about 15 to 20 minutes. Now fold in 1½ pints of unsweetened, heavy whipped cream.

Let chill overnight. Serve.

– GP

PAVÉ AU CHOCOLAT

From the recipes of Lee Leruth, who worked in the kitchen of the Restaurant La Maree in Paris in the summer of 1972.

1 8-inch cake pan, lined with paper
12 eggs, separated

12 oz. sweet butter
12 oz. sweet dark chocolate

Melt chocolate – fold beaten yolks into melted chocolate. Then fold in melted sweet butter. Whip whites until they are stiff then fold into the above. Pour mix into mold and chill overnight.

Serve with sweetened whipped cream. – WL

LA TARTE TATIN AUX POIRES
(Hot Pear Tart)

1 cup sugar
¼ lb. unsalted butter
9 pears, peeled, cored and quartered
1 14-inch circle puff paste dough approximately ⅛-inch thick (available in store from Pepperidge Farm)

1 12-inch silverstone sauté pan

Spread 1 cup sugar on bottom of silverstone pan. Arrange pears in flower pattern on top of sugar. Cut butter in small slices and place on top of pears. Place in 450° oven for 30-35 minutes. Remove from oven and place puff paste dough on top. Return to oven for approximately 20 minutes or until dough is very crispy and brown. Remove from oven and turn tart upside down on pie sheet pan. (Pears should have coating of caramel sugar and be a beautiful brown color if done properly.) Let rest for 10 minutes for caramel to cool slightly and serve with fresh whipped cream. – LED

ALMOND COOKIES

¼ cup butter
½ cup sugar
¼ cup egg whites

⅓ cup chopped almonds
¼ tbsp. almond extract
¼ tsp. vanilla extract

Cream butter in a bowl with sugar. Add egg whites, mix well with rubber spatula, blend in finely chopped almonds, almond extract, and vanilla extract. Preheat oven to 425°. Smear baking sheets with soft butter. Drop 1 tablespoon globs of batter on sheets; space them 3 inches apart. With back of spoon smear out each glob into thin 2½-inch disk. Bake for 4 minutes; when done use metal spatula under cookie. Lift over a small glass dish and form into a cup. Let cool off. On glass dish, arrange cookie with mocha sauce then scoop hazelnut mousse in cookie and decorate with whipped cream and glazed cherry.

Served 6.

– GP

MOCHA SAUCE

½ lb. butter
¼ cup sugar
2 pkgs. Sanka instant
    coffee

¼ cup brandy
½ pt. whipping cream

Melt butter, add sugar, and whip until sugar has dissolved. Dissolve Sanka coffee in brandy and add to warm butter mixture. Let cool at room temperature, then add cream (not whipped) to mixture. Keep sauce at room temperature and don't chill.

– GP

HAZELNUT MOUSSE

6 oz. egg yolk
2 oz. sugar
½ oz. gelatin
¼ cup brandy

1 cup milk
6 oz. hazelnut paste
1 pt. whipped cream

Add all ingredients (except cream and hazelnut paste) together. Whip in double boiler until thick. Cool in icebox. Whip cream until stiff peaks form. Then fold whipped cream and hazelnut paste into cooled mixture from refrigerator. Cool for 1 hour then serve.   – GP

APPLE STRUDEL

1 cup flour
1 egg
1 tsp. salt
1 tbsp. butter
1 tbsp. oil
about ½ cup lukewarm
   water

2 lbs. apples
1 cup raisins
1 cup bread crumbs
½ cup melted butter

Place flour, egg, salt, butter, oil, and water in a bowl and mix to a smooth dough. Allow the dough to rest in a warm place for about 30 minutes.

Peel, core, and slice apples very thin.

Roll dough into a square piece, as thin as possible. Take a clean cloth sprinkled well with flour and place the rolled dough onto it. Now start pulling the dough from the sides until it's transparent. Sprinkle the dough with bread crumbs, melted butter, sliced apples, and raisins. Now roll the dough into a roll. Place gently on a baking sheet. Brush with butter and bake at 375° for about 30 to 35 minutes. Brush again and sprinkle with cinnamon sugar.   – JLA

SPONGE CAKE WITH AMARETTO AND CHOCOLATE

⅔ cup sugar
7 eggs
¾ cup all-purpose flour

3 tbsp. cornstarch
2 tsp. grated lemon rind

In a bowl, mix eggs and sugar. Heat over hot water to 115°, beating until doubled in volume. Sift flour and cornstarch together 3 times. Carefully fold the flour, cornstarch and lemon rind into the egg mixture. Pour into 2 greased and floured 9-inch cake pans. Bake at 425° until set and springy. Remove from pans and cool on cake racks. ·

AMARETTO AND CHOCOLATE FILLING:

3 cups whipping cream
1 tsp. LeRuth's Vanilla
   Bean Marinade

6 oz. semi-sweet chocolate
   chips
¼ cup Amaretto

Heat cream to 180°. Stir in Vanilla Marinade and chocolate chips. Remove from the heat. Stir to melt, then chill overnight. Put half of the sponge cake on an upturned cake pan and sprinkle with half of the Amaretto. Whip the chocolate-cream mixture until stiff. Spread a quarter of the mixture on the cake. Add top layer of cake and sprinkle with the remaining Amaretto. Ice top and sides of cake with chocolate-cream filling, reserving some of it to pipe through a pastry bag for finishing decorative touches.

                                                       – WL

Index

Demi-Glace
  Demi-Glace, 104
Desserts
  Apple Strudel, 322, 339; Bananas
  Foster, 331; Black Forest Cake, 328;
  Bread Pudding with Rum Sauce, 318,
  321; Budino (Cup Custard), 334;
  Cannoli, 316; Charlotte Russe, 307;
  Cheese Cake, 330; Chocolate Pecan
  Pie, 332; Coconut Mousse, 330;
  Coconut Tart, 332; Crêpes, 315, 323;
  Estelle's Brownies, 329; Estelle's Pecan
  Pie, 329; Flo's Coffee Cake, 336; Flor-
  entine Cookies, 315; Hazelnut Mousse,
  340; Kahlua Cake, 312; Lemon Tart,
  329; Mile High Ice Cream Pie, 306;
  Onion Cake, 26; Orange Mousse, 336;
  Pecan Pie, 307; Petits Four Florentine,
  320; Profiteroles Au Chocolat, 313;
  Sponge Cake, 324; Sponge Cake with
  Amaretto and Chocolate, 338
Dressings
  Avocado Dressing, 74; Belle Rives
  French Dressing, 80; Buttermilk
  Dressing, 75; Celery Seed Dressing,
  71; Chinese Dressing, 80; Cole Slaw
  Dressing, 71; Crabmeat Dressing, 128;
  Fruit Salad Dressing, 67; Green
  Goddess Dressing, 80; Italian Dressing,
  75; ProvenceDressing, 74; Roquefort
  Dressing, 99; Russian Dressing, 81;
  Thousand Island Dressing, 69; Vinai-
  grette Dressing, 103
Duck
  Duck Breast a la Révolution, 233;
  Duckling Bernard, 227; Duckling with
  Cherries, 229

Egg
  Egg-Cheese Soup (Stracciatella), 49;
  Eggs Hussarde, 100; Eggs St. Charles,
  208; Huevos Rancheros, 284
Eggplant
  Eggplant a la Bayou Teche, 276;
  Eggplant Soup, 76; French-Fried
  Eggplant, 275; Fried Eggplant Fingers,

33; Stir-fry Eggplant in Meat Sauce,
288; Stuffed Eggplant, 147, 151, 280;
Szechuan Style Eggplant, 292
Eggrolls
  Egg Rolls, 31; Spring Rolls, 34
Endives
  Endives Flamande, 281
Escargot
  Escargot Bourgiognonne, 37; Escargot
  in Red Wine, 41
Etouffée
  Chicken Etoufée, 230; Crawfish
  Etouffée, 123, 124; Redfish Etouffée,
  165; Shrimp Etoufée, 150

Fennel
  Fennel, 295
Filet Mignon
  Grilled Filet Mignon, 197
Fish
  Catfish with Mustard, 130; Cod Fish
  Cakes, 124; Drum in Lime Butter, 144;
  Eggs St. Charles, 208; Fish Fumet,
  106, 109; Fish Mousseline, 170; Fish
  Soup, 54, 57, 77; Fish Velouté, 108,
  180; Flounder Fillet in Butter, 163;
  Fried Catfish, 122; Pompano Grand
  Duc, 176; Pompano Meunière, 121;
  Pompano Papillote, 153; Pompano
  Vermouth, 175; Quenelles, 168;
  Redfish Au Poivre, 118; Redfish Au
  Sauterne, 154; Redfish Etouffée, 165;
  Redfish Froid, 24; Redfish Herbsaint,
  149; Redfish Kottwitz, 150; Redfish
  with Basil, 178; Redfish with Crab-
  meat, 148, 156; Redfish with Crawfish
  and Scallops, 140; Red Snapper Carib-
  bean, 163; Red Snapper Chevillot,
  126; Salmon, 169, 176; Seviche, 42;
  Smoked Fish with Pasta, 166; Terrine
  of Catfish, 142; Venetian Style Sole,
  157; Véronique Trout, 126
Flounder
  Flounder Fillet in Butter, 163
Fritters
  St. Joseph's Fritters, 335

Seafood Sauce Piquant, 58; Shrimp Barataria with Veal, 220; Shrimp Bisque, 57, 95; Shrimp Marinade, 109; Shrimp Remoulade, 30, 32, 46; Shrimp Stew and Squid, 169; Singing Shrimp, 30; Soft-Shell Crabs, 140, 181; Stuffed Crab a la Pontchartrain,; Stuffed Lobster, 172; Stuffed Lobster Toulouse, 152; Stuffed Shrimp, 167; Stuffed Squid, 143; Trout Marguery, 129, 141; Trout Meunière Amandine, 130

Sherbet
Strawberry Sherbet, 322

Shrimp
Butterfly Shrimp, 148; Crystal Shrimp, 164; Curry Shrimp, 174; Grapefruit and Shrimp, 161; Grilled Shrimp, 154; Lettuce Blossom Shrimp, 131; Qun Ming Shrimp, 133; Salt and Pepper Shrimp, 129; Shrimp and Pernod with Pasta, 260; Shrimp Barataria with Veal, 220; Shrimp Bisque, 57, 95; Shrimp Creole, 125, 134, 182; Shrimp Etouffée, 150; Shrimp Jambalaya, 121; Shrimp Kew, 159; Shrimp Madeleine, 25; Shrimp Marinade, 109; Shrimp Remoulade, 30, 32, 46; Shrimp Toast, 151; Shrimp Vermicelli, 173; Shrimp Victoria, 162; Singing Shrimp, 30; Squid and Shrimp Stew, 169; Stuffed Shrimp, 167

Sole
Fillet of Sole Florentine, 141; Oysters with Sole, 125; Sole Au Sauterne, 138; Venetian Style Sole, 157

Soufflé
Apricot Soufflé Glace, 308; Chocolate Soufflé, 312; Crab Soufflé, 170; Garlic Soufflé, 35; Lemon Soufflé, 334; Lemon Tequila Soufflé, 313

Soups
Army Bean Soup, 89; Avocado Soup, 56; Basic Chicken Stock, 273; Bean Soup, 74; Beef with Watercress Soup, 48, 88; Cauliflower and Ginger Soup, 49; Cauliflower Soup, 61; Chicken Asparagus Soup, 93; Corn and Oyster Soup, 88; Crab Soup with Saffron, 78; Cream of Asparagus Soup, 56, 62; Cream of Celery Soup, 81; Creole Onion Soup, 96; Egg-Cheese Soup (Stracciatella), 49; Eggplant Soup, 76; Escargot Soup, 54; Fish Soup, 54, 57, 77; Hot and Sour Soup, 67; Leek Soup, 62; Margie's Oyster Soup, 90; Minestrone, 51; Mirliton Soup, 91; Mussel Soup, 88; Oyster and Artichoke Soup, 76; Oyster and Truffle Soup, 52; Oyster Broth, 55; Oyster Soup, 48, 87; Red Snapper Soup, 52; Salsify Cauliflower Soup, 87; Turtle Soup, 63, 70, 73, 90, 94; War Won-Ton Soup, 65; Zucchini Soup, 83

Spinach
Spinach Mold, 293

Squid
Shrimp Stew and Squid, 169; Squid a la Bretonne, 158; Stuffed Squid, 143

Steak
Green Pepper Steak, 211; Ming Steak, 220; Pepper Steak Robert Aymes, 188; Steak Au Poivre, 187; Steak Diane, 216

Stracciatella
Stracciatella (Egg-Cheese Soup), 49

Strawberry
Strawberry Sabayon, 319; Strawberry Sherbet, 322

String Beans
Dry-fry String Beans Szechuan Style, 278

Strudel
Apple Strudel, 322, 339

Stuffing
Corn-Goose Breast Stuffing, 226; Rice and Almond Stuffing, 294

Sweet Potatoes
Candied Sweet Potatoes, 277; Sweet Potatoes and Veal, 207; Yams, 282

Sweetbreads
Sweetbreads Madeira, 192